Rediscovering Interlanguage

APPLIED LINGUISTICS AND LANGUAGE STUDY

General Editor
Professor Christopher N. Candlin, Macquarie University

Error Analysis
*Perspectives on second
language acquisition*
JACK C. RICHARDS (ED.)

Stylistics and the Teaching of
Literature
HENRY WIDDOWSON

Language Tests at School
A pragmatic approach
JOHN W. OLLER JNR

Contrastive Analysis
CARL JAMES

Language and Communication
JACK C. RICHARDS AND RICHARD
W. SCHMIDT (EDS)

Learning to Write: First Language/
Second Language
AVIVA FREDMAN, IAN PRINGLE AND
JANIC YALDEN (EDS)

Strategies in Interlanguage
Communication
CLAUS FAERCH AND GABRIELE
KASPER (EDS)

Reading in a Foreign Language
J. CHARLES ALDERSON AND A.H.
URQUHART (EDS)

Discourse and Learning
PHILIP RILEY (ED.)

An Introduction to Discourse
Analysis
New edition
MALCOLM COULTHARD

Computers in English Language
Teaching and Research
GEOFFREY LEECH AND
CHRISTOPHER N. CANDLIN (EDS)

Language Awareness in the
Classroom
CARL JAMES AND PETER GARRETT

Bilingualism in Education
*Aspects of theory, research and
practice*
JIM CUMMINS AND MERRILL
SWAIN

Second Language Grammar:
Learning and Teaching
WILLIAM E. RUTHERFORD

The Classroom and the Language
Learner
*Ethnography and second-language
classroom research*
LEO VAN LIER

Vocabulary and Language Teaching
RONALD CARTER AND MICHAEL
McCARTHY (EDS)

Observation in the Language
Classroom
DICK ALLWRIGHT

Listening to Spoken English
Second Edition
GILLIAN BROWN

Listening in Language Learning
MICHAEL ROST

An Introduction to Second Language
Acquisition Research
DIANE LARSEN-FREEMAN AND
MICHAEL H. LONG

Language and Discrimination
*A study of communication in
multi-ethnic workplaces*
CELIA ROBERTS, TOM JUPP AND
EVELYN DAVIES

Translation and Translating:
Theory and Practice
ROGER T. BELL

Process and Experience in the
Language Classroom
MICHAEL LEGUTKE AND HOWARD
THOMAS

Rediscovering Interlanguage

LARRY SELINKER

LONGMAN
LONDON AND NEW YORK

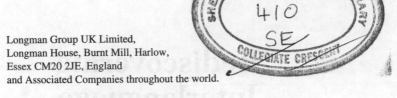

Longman Group UK Limited,
Longman House, Burnt Mill, Harlow,
Essex CM20 2JE, England
and Associated Companies throughout the world.

Published in the United States of America
by Longman Inc., New York

First published 1992
Second impression 1994

British Library Cataloguing in Publication Data
Selinker, Larry
Rediscovering interlanguage. – (Applied linguistics and
language study).
1. Foreign language skills. Acquisition
I. Title II. Series
401.93

ISBN 0–582–06401–5

Library of Congress Cataloging-in-Publication Data
Selinker, Larry, 1937–
Rediscovering interlanguage / Larry Selinker.
p.   cm. — (Applied linguistics and language study)
Includes bibliographical references and index.
ISBN 0–582–06401–5
1. Interlanguage (Language learning) 2. Second language
acquisition. 3. Contrastive linguistics. I. Title. II. Series.
P53.S395   1991   90–24335
401'.93—dc20   CIP

Set in 10/12pt Ehrhardt

Printed in Malaysia by CL

Contents

Contents

To Peter Strevens and S. Pit Corder

Who introduced me to British applied linguistics in 1966 and 1968 respectively, encouraging me to pursue interlanguage and, thus, affecting all of this. They will be missed.

'A field is in constant dialogue with its founding texts.'

Dominic La Capra
Historian

'I should not like my writing to spare other people the trouble of thinking. But, if possible, to stimulate someone to thoughts of his own.'

Ludwig Wittgenstein
Philosopher

'Without magic, the end will be tragic.'

Billie Holliday
Singer

Foreword

As recently as twenty-five years ago, it was literally possible to read everything – books, journal articles, unpublished papers – that was considered to be within the purview of the field of linguistics as it was then delimited. Since that time we have witnessed the obliteration of those old boundaries and, concomitantly, a veritable explosion of research within sub-areas of the newly constituted discipline. Both developments – the broadening and the deepening – have led to a continuing need throughout the field for vastly more bookshelves and file cabinets.

The picture is very similar, though obviously of smaller proportions, for second language acquisition (SLA). The more daunting the sheer necessity of sustaining a grasp of unfolding research in SLA, the more difficult it becomes to give contemporary SLA events their proper historical perspective. If limitations of time and energy now dictate that one can read only a small fraction of the literature that falls within the purview of the field, then comprising that fraction will tend to be largely what has just been written: items considered to be on the 'cutting edge' of progress in that field. And similarly, of course, no more than a readable fraction of the literature – again of the cutting-edge variety – will understandably serve to *inform* what has just been written. It is a professional state of affairs that has both its excitement and its despair, as when, for example, the temptation to save time by incorporating into one's own work, without checking, another's reported findings can bring about the eventual wide dissemination of flawed research.

Historical perspective, then, is often the first casualty of our familiar obsession with making progress by breaking new ground, by having what was conceived only yesterday give way to what will likely last only till tomorrow. But in this fascinating book by Larry Selinker, historical perspective comes back into focus and contemporary SLA is once again put in touch with its roots. Indeed, the author's work over the years is to such an extent co-extensive with the life of the entire field that in a very real sense he himself can serve as one of his *own* roots. There is thus no one around better equipped to render us this service.

The beauty of the book, however, is that it shows us the value not of mere ritual obeisance to scholarly work of previous generations but, in the true Talmudic spirit, of awareness that new wisdom is to be gained by *constantly* examining the new in the light of the old, or in the light of our 'founding texts', as the author so aptly puts it. I am often reminded, for instance, of how much contemporary linguistics owes to *its* founding texts – the lamentably much-ignored works of the traditional grammarians, to cite one example. One of the most astonishing books of earlier years that I can recall reading is Otto Jespersen's *The Philosophy of Grammar*, originally published in 1924. In various chapters one can clearly discern Jespersen's anticipation of the modern principles of underlying grammatical structure, of case grammar, of ergativity, of generative semantics, of the function of English *do*-support (as maintaining the post-subject position of lexical verb), of Chomskyan UG, and so on. Well, Larry Selinker redirects our attention to a few astonishing texts in the SLA tradition and shows us how they may be woven into the general fabric of interlanguage (IL) study. In his own words, 'I suggest a methodology which allows us to relate crucial material in founding texts to current IL concerns and current concerns to a realization of the potential of these texts' (p. 3). We are thus able to see the links between Harris and Van Buren, between Nickel and Tarone, between Weinreich and Kellerman, etc.; and we begin to understand the importance of the work of Fries, of Lado, of Ferguson, of Nemser, of Drubig, and especially of Corder. To encounter the author's transcendent vision of the unfolding of the field, mediated through its founding texts, amounts to a catharsis, a cleansing of our professional emotions, as it were.

The humanist Daniel Boorstin once said that the great obstacle to progress is not ignorance but the illusion of knowledge. What Larry Selinker's book teaches us is that in order to dispel that illusion, gain true knowledge, and have a sense of where we are going, we must, as a field, always know whence we have come.

William E. Rutherford

Acknowledgements

The impetus for this book came from Peter Strevens. Over the years he cajoled me many times to 'take on the whole interlanguage show' and to try to 'link things together through time'. He kindly insisted, over a long period of time, that I had the wherewithal to do this job; he graciously read pieces along the way, constantly giving needed encouragement since, like many authors before me, I did not know what I had taken on. His insistence that language teaching studies have much to contribute to second language acquisition thought has stood me in good stead in this volume.

The other great influence on this volume came from my 'intellectual father' in interlanguage and second language acquisition, S. Pit Corder. I owe to Pit the context, in the Edinburgh Department of Applied Linguistics in the late 1960s, that led to the formulation of the original 'interlanguage hypothesis'. Detailing his many contributions to this field, culminating with the list at the end of Chapter 6, has been pure joy. As stated at the end of that chapter, how could we possibly manage without all he created? All will agree then that much is owed to Pit intellectually, but not many know that we also owe him much for his ability to set up a context for creative work for younger scholars. This was certainly true for me in those formative years, 1968–1969. Without Pit's personal hospitality and intellectual input, there would be no interlanguage hypothesis. It is as simple as that.

The detailed analysis of his work in Chapter 6 serves as my final goodbye to Pit.

I am glad that I visited Pit and Nancy in retirement. It renewed the old excitement, seeing Pit's continued insights into language acquisition questions, though interestingly in a more local context than before. He was concerned with the attempted second language acquisition of his colleagues in retirement in Braithwaite, that pretty village in the Lake District. It's a pity that we found no forum to capture that material. I am also glad that I was able to meet with Peter and Gwyn several times in the past two years. Peter and I continued to discuss matters of mutual interest; his thoughts on fossilization written in an extended letter have been at times a sub-text for me here. Some years ago, in the first attempt at this volume, I wrote most of the dedication to Peter and Pit that appears at the front, so, in general terms, they knew what was in my attempt to reframe interlanguage. It is a pity that neither survived to see this project through to its fruition, to see whether, in the final analysis, I had finally 'gotten it right'.

To thank others – early on I knew I had made the right choice to go with Longman. Chris Candlin has been a most helpful and insightful editor, carefully going through the entire manuscript twice and some parts three, and even four times! Whatever clarity is finally achieved in this volume is due largely to his intelligence and diligence.

Trying to figure out what is second language fact and what is not led to the discovery of 'interlanguage'. I came to this concept from a long apprenticeship, of some eight years, intermittently doing a number of seemingly unrelated activities, most particularly teaching English in the USA and overseas and being trained at two univerities in Washington, DC, American and Georgetown, in the fields of language teaching methodology, contrastive analysis and bilingualism, all within a framework of general linguistics. In thinking of future graduate training related to interlanguage and second language acquisition, it might be useful to share some of these experiences. I began general linguistics in a structural point of view and language teaching methodology in a pattern practice point of view at American with Ken Croft, Harry Freeman and Hugo Mueller. At Georgetown, Bob Di Pietro got me started in the theory of SLA by teaching the empirical tools of doing contrastive analysis and bilingualism. In the papers I did for Di Pietro, I looked in depth at Israeli–Hebrew data in a bilingualism framework and American–English data in a contrastive framework with Israeli–Hebrew data; these in turn pushed me into a contrastive empirical look at Hebrew–English data, and the notion that three, not two systems are involved in second language acquisition. From Charles Ferguson I learned the all-important skill, the crucial skill, of thinking critically about linguistics as a discipline. All of this was reinforced by David Harris's and Robert Lado's courses on language testing, Fred Bosco's course on the philosophy and practicality of Fries-type teaching methodology, and Chuck Kriedler's course on English structure. Importantly for the notion of training future students in our field, it may be useful to note in each course, as I saw it, a parallel perspective leading to empirical work. In my view, the most important teaching tool at

Georgetown at the time is one I recommend we consider reinstating: each student 'has a language', to which they keep coming back for projects in various courses. Additionally, given the tenets of structural linguistics, there was an emphasis on learning to handle large linguistic texts. (Harvey Sobelman assigned as term project the infamous 500-sentence problem on Isthmus Zapotec (Nida 1949).) Training in analysing extended texts in one language from several points of view seems currently lacking in our training of graduate students. I maintain that experience with extended texts is an important strand in deciding second language fact (cf. Selinker and Douglas 1985 and 1989) and we should consider reinstating it in our applied linguistics teaching.

Interlanguage emerged further from extended discussions with colleagues in two universities, Edinburgh and Washington, trying further to figure out what is second language fact in light of the experimental language transfer results described in Chapter 7. In those formative years of 1966–72, I was fortunate to be among an extraordinary group of students and colleagues. Here, I wish to thank them all for putting up with my constant and probably annoying questioning. At Edinburgh: David Abercrombie, Patrick Allen, Dick Allwright, Gill Brown, Keith Brown, Roger Campbell, Ruth Clark, Pit Corder, Clive Criper, Bill Currie, Alan Davies, Chris De Linde, Les Dickinson, Tony Howatt, Bet Ingram, John Laver, John Lyons, Jagdish Jain, Mahavir Jain, Catherine Johns, John Marshall, Ian Pearson, Myint Su, Elaine Tarone, Jimmy Thorne, Peter Trudgill, Sandy Urquhart, Paul Van Buren, Roger Wales and Henry Widdowson. At Washington: Chris Adjemian, Jim Armagost, Del Bennett, Robert Bley-Vroman, Ernie Clifton, Ken Coulter, Harold Edwards, Uli Frauenfelder, Cheryl Goodenough, Sandra Hamlett, Stephanie Harris, Jim Hoard, Tom Huckin, Helen Kline, John Lackstrom, John Lawler, Jeanie Lee, Fred Lukoff, Fritz Newmeyer, Ralph Patrick, Keith Sauer, Michael Seitz, Elaine Tarone, Bill Tiffany, Louis Trimble, Ken Watkin and Dick Weist. As this list shows, Elaine Tarone was at both universities and has a very special place in my development. In my mind's eye I see Tarone and Adjemian arguing in class, staking out positions, positions mirrored today in the UG/contextual SLA debate and the single competence/multiple competence debate. One should note, also, that in a brief paper (Watkin 1970), Ken was the first to use the phrase 'IL Hypothesis'; that paper seems also to have been the first empirical attempt to study the phenomenon of fossilization. During my Edinburgh time, Dave Reibel of York pushed me towards explicitness in the early interlanguage papers, though I soon realized that there is a certain profit to 'purposeful ambiguity' as a spur to research. In the early 1970s I also had the extreme good fortune to discuss IL matters with Gerhard Nickel, the editor of IRAL where the IL paper was first published (Selinker 1972). I thank Gerhard for his strong support of IL research, long before it became fashionable; this can be seen from the error analysis chapters here where the important PAKS material is discussed.

My colleagues have been very helpful. Bill Rutherford and Sue Gass read a very early draft and provided much-needed encouragement and detailed comment at that crucial stage. I thank Bill for offering to write the Foreword here. Over the years, other colleagues have discussed with insight one part or another of this manuscript: Charles Alderson, Roger Andersen, Lyle Backman, Pete Becker, Ruth Berman, Dan Douglas, Sue Gass, Eric Kellerman, Wolfgang Klein, B. Kumaravadivelu, Usha Lakshmanan, Clive Perdue, Catherine Pettinari, Dennis Preston, Mike Sharwood Smith, Jackie Schachter, John Schumann, Merrill Swain, John Swales, Elaine Tarone, Leo van Lier and Henry Widdowson. And, at key points, Judy and Roger Winn-Bell Olsen provided important perspective and encouragement.

But in this volume I owe most to my co-authors, co-presenters and co-editors over the years: Guillermo Bartelt, Charley Basham, Ann Beck, Robert Bley-Vroman, Dan Douglas, Guy Dumas, Ahmed Fakhri, Sue Foster, Uli Frauenfelder, Sue Gass, Victor Hanzeli, Tom Huckin, Eric Kellerman, B. Kumaravadivelu, John Lackstrom, Usha Lakshmanan, John Lamendella, John Lawler, Carolyn Madden, Dave Miller, Joan Morley, Judy Winn-Bell Olsen, Robert Phillipson, Dennis Preston, Betty Robinette, P.J.N. Selinker, Mike Sharwood Smith, Eva Stahlheber, Merrill Swain, Elaine Tarone, Russ Tomlin, Mary Todd Trimble, Louis Trimble, Henry Widdowson and Devon Woods. I have been very lucky. In the time-consuming process of co-producing publishable materials, I have learned much from these colleagues. From my point of view, happily, there is no way I can totally disentangle my work from theirs.

At the University of Michigan Pete Becker provided philosophical anchoring concerning interlanguage "particularity". [See his masterful lecture (Becker, 1988) where he traces this insight to his teacher, Pike.] I also wish to acknowledge the many kindnesses of Patsy Aldridge, Mary Evich, Ahmed Ferhadi, Melonie Grasty, Gemma Lum, Dan Madaj, Rosemary Tackabery and Sheila Williams while struggling to complete this manuscript. And to Mike Selinker and

Jason Reyes go my thanks for getting the book finalized, at long last.

I hope I have forgotten no-one. I know they won't all agree with all that appears here; what I wish for is that they are pleased overall with this attempt at reframing the debate.

Finally, I wish to thank posthumously Nahum Glatzer, my undergraduate advisor at Brandeis University. He taught me the Talmudic way of looking at texts. He died near the end of this writing. Wisdom *is* possible.

Larry Selinker

The Publishers are grateful to Oxford University Press for permission to reproduce copyright material in Table 8.1 which is taken from the English Language Teaching Journal 'Talking Shop', April 1983, 37.2, pp. 129–37.

Abbreviations

CA	Contrastive Analysis
EA	Error Analysis
IL	Interlanguage
SLA	Second Language Acquisition
MLA	Multiple Language Acquisition
NL	Native Language
TL	Target Language
CLI	Cross Linguistic Influence
L1	First Language or NL
L2	Second Language
N/N	Native/Native
N/NN	Native/Non-Native
NN/NN	Non-Native/Non-Native
NS	Native Speaker
NNS	Non-Native Speaker
R/G	Rhetorical Grammatical
ESL	English as a Second Language
EFL	English as a Foreign Language
ELT	English Language Teaching
EST	English for Science and Technology
ESP	English for Specific Purposes
EAP	English for Academic Purposes
EOP	English for Occupational Purposes
EVP	English for Vocational Purposes
SAE	Standard Average European
LPS	Latent Psychological Structure
UG	Universal Grammar

Introduction: Scope of the study

Since Corder's seminal 1967 paper 'The Significance of Learners' Errors', there have been literally hundreds of empirical studies about interlanguage (IL) in second language acquisition (SLA). In order to integrate these studies, it is time to rethink and reframe the interlanguage hypothesis. This volume attempts to follow several threads of thought which are initially discussed in this Introduction.

Rethinking several older literatures, this work shows that in some important sense for a very long time hints of the notion interlanguage have been in many of the writings about learning a second language, albeit buried and unnamed. The attempt painstakingly to gain insights from the wisdom of older literature for today's questions leads to a rethinking of crucial earlier texts, or *founding texts*. Our ultimate goal in explicitly contemplating our founding texts would be to seek general laws of second language acquisition.

To show the need for rethinking the foundations of our field, we need only note that in SLA, TESOL ('The Teaching of English to Speakers of Other Languages') and other applied linguistics disciplines, negative phenomena regularly occur, such as:

(a)   students do not learn the history of their field
(b)   colleagues constantly re-invent the wheel
(c)   bandwagons regularly appear.

Trend (a) is expressed most often by those who teach new students in the areas of SLA and language teaching methodology. It would be embarrassing to detail trend (b). Concerning (c), it has been pointed out numerous times that bandwagons exist not only concerning teaching but, unfortunately, in research as well. In these pages we discuss several cases. Teachers and researchers deplore these trends but find that there is little one can do about it. Historical depth related to current questions is usually unavailable in the literature. One would like to know why our field is not more conscious of where its history fits into current work.

In this volume we re-examine founding texts with the aim of

reframing the IL hypothesis and tie together ideas over time with current IL thinking. Here we take the historian La Capra's quote above quite seriously, that 'A field is in constant dialogue with its founding texts.' In making this dialogue explicit here, we not only hope to help obviate the above negative trends, but we discover that there are certain needs that must be included in our current theoretical and empirical work. Prime among them is our need to include more carefully contrastive thought in SLA work. For example, a reframing of contrastive analysis (CA) data from founding texts leads us to recognize the depth and importance to IL concerns of Weinreich's (1953) notion of interlingual identifications, the suggested mechanism that unites units across linguistic systems. Also, we need an understanding of how to decide what is and is not IL fact and where IL variation, language transfer, fossilization and universal linguistic processes fit in.

We show here that one can often read into earlier work not only some sort of 'in-between' language or grammar, but also hypotheses that are *not* part of the current debate. Earlier sources presented in this volume have discussed (and at times actually named) important concepts necessary to current SLA thought, e.g. permeability, transferability, and language transfer as a selection process. Though not named, the phenomenon of fossilization is described. Yet current discourses rarely referred to unsettled theoretical questions as they are discussed in these earlier texts. In this volume we attempt primarily painstakingly to gain insights for today's IL and SLA questions from the wisdom of these crucial earlier texts, these *founding texts* of our discipline.

In order to see the wisdom of these founding texts as related to current concerns, I suggest we first borrow methodologically from Talmudic studies the notion of a close study of basic texts and commentary upon them. The Talmudic spirit teaches that one should always question basic premises and never accept things at face value. Adherence to this principle would make bandwagons impossible. Wisdom *is* possible, but only through the careful study of certain previous texts as well as learning from the previous commentary upon them. One criterion, then, that we use here for determining founding texts is that of continual discovery, the notion of constant enlightenment that one receives from studying a founding text such as Weinreich (1953). (My previous experience with this approach appears in Bley-Vroman and Selinker 1984 concerning research methodology in considering 'highly valued' texts in language for specific purposes.)

However, we must be careful. In previous dialogues with founding texts, we have read them too literally. We have focused our attention on their defects, defects which are so obvious in hindsight. A focus on defects leads to the infamous 'baby and bathwater syndrome', where because of these a whole body of literature can be thrown out. The most notorious example of throwing out a field in a very bandwagon-like way is the painful example of CA in the early 1970s; this example is discussed in the first chapter in some depth. In order to avoid too narrow a focus, a procedure is needed to look more carefully at the founding texts of our discipline. I suggest a methodology which allows us to relate crucial material in founding texts to current IL concerns and current concerns to a realization of the potential of these texts. To link IL concepts together through time, the methodology suggested here is that of a *purposeful misreading* of founding texts in our field. It is important to note that included here are some texts in other fields from which we have borrowed, for we have borrowed much in SLA. We gain the insight of 'purposeful misreading' from Harold Garfinkel.

Garfinkel has seen wholesale borrowing from his field, ethnomethodology (Garfinkel 1967), into other fields. He believes that the borrowing of ideas wholesale from other fields into one's own may mask the fact that central variables can be different across fields. In a 1980 seminar at the University of Michigan on SLA, he suggested that one must purposefully misread borrowed texts in terms of underlying assumptions and needs *in one's own field*. One purposefully misreads, then, texts from other fields through the prism of key concepts in one's own field. To take as an example the SLA and IL case, Garfinkel pointed out that concepts central to SLA and IL are *not* usually found in some of the fields from which we borrow in terms of theory or research methodology. He had in mind concepts central to SLA such as change over time (possible acquisition) and non-change over time (possible fossilization). He cautioned that if we decide to apply research methodologies from other fields to SLA problems (as we do), we need to adapt these methodologies to be sure to include in a key way these central SLA variables. Such cases are discussed in detail in this volume.

In terms of how purposefully to misread a founding text in CA, Lado (1957) is presented as an example. The traditional difficulty, we maintain, has been reading Lado too literally. For example, Lado's frequent statements that 'the learner *will* do X or Y' have caused difficulty for many readers. Thus, it has been to dismiss his work as was done in the 1970s. This dismissal, however, fails to notice that

Lado continues to have a crucial and continuing influence, either as synthesis or as antithesis. The purposeful misreading technique in this case recognizes IL variation and includes statements such as: 'a learner *might* do X and/or Y under Z conditions'. It turns out that we then achieve current and useful SLA hypotheses, including some that may not have been explicitly stated in the literature. Exemplars of this procedure regarding Lado (1957) are provided in Chapter 1.

Purposefully misreading earlier texts from the CA, error analysis (EA) and bilingualism literatures generate testable hypotheses and many exemplars are presented below. Specifically, concerning the CA literature and reinterpreting it as we do in detail in Chapters 4 and 5, we see that the best CA studies provide 'predicted IL data'. That is, we can now look at classical CA studies as if they were trying to generate predicted IL data, often in terms of underlying or deep grammatical transfer. This point is taken up in Chapters 4 and 5.

This volume is *not* intended to be mere history per se; this is not a book of the past. The claim made here is that in order to understand IL in SLA, we must use the past in the particular way suggested above. I do not want to give the impression that I am the first in SLA to indulge in this exercise. Corder, for example (Chapter 6, below), uses EA in an idiosyncratic way. He reinterpreted CA by explicitly exploiting the CA/EA/IL link, stating that the hunches that the investigator may wish to test through specifically designed elicitation procedures 'will derive from the two systematic techniques . . . mentioned: formal error analysis and contrastive analysis. These are complementary.' He provides a 'logical sequence of procedures' in the investigation of IL, showing how the three areas are linked. In studying his analyses we see that Corder has done for research methodology what we are trying to do in this volume on a different scale. As a result of this procedure, Corder's reinterpretation of EA concludes that EA is a basic learning strategy on the part of the learner and a convincing place for us to start studying the transfer from one IL to the next learned, what we have described in Chapter 6 as: IL1, IL2 . . . ILn. These conclusions can now be empirically tested.

In my vision of IL and SLA, founding texts exist in *six* areas: contrastive analysis (CA) discussed in Chapters 1, 4, 5, 6, 7 and 8; bilingualism discussed in Chapters 2, 3, 7 and 8; error analysis (EA) discussed in Chapters 4, 5, 6, 7 and 8; experimental CA discussed in Chapter 7; theoretical linguistics, discussed *passim* throughout this volume; and experimental, especially mathematical, psychology discussed in Chapter 8. Note that by founding texts in IL and SLA, we also mean *texts from other fields* from which we have borrowed. In Chapter 8 we also face the issue of how we determine IL fact.

Specifically concerning contrastive thought, the founding texts for me are those by Fries and Lado (Chapter 1), Weinreich (Chapter 2), Harris (Chapter 4), numerous CA scholars (Chapter 4), EA scholars, especially Coulter and the PAKS group led by Nickel (Chapter 5), Corder and Van Buren (Chapter 6), Nemser and Briere (Chapter 7) and the Osgood transfer material (Chapter 8). Additionally, I have applied purposeful misreading to the detail of several of my own earlier bilingual, CA and IL texts as reframed and updated IL data (Chapters 3, 5 and 7).

It has been a worthwhile experience to struggle back through our roots, to draw more than fifty years of literature together, looking at this literature through the prism of current work and at current work through its prism. Because of the rhetorical process of 'invention' inherent in the writing process, I now understand much more of all this than before. Particularly, what I have slowly begun to realize over the years is that in studying IL and the influences that shape it, we have never left, and cannot leave, some fundamental insights inherent in CA. I do not think that this has been digested and written about, or, rather in terms of invention, has been written about and digested. I wish you the patience to go through this continuing intellectual adventure with me.

We begin with C.C. Fries . . . .

1 Beginnings: Fries/Lado

Practical teaching concerns

One can say that the Contrastive Analysis (CA)/Interlanguage (IL) experience began with the following insight. In a much-quoted sentence, C.C. Fries wrote in 1945:

> The most efficient materials are those that are based upon a scientific description of the language to be learned, carefully compared with a parallel description of the native language of the learner.
> (Fries 1945, p.9)

In this chapter we describe briefly some of Fries's contributions and then consider the work of his colleague, R. Lado. One link we will explore is the important connection between Lado and scholars in a neighbouring field, bilingualism. Thus, in Chapter 2 we will discuss in some detail the relevant contributions to CA/IL thought of a pioneer in several branches of linguistic study – Uriel Weinreich. Then we will move on to a study of the question of what is 'comparable' across languages, more precisely across linguistic systems. We will do this because, we will argue, this latter insight is important to IL and thus to second language acquisition (SLA) thought. Later in the book we will pause for a detailed look at the continuing discovery of IL and the forces that shape it. We will move towards a consideration of the ongoing process of comparison in applied linguistics and SLA, specifically at several recent attempts to understand IL and IL learning through one or another comparative endeavours.

Beginning with Fries, then, the above quotation often appeared in the 1950s and 1960s at the beginning of MA and PhD theses to justify the writing of a particular CA study. The intellectual link between this quotation and CA was made explicit by Lado when he pointed out that for effective teaching materials, implied in Fries's statement is 'the fundamental assumption' of CA work that 'individuals tend to transfer the forms and meanings, and the distribution of forms and meanings of their native language and culture to the foreign language and culture' (Lado 1957, p.2). The direct link, then, between Fries's thought and CA – and thus IL and SLA – is established. The strongest motivation for doing CA from its earliest days involves applied work, namely, in considering what the best teaching materials might be, one has to look carefully at the learner from the point of view of *possible* transfer. This is still, I would maintain, a useful current position. So one strong motivation for doing a CA in applied linguistics has always been to learn something important about transfer, 'negative transfer' (in this view of things) being traditionally associated with the making of 'errors'. Later in this chapter we will come back to Lado's seminal work and we will be returning to considerations of language transfer (in Sharwood Smith's phrase (1982): 'cross-linguistic influence' or CLI) at various points throughout the volume.

Fries, in the 1945 classic *Teaching and Learning English as a Foreign Language*, was primarily concerned with the 'first stage of language learning' and the '*end* to be attained' in that stage (p.8, emphasis in original). 'That end,' in Fries's words, 'is the building up of a set of habits for the oral production of a language and for the receptive understanding of the language when it is spoken.' On the next page, Fries states that to gain that end 'within a reasonable time' one of the key ingredients is 'proper' teaching materials, the 'most efficient' ends being those gained by the method described in the quote in the first paragraph above. Fries's explicit aim was to develop teaching materials which would lead the adult learner towards making the sound system and structural system of the language to be learned 'automatic habits' and 'unconscious habits' (p.3), using only enough vocabulary to make the systems work. (For further discussion of this point, see Morley *et al.* 1984.)

The teaching materials contemplated by Fries/Lado and colleagues, since they are based on a careful comparison of the native language (NL) and the target language (TL), obviously have to be language specific. In light of this, Fries framed an important truism, one which was to have substantive import on the development of our field, especially since enchantment and disenchantment with CA have been dominant themes in SLA and IL thought: 'Foreign language teaching is always a matter of teaching a specific "foreign" language to students who have specific "native" language background' (Fries 1945, Preface). How this approach fits in with current attempts to integrate SLA thought into considerations of universal grammar (UG) will be discussed subsequently, but here suffice it to restate that the applied/practical impetus for doing CA over the years has to be clearly emphasized.

In a later discussion in the Japanese context, Fries and Fries (1961) made all of this even more explicit. In order for the Japanese student to 'learn English well', he 'must have' English teaching materials which are 'especially adapted to his linguistic needs'. They then make a statement which has important ramifications for SLA prediction:

> The proper selection and *contrastive* arrangement of the English patterns to meet the special needs of Japanese pupils at the very beginning will determine whether the teaching will be effective and the learning easy or the pupils will be so confused that the teaching will be very difficult and a satisfactory learning almost impossible.
> (Fries and Fries 1961, p.1, emphasis added.)

Today, although we would not accept such claims as to ease and difficulty of learning without empirical evidence from an input study, we can nevertheless clearly see the link between practical concerns and SLA thought inherent in a Fries approach to CA. It is important here to preview the following: a conclusion such as that just quoted – whatever its current lack of empirical evidence – now becomes, for the record, an important hypothesis available for empirical testing on some learners under some (as yet unspecified) conditions.

The contrastive approach is presented by Fries for use with Latin-American students, the earliest students dealt with in a systematic fashion (for more detail see Morley *et al.* 1984). On p.25 of Fries (1945), for example, one of the steps used in considering each TL-English sound is to 'isolate' for the Spanish-speaking learner 'the most similar sounds in Spanish words, as "perro" for [ɛ] or "mismo" for [z] or "dedo" for [ð]'. Or on p.33, in discussing 'word order patterns that English uses to express fundamental relationships', Fries refers to the fact that Spanish speakers must not, as they 'frequently do', say 'station bus' when they mean 'bus station', and 'must develop a habit of placing single word modifiers of substantives before the words they modify'. Neglecting for now the troublesome word 'habit', this point is then linked to an extensive discussion of the selection of patterns to be taught and learned productively versus those to be learned receptively. The relationships to IL of considerations of perception vs production involve a host of issues that are still with us (see, e.g., Gass and Selinker 1983a, *passim*, and Selinker 1984, fn 2).

On pp.39 and 40 of Fries (1945) he provides detailed examples of the fact that 'practically no words of one language ... ever cover exactly the same areas of meaning and use as those of another language'. He contrasts, for example, the English word 'table' with the Spanish word 'mesa', pointing out that 'mesa' is not used for a 'table of figures', nor for a 'table of contents' nor for a 'time table'. And then, elegantly I would claim, he gives examples where mesa 'is used in many connections for which we do not use the word table'. He then gives seventeen examples of the use of the English word 'time' for which there is 'no simple Spanish word'. And there is much more in this vein in Fries's writings. What we have are useful CA facts which, in terms of the essence of our discussion here, become useful hypotheses for understanding and testing IL in various SLA contexts.

One point to note is that Fries is not known for having undertaken detailed CAs himself and that is most likely why histories of CA and SLA usually fail to mention him. In hindsight it is easy to criticize Fries's approach to CA and SLA (and we do criticize Fries – see Morley *et al.* 1984), but here I wish only to reveal for the reader something of Fries's crucial place in the CA/IL chain, as well as to lend at least some of his conclusions the respect of being reasonable CA hypotheses that can be empirically studied.

A technology of contrastive analysis

It was clearly Lado (1957), however, who carried this approach into a 'technology of CA', which, as we shall show below, provides us with useful current tools and, where certain key issues are first carefully explored in the literature, issues that are still with us today. In Lado's work the comparison of the learner's NL to the language to be learned was explicitly hypothesized as a predictor of learner errors. Importantly for SLA thought, this is sometimes true, and from subsequent attempts to validate this hypothesis arose error analysis (EA), one of the immediate precursors to IL and SLA. It appears then that from Fries's insight that the best and most efficient teaching materials arise out of a comparison of the NL and TL, one derives the notion from Lado that such a comparison is able to predict transfer and thus errors which learners will make, which for Lado equal the 'problems' or 'hurdles' learners will encounter.

We find in Lado the conclusion that *before* one can prepare the best and most efficient teaching materials, one has to discover the learning difficulties through such a comparison: 'The most important new thing in the preparation of teaching materials is the *comparison* of native and foreign language and culture in order to find the *hurdles* that really have to be surmounted in the teaching' (Lado 1957, p.2, emphasis added). Lado goes on to state that 'it will soon be considered quite out of date' to do such things as begin to write a textbook without having 'previously compared' the NL and TL, i.e. in classical CA terms, the 'two systems involved'. Lado (1957, p.2) further states that 'the linguistic comparison is basic and really inescapable if we wish to make progress and not merely reshuffle the same old [teaching] materials'. As we shall see in succeeding chapters, the proposing of IL comes directly out of the empirical attempt to undertake such comparisons and to test these comparisons in light of the phenomenon of language transfer. Researchers now realize (cf. Gass and Selinker 1983a, *passim*, and Kellerman and Sharwood Smith 1986, *passim*) that language transfer as a 'selection process' should not necessarily be equated either with the making of errors in a second language nor with learning problems in attempting to acquire that particular TL. The reader should also note that neither of the latter two concepts, errors and learning problems, should necessarily be equated with the other.

We note that Lado (1957) is considered a seminal work. For example, James (1980, p.8) states, 'For me, modern CA starts with' this book. Importantly, Lado is not only historically significant but is quite relevant in many ways to continuing concerns in SLA and IL studies. We have noted this before: '. . . we have been able to infer from the Toronto French-immersion data we have looked at, that these . . . individuals are using in their IL, grammatical structures . . . [which] are, to some degree, similar to the "rules" described by Lado [1957]' (Tarone *et al.* 1976, p.99). My point here is that in empirically studying IL and the influences that shape it, SLA thought has never abandoned some fundamental insights inherent in CA. One of the reasons we have to go 'back again' to classical CA for insights appears in sentence two of the Preface to Lado (1957); Lado's point is that the results of CA prove of 'fundamental value' to 'language learning experiments' (see also his p.7, 'Significance for Research'). We are sure that this is the case and have also noted this before: in the Introduction (Chapter 1) to Gass and Selinker (1983a), after a careful review of what is known about the phenomenon of language transfer in language learning, we conclude that: 'For us, one important preliminary step to understanding language transfer is, at the very least, a native language–target language comparison, which often leads to insightful hypotheses concerning language transfer phenomena' (Gass and Selinker 1983a, p.6). Several chapters in that volume and in that of Kellerman and Sharwood Smith (1986) demonstrate, in a very current way, the truth of Lado's insight.

On balance, however, Lado surely promises too much when he states in his Preface that language teachers 'who understand this field [i.e. CA] will acquire insights and tools for . . . diagnosing student difficulties accurately'. This is where classical CA began having problems. These problems unfortunately led to the ten-year effort (called the 'baby and bathwater syndrome') of attempting to discard the entire enterprise of CA. This effort has failed and, as we shall show in these pages, CA has made a comeback. But here one has to ask: Does 'diagnosing student difficulties accurately' mean accurately diagnosing 'all difficulties' or only the major ones? And if the latter, which are they and how does one decide? How does this conclusion then relate to individual differences which Lado himself brings up (p.72)? In the final analysis, one has to ask: Why is Lado's claim stated so strongly? This is not nit-picking; this sort of claim led many teachers and researchers totally to stop paying attention to the insights of CA.

In order to understand IL and the forces that create it, we have to strive for some balance, for it is a fact that CA predictions sometimes work. In this regard I have pondered long and hard the following assumption, that by doing CA '. . . we can predict and describe the patterns that will cause difficulty in learning, and those that will not cause difficulty . . .' (Lado 1957, Preface). My concerns with this statement mirror those above. I wonder why this strong assumption was made in the first place. I have asked people who were there and who cannot really explain the strong categorical tone, even in hindsight. One has to ask: When, and especially why, did the notion of CA as predictor of errors, learning problems, difficulties, interference, hurdles, what have you, begin to take over the research endeavour? Where did these scholars go wrong? Why would one have believed in the first place (as I surely did for a time) that by comparing abstract linguistic structures one would necessarily learn about 'the patterns that will cause difficulty in learning' a second language. This is not a trivial point. Why would a whole generation of linguists and applied linguists, actively involved in second language learning and teaching in many parts of the world, have believed this as accepted fact? The only conclusion I can come to is sociological, related to a dominant pseudo-issue of the times, of whether or not linguistics is a 'science'. My conclusion is that the hope was there that had Lado's categorical statements been right, i.e. had CA predictions been unequivocally borne out by the empirical CA study for which Lado himself was calling (see below), then linguistics would have become a 'real science'. We must continually be aware of this pseudo-goal, for unfortunately one sees this same trend now with some experimental SLA. I can recall a discussion with Lado, about 1964, where the section of CA structuralist studies called 'residue' (= unexplained phenomena) was apparently growing with each study. This was certainly puzzling since some CA predictions were indeed being empirically borne out. As we shall see throughout this volume, this continues to be a central area for understanding IL and IL learning in SLA.

We must note again that it is unfortunate that the extreme claims of CA as SLA prediction led many to abandon CA entirely because of those cases when the predictions of errors, especially, did not come true. But in the context of the discussion here, we can easily proceed since our mission is to try to show why, in order to understand IL one must understand CA. If it is true, as we will argue throughout this volume, that in order to understand IL one must understand CA, then Lado deserves much credit for looking at CA as a technology for the SLA issues it continues to raise.

Techniques for comparison

In the Preface to Lado (1957), 'techniques for comparison' are mentioned and much of the book is devoted to spelling these out. We are fortunate here for it is a related point of this discussion that most SLA scholars do in fact compare linguistic systems as a central part of their SLA work. For example, they compare either ILs with NLs or with TLs, or Native/Non-Native (N/NN) interaction with Native/Native (N/N) interaction, or in fact make some other important SLA comparison. If this is so, then it is a good thing to have this technology in place. We will look at Lado's techniques of comparison in a moment.

On p.1, Lado introduces the work of scholars in the neighbouring field of bilingualism, by stating that a 'practical confirmation' of 'the fundamental assumption' of his book (quoted above) has come from such scholars. He specifically states that 'practical confirmation of the validity' of this basic assumption has come from the work of Weinreich (1953) and Haugen (1953). Is this a fair reading of the evidence? Lado states that researchers in bilingualism 'report that *many* linguistic distortions heard among bilinguals *correspond* to describable differences in the languages involved' (Lado 1957, p.1, emphasis added). They did so report, but the emphasized words raise two central issues: a) the hedging issue of *many* leads to the conclusion that classical CA statements were in general statistical in nature without statistical controls (see Selinker (1966) and the discussion below of hedging used in classical CA), and b) the *correspond* issue leads to the conclusion that domains of inquiry were confused in classical CA. This latter issue was raised by Weinreich himself and is discussed in Chapter 2.

In brief this issue is best understood in terms of the Saussurean distinction (Saussure 1922) of 'langue/parole' in that (as we shall see in the next chapter) Weinreich points out that quite often the speech of bilinguals (one domain of research) relates well to abstract linguistic categories (a different domain of research), but quite often it does not. As pointed out above, this lack of correspondence between language transfer and linguistic categories remains an issue unresolved in SLA (and in general linguistic inquiry as well). But even so, in this context we must specifically ask: Is the work of Weinreich and Haugen 'practical confirmation' of the work of CA? It is not, for reasons stated above, and in particular because the phrase 'many correspondences' dodges issues of IL fact. The problem here is that there is a second issue regarding domains of inquiry. Dulay and Burt (1973), in a very useful paper, point out that Lado has made a fundamental error here by 'equating' the domain of inquiry for his CA (in more current terms, a developing IL in SLA), with the domain of inquiry studied by Haugen and Weinreich (i.e. those individuals who have established competence in two languages from birth or from early childhood). Though the domain of SLA and the domain of bilingualism appear overlapping, they are surely not identical. Importantly, from a research point of view, claims, in general, made in one domain cannot automatically be transferred to another. (See Chapter 8 for further discussion of this point.)

Lado, interested in being empirical, makes the important distinction (p.7) between those elements of the TL which the student has to learn and the student's current linguistic knowledge. Here he asks a research methodology question: 'How can we design a meaningful experiment on the effectiveness of an oral technique if we do not know specifically what the student *is to learn*, and what he *already knows* because it is *the same* as in his native language?' (Lado 1957, p.7, emphasis added). My view is that Lado has made here a central distinction which appears over and over again in various guises in the SLA literature, but that the equivalence he creates is false: between what the learner 'already knows' and what 'is in his native language'.

As pointed out above, learners do not always transfer to their IL what is in their NL (Gass and selinker 1983a, *passim*), and common sense states that learners may know things important to SLA (e.g. universal grammatical knowledge, knowledge from a third language, cognitive abilities) that cannot be directly related to their NL competence. Lado overstates his case yet again, and perhaps this is where a whole generation of contrastivists (myself included) went astray. To assume that in creating an IL (to put things in more current terms) all that a learner 'already knows', as s/he goes about the process of acquiring an L2, is 'the same' as that which is in his or her NL – as many contrastivists have said at different times – flies in the face of empirical evidence and unfortunately, as a reaction, led for a while to the diminution of language transfer as a force in SLA (Gass and Selinker 1983a, Introduction and *passim*).

Ironically, but understandably, it is Lado's work itself which in part leads to the impetus for creating the database to refute conclusions such as his own just quoted above. Lado's emphasis on empirical studies in CA inspired a whole generation of contrastivists to undertake such studies and to pay attention – careful attention – to their results. As we shall see, 'residue' in CA studies leads to research failure for the general SLA predictions made by contrastivists, but research success in inspiring work directly leading to the continuing discovery of IL.

Most of Lado's work is taken up with providing the first complete statement of the technology of CA, what Lado (p.8) calls: 'working techniques to carry out specific comparisons of two systems of pronunciation, grammatical structure, vocabulary, writing, and cultural behavior'. Each of these is presented in a detailed chapter (2 to 6, respectively), the most detailed – given the structural linguistics of the day – being the chapter on phonology. An important contribution here is that Lado clearly separates out the doing of CA from its application. In his organization of the material presented, he suggests 'three stages' (p.12) of presentation: (a) linguistic analysis of NL/TL sound systems; (b) comparison of these sound systems; and (c) an applied 'description of troublesome contrasts'. Of course, contrastivists discovered over the years that stages (a) and (b) cannot easily be separated (if they can be separated at all); for what is compared and contrasted often, if not always, depends on what is analysed linguistically and how the categories are in fact established. This theme is developed in Chapters 2 and 3. But (c) can clearly be separated out; workers in 'theoretical CA' have indeed separated out description and comparison, on the one hand, from application on the other (cf. e.g. Fisiak 1980 and the review by Gass, 1982).

Contrastive phonology

In Lado's treatment of phonology there is no need to raise the thorny issue we will deal with throughout this book, that of the exact comparability across linguistic systems, since structural linguistics provided the unit to be compared and contrasted: the *taxonomic phoneme*. With the exception of the well-known problem of defining the phoneme in terms of phonetic parameters, Lado deals with the question of 'phonetic similarity between sounds in two languages' (p.15), in an 'admittedly' arbitrary way 'because sounds that are different in one language may be heard as similar in another'. (In the next chapter we will discuss this problem of the break-up of structural patterning by bilinguals.) Lado's usefully detailed suggestions on how to undertake phonological comparisons across linguistic systems are illustrated on p.13 when he provides 'at least three checks' for the comparison of each phoneme:

(1) Does the NL have a phonetically similar phoneme?
(2) Are the variants (the allophones) of the phonemes similar in both languages?
(3) Are the phonemes and their variants similarly distributed?

Lado answers each of these questions 'structurally', i.e. whether or not a particular feature makes a phonemic difference or not. If it does not, then the phoneme and all its distributional allophones should be transferred. Lado's example (pp.14–15) of the English and Spanish phonemes /d/ seems to bear him out, and this is interesting. First, when one looks at English and Spanish /d/, one sees similar phonemes. Thus, one would predict no learning problem. Looking closer, one sees that Spanish /d/ 'has two well-defined variants, a stop variant [d] . . . and a fricative variant [ð]', both distributed differently. Also, note that the latter 'resembles English /ð/'. Lado then describes his extensive experience with Spanish speakers in English, and I have certainly heard Spanish speakers on occasion do what Lado claims: he states that Spanish speakers produce in their English the [ð] variant 'between vowels and after /r/'. Importantly, these are environments in which the variant discussed 'normally occurs in Spanish', and Lado's levels of questions allow him to arrive at these insights. Based on these insights, and others to be discussed below, we come to an important question that we have begun to answer in SLA: Why is it that NL structural features do in fact sometimes correspond to forms in IL? The sort of answer to the question posed would, however, be of a deeper sort than constraints on language transfer, no matter how valuable such insights might be.

It would be in the nature of the response to the question, 'Why does fossilization occur?', a proposed answer having to do with 'identity'. To my knowledge, such answers have not yet been proposed in IL studies and SLA.

Concerning Lado's question 3 above, on p.17 he deals with an interesting case: 'In comparing French with English we would find that French /ž/ as in "jamais" has a parallel English phoneme /ž/ as in "measure".' Lado claims (rightly I believe) that we would find that the variants of these phonemes 'would not cause any particular difficulty'. If we left it there and did not ask Lado's third question above, i.e. are the phonemes similarly distributed, we would miss important CA, and possibly IL, information. Concerning the phoneme in question, '. . . we would notice that in French it appears at the beginning of words and in English it does not. English speakers *will transfer* their /ž/ phoneme with its limitations into French and will *thus have difficulty* with learning the word initial /z/ in that language' (Lado 1957, p.17, emphasis added). What is factually true here? First, the phonemes /ž/ exist in both NL and TL; second, the variants as phonetic segments seem to cause no learning difficulty; third, they are in fact distributed differently; fourth, at times, learners whose NL is English do have trouble pronouncing initial French /z/, i.e. in attempting to acquire French they at times produce [dǰ] for [ž] where a NS of French would produce and would expect [ž]. Fifth, this situation is both a little more complex and a little less complex, since there are alternate, non-allophonic pronunciations of initial [ž-] as in [šwi-] for 'je suis' in rapid speech, non-complicating because initial [šw-] is regularly produced by English speakers with no difficulty. But one cannot deny that some sort of CLI influence is at work with those English speakers who 'substitute' [dǰ] for [ž]. But what exactly is it? Some French teachers have claimed that this substitution is the result of the writing systems 'interfering'. Lado does take up this possibility in his chapter on writing systems, but with other examples. To complexify matters, Briere *et al.* (1968) have pointed out that what might be going on in cases like this should be related more to syllable structure than to words, as in Lado's proposition. Even with this amendment, we still have CLI that can be related to structural differences, of some sort, across linguistic systems.

But, in a contradictory fashion, Lado here hedges the general claim somewhat concerning 'sequences of sounds' by stating (p.17): 'By following through on this matter of distribution of each phoneme we would eventually locate *all* the sequences of phonemes that *might* cause difficulty' (emphasis added). In a positive 'purposeful mis-reading' (see Introduction above) of Lado that removes the word 'all' in this quote and underscores 'might', we find one of the strands leading to IL, in harmony with Lado's strong empirical bent discussed above.

Contrastive grammar

Lado's grammatical chapter (Three), which includes morphology, is particularly important since it studies the area of language most worked on in SLA and provides insights related to the influential teaching technique, 'pattern practice'. In Morley *et al.* (1984) we detail this concept (and misunderstandings of it) in the work of Fries. Lado's work (growing directly out of Fries) on grammatical CA builds on the structural linguistic notion of 'system' and 'grammatical pattern'. As Lado puts it (p. 57): 'Each pattern has a number of features which are the same as some features of other patterns and different from others'. He focuses on 'things which cannot change in English but might normally change in another language'. This is one of the conceptual bases of CA and one we will come back to. Lado has in mind features which do at times turn up, as we have found out, in ILs. He invites us to look at features of English, such as the fact that the word 'the' does not change for number or gender; the word 'light' does not change for number '... when it is a modifier, and it does not change for gender'; the verb 'show' does not change for number '... except in the present tense', etc., contrasting these with 'similar' features in other languages. Lado also intends the doer of CA to concentrate on Fries's quintessential areas of study: word order and function words. IL research has shown that they are both of extreme importance in SLA and, though we return to this theme later, we have already mentioned above an example of where a Lado prediction on L2 word order has shown up in IL studies.

In discussing grammatical transfer, Lado (in the tenor of his times) unfortunately produces (p. 58) a theoretical linkage which has caused a lot of trouble, linking up the concept 'transfer' with the concept 'habit'. In fact, Lado even uses the term 'transferred habits' on the same page. Lado states that 'we understand that the use of a grammatical structure by a speaker depends heavily on habit'. In a sentence widely quoted, he then states that, 'We know *from the observation of many cases* that the grammatical structure of the native language *tends to be transferred to the foreign language*' (emphasis added). There are several points to be made here. First, the phrase 'transferred to the foreign language' is clearly not right. How could NL forms be transferred (even when shown beyond a doubt that they have been transferred) to the TL? In Andersen's (1983) terms, the transfer must be to 'somewhere' and the TL, as spoken by native speakers of that language, is something other than what learners transfer to. The TL is what NSs of the language to be learned speak. It is, for example, the French that NSs of French speak, not what learners, who speak other languages natively, produce when attempting to express and negotiate meanings in French. Inherent in the sentence just quoted from Lado, for me, is the notion of a third system in addition to the NL of learners and the TL to be learned – what in 1969 I first called 'interlanguage' (Selinker 1969, fn 4).

A second point to be made about the sentence quoted in the last paragraph is a happy one: we have moved from the uncontrolled 'observation of many cases' in CA to various types of empirical studies in SLA; SLA, as currently conceived, must have a strong empirical base. Third is a related point, a hard lesson for some to learn, myself included. The 'observation of many cases' may just be misleading. One may end up seeing what one wants to see. Fourth, even with the word 'tend', the conclusion may prove false, since inherent in the notion 'tendency' is a statistical view of things and one is taking tremendous chances in making statistical claims without statistical controls. This point is taken up in detail in Chapter 5. Fifth – and this point was obscured for close to a decade – one can at the same time hold the following two intellectual positions without inherent conflict: (a) that 'language transfer' as CLI does exist and is central to SLA and IL learning, and (b) that language transfer and the theory underlying the concept 'habit' are not by necessity connected. In other words, one can believe in language transfer without being a behaviourist. One wonders why this was not always clear.

Concerning grammatical structure, Lado then (p.59) attempts to link up, in his CA framework, transfer and habits with the concepts 'ease' and 'difficulty' in learning the grammar of a TL. The argument is elegant and it is a shame it turned out to be wrong. The learner, in this CA framework, tends to transfer the habits of his NL structure to the TL which is the 'major source' of ease or difficulty in learning a foreign language. Here is where CA comes in: the structures which are 'similar will be easy to learn because they are transferred and *may* function satisfactorily in the foreign language' (emphasis added). The hedging word, 'may', in this case, should have served – without clearly specified constraints – to show the potential vacuousness of this extreme position. In principle, how can something that only *may* happen under unspecified conditions be '*the* major source' of anything? Concerning 'difficulty', the structures that are 'different' between NL and TL 'will be difficult because when transferred they will not function satisfactorily in the foreign language and will therefore have to be changed' (p.59). Lado's wording is more certain here, which makes the claim, as stated, hard to understand. As has since been pointed out many times (cf. Gass and Selinker 1983a, *passim*), it depends. Some things that are different do not appear to be difficult; some things that are transferred do not function unsatisfactorily in NN/N interaction, but are even preferred (e.g. a chic French accent in English); even if something has to be changed, given the reality of fossilization, the learner may not be able to change it and still may (or may not) function satisfactorily in the TL situation. Again, it depends. Lado's argument concerning 'ease' in learning the structure of the TL is no different, only reversed. I repeat: I believe the argument is elegant; it unfortunately flies in the face of empirical reality. We shall try to make sense of all of this in terms of what is known, as this book develops.

One should note that Lado (1957) consistently touches on issues with which we have not yet learned how to deal satisfactorily. On p.59, for example (following earlier insights by Fries), he points out that there are important differences, in an applied CA sense, between 'production' and 'recognition' in terms of 'the effects of native language transfer'. Lado points out, correctly I believe, that the effects of NL transfer 'are not identical when the learner speaks the foreign language and when he listens to it'. His example is a clear and simple one: the Spanish-speaking student who says in his English 'Can he speaks' does not necessarily have a 'listening' (also called 'recognition') problem in English 'since when native speakers omit the "s" the learner will recognize the question equally well'. This distinction between comprehension and production in SLA is one that keeps reappearing in the literature in various guises and is another problem to which we will be returning at various points in the book. The chain of reasoning from comprehension to production is, as Long (1985) points out, a complicated one. Gass (1988) shows that there are many tricky issues in making this comparison at all.

Lado presents much useful detail (pp.59–66) relating to grammatical differences between languages, and (reinterpreting Lado) possible NL effects on IL structure, 'possible' since, as suggested above, we can now take such CA statements as the best source of hypotheses about language transfer as CLI. In terms of function words, for example, we know that the English word 'do' exhibits different formal characteristics in English ILs to that which would be expected in English TL norms (cf. e.g. Schumann 1978, Huebner 1983). We can thus reinterpret Lado (p.60) as claiming that a Japanese learning English may make an 'interlingual identification' (see next chapter) between 'do' in English questions and 'ka' in Japanese questions, creating an area worth investigating. Lado does in fact make specific predictions which should be testable. With the above example, he claims that, 'A Japanese speaker learning English expects to find a function word equivalent to [ka] and he finds it in "do", but only in part' (p.60). Since the Japanese word is 'fixed at the end of the sentence' and the English word is not, the Japanese learner, it is hypothesized, 'expects to find' an equivalence, but not a total one, word order being 'not significant in the same sense'. As one can see, there are several testable things here – what occurs in Japanese–English ILs, what expectations are involved, their inter-connections, and so on.

Another type of grammatical claim in Lado (1957) appears on pp.60–1, when discussing English vs Chinese word order; he states that 'a Chinese speaker learning English has to learn to place after the head (noun) those modifiers that are phrases or clauses'. It seems to me that this is theoretically a different sort of claim to the one in the previous paragraph. There, transfer is discussed in terms of what a learner 'may do'; here, transfer is discussed in terms of what a learner 'has to do' in terms of TL structure to gain a correspondence of some sort. The latter claim may relate to Swain's (1985) interesting notion of the learner having to produce 'comprehensible output' in order to progress beyond a certain IL stage. Such output is achieved by the learner trying to become more and more 'precise' in TL (especially NN/N) interactions. Studying what the learner 'has to' do is more TL-related than studying what the learner 'may do'.

On p.62 Lado produces what to me seems to be even a different sort of theoretical claim, one which I believe is also testable. In contrasting word order to signal English questions and intonation to signal Spanish ones, he states that: 'In this case, the Spanish speaker *has considerable trouble mastering* the word order pattern of the English sentence, and the English speaker in turn *has considerable trouble using* the intonation pattern as the signal for the question in Spanish' (Lado 1957, p.62, emphasis added). First, of course, 'considerable trouble mastering' is a different sort of claim from 'considerable trouble using'. When one can be said to have 'mastered' an L2 structure is a research question going back to Fries (1945, Chapter 1), and a question that is clearly still with us. The notion of looking at actual SLA use appears to be a more current concern and is usually studied under the rubric of 'communication strategies' (cf. Faerch and Kasper 1983; Bialystok and Kellerman 1987, and the references cited). In terms of data relevant to SLA theorizing, Widdowson's (1978) distinction between grammatical 'usage' (what the result of drills in classrooms is presumably all about) and language 'use' in context (in this case, IL use) is quite valuable. One may logically have trouble mastering what one does (and does not) have to learn in order to interact with speakers of the TL, and once again neither of these may be clearly relatable to CLI. Thus, different sorts of empirical studies are called for in each case raised originally by Lado.

Theoretical claims

We have here, then, at least three generally distinguishable sets of theoretical claims resulting from CA: (1) the learner in an SLA situation 'expects to find' some 'equivalent' in the TL to NL structures, productively, receptively or both; (2) such a learner 'has to learn' to produce something different from his NL in his attempt at learning the TL; and (3) such a learner 'has considerable trouble' (in some way) with a TL pattern which is different from the NL. I have tried to show that each of these involves quite different claims and, furthermore, quite different psycholinguistic relationships to a particular CA in terms of possible language transfer. These, and other, claims are not as clearly separated in Lado's book as one might wish, but to Lado's credit, they have all spurred empirical research in SLA. These relationships will be established as we move through this volume.

The reader should note that this claim becomes difficult to pin down in the absence of particular empirical studies in the relevant research domains concerned. For example, in contrasting word order in English vs inflection in Latin, Lado relates to the functional category, indirect object. He presents several facts showing differences within this same function. He concludes (p.63) 'The English speaker learning Latin *finds a great deal of difficulty* in grasping the subject and indirect object from the inflection of the words in the sentence' (Lado 1957, emphasis added). I can certainly remember 'difficulties' with word order/inflection differences in Latin (vs English) in high school. Unfortunately, I do not have any data, but what could be factually true here? (a) I do not think this difficulty would be a question of production since writing original materials in

Latin was not something we did very much; (b) I do remember this as a question of grammar in learning to do declensions, but if this is (ir)relevant to transfer, then how? (c) In terms of reading Latin texts, I feel sure that I must have confused some cases with others, but . . . . One can make useful hypothesized statements without empirical data, but should be wary of stating categorically what a particular group of learners 'finds difficult' independently of such data.

Another example of Lado as a basic source in SLA is when he leads us (pp.64–5) to a consideration of gender differences, in this case Spanish, English and French. Lado provides the CA information that English and Spanish each have a 'full gender system', but says that it is a mistake to think there will be no learning problems here and goes on to suggest possible examples, such as 'remembering the class to which each item belongs'. We know from IL studies (Tarone *et al.* 1976) that learners regularly do have trouble with TL gender and appear to fossilize in this domain. Gender in IL is quite interesting since getting gender 'right', in TL terms, appears to be a hard thing for many learners to do but getting gender 'wrong' in the TL does not seem to affect getting one's meaning across very much. Importantly, though, gender seems to be one of those 'small' important facts that NSs of a TL use to recognize outsiders to the group. Finally, gender is interesting in IL learning because there is a small set-number of classes for the learner to be concerned with – for example masculine, feminine, neuter. Thus, tight experimental studies of the statistically based kind, well known in sociolinguistics, are possible. In fact, based on Lado's inspiration, this has already been done. Tarone *et al.* (1976), for example, provided a detailed study of systematicity, variability, and stability over time, from the Toronto French-immersion data, based on the theoretical principle of 'per cent correct'. The reader may be interested to note, however, that based on relistening to the tapes cited in Tarone *et al.* we realized that a number of the students were producing in their English–French IL the phonetic segment [lə] for French le and la. If getting meaning across is the main consideration, this is not a bad strategy for English-speaking students learning French. I have tried it myself and find it most effective in apparently reducing 'cognitive load'. This study was based, however, on the concept 'per cent correct' and Bley-Vroman (1983) has found difficulties with this concept, producing a theoretically challenging argument, with which we must attempt to deal in Chapter 8 here. All of this can be directly traced to Lado's work.

Summary

To summarize so far, a careful rereading of seminal works by Fries and Lado is helpful in understanding an important theoretical strand informing us, in part, how we have reached our present point in SLA and IL studies. Additionally, there is much in both authors that is relevant to ongoing concerns, especially if one takes Lado not as a dogma (for it clearly fails when interpreted that way) but as a source of testable hypotheses in SLA about the structure and function of ILs, especially concerning the phenomenon of language transfer.

To conclude, we need to reinforce the view that one dimension of Lado was indeed deeply empirical and that this has by and large been missed in the critical literature. On p.72, Lado (1957) presents a series of important thoughts: 'The list of problems resulting from the comparison of the foreign language with the native language ... *must be considered a list of hypothetical problems* until final validation is achieved by *checking* it against the actual speech of students' (Lado 1957, p.72, emphasis added). In retrospect, I am convinced that this is where IL studies began for me; Lado, as teacher, told us to go out and look. I will take this point up again when discussing the discovery of IL in Chapter 8. It turns out that this empirical dimension is quite realistic, including in its concern the reality of individual differences: 'In this kind of validation we must keep in mind of course that not all speakers of a language will have exactly the same amount of difficulty with each problem. Dialectal and personal differences rule out such a possibility' (*ibid*. p.72). Variation in second language acquisition is now quite accepted (see, for example, Tarone 1979 and the various studies in Gass *et al.* 1989a and 1989b). Lado's statement pre-dates modern sociolinguistics; Robert Lado was way ahead of his time.

Points for discussion

(1) In this volume we are interested in interlanguage reframed (Goffman, 1974) and in the ongoing process of reframing interlanguage. How does the reconsideration of Fries and Lado presented in this chapter affect your views of these original interlanguage statements (from Selinker 1972):

   (a) There are intermediate stages between native language and target language which are observable in a language learner's linguistic output.

   (b) There are interlingual units of identification which might not equal the classical units of grammatical and phonological study.

(c) Successful second language acquisition 'for most learners' is the reorganization of linguistic material from an interlanguage to identity with a target language.

(d) The qualification 'for most learners' in (c) is necessary since most adults (perhaps a mere 5 per cent) who seem to achieve native speaker 'competence' have *not* been taught this performance through explanation and instruction but have somehow overcome language transfer and fossilization and reactivated latent language structures.

(2) As mentioned in this chapter, Fries said: 'Foreign language teaching is always a matter of teaching a "specific" foreign language to students who have a specific "native" language background'. How does this obvious truism relate to your own language learning experiences? Have the textbooks you have used, for example, specified contrastive information between the language you are learning and your native language? Has such information proved useful? If so, how?

(3) As noted above, Fries also said: 'The proper selection and *contrastive* arrangement of the English patterns to meet the special needs of Japanese pupils at the very beginning will determine whether the teaching will be effective and the learning easy or the pupils will be so confused that the teaching will be very difficult and a satisfactory learning almost impossible.' If you have had teaching experience with a contrastive approach, describe from your own experience with 'satisfactory' second language teaching materials how students actively remembered contrastive items related to apparent 'ease' or 'difficulty' in learning the required material. Now describe a relevant 'unsatisfactory' experience.

(4) Specifically concerning Japanese students learning English, Fries stated, as noted above, that the Japanese student '. . . must have, therefore, a set of English materials especially adapted to his linguistic needs, if we want him to learn English well. Such especially adapted materials are most important for the first stage of learning' (Fries 1945). How do such notions as 'stage of learning' and 'first stage of learning' affect the basic contrastive notions discussed in this chapter?

(5) Take a well-known phonological example, such as 'l' and 'r' in English and Chinese or Japanese, and arrange the contrastive data as Lado has suggested: first, ask if the native language has a phonetically similar phoneme. Next, ask if the variants (the allophones) of the phonemes are similar in both languages. Then ask if the phonemes and their variants are similarly distributed.

Rethink these three levels of checks for predicting pronunciation problems. Did they work for the example you have chosen? Might you now wish to revise them? If so, how? How does this approach now fit in with your language learning and teaching experiences?

(6) Reconsider your attempts to learn second language gender in light of the discussion in this chapter. Has the arbitrariness of categories been a problem for you? Now consider multiple language acquisition. Reflect on the following: say you have gone from English, with a minor gender system, to a language with a major gender system, say French. Then you began to learn a third language with a major gender system, say Hebrew. Has the transfer been from your native language to the third language or from the *second* language to the third, i.e. from a first interlanguage to a second?

(7) Discuss some of the major theoretical claims presented in this chapter from the point of view of their reasonableness, as well as from the point of view of your own second language acquisition experiences. For example, consider the three generally distinguishable sets of theoretical claims resulting from CA: that the learner in an SLA situation expects to find some structures in the TL equivalent to NL structures; that a learner has to learn to produce something different from his NL in his attempt at learning the TL; and that a learner has considerable trouble with a TL pattern which is different from the NL. Exactly how do each of these involve different claims regarding interlanguage and second language acquisition?

(8) Finally, discuss some of the major theoretical claims presented in this chapter from the point of view of learning strategies. Choose a source from the literature, such as Oxford (1990) or Cohen (in press). Given the conclusions drawn here, decide which sorts of learning strategies are assumed by Fries and Lado to take place on the part of learners, and compare these with those suggested by more recent sources which are based on empirical evidence.

2 Towards interlanguage: Uriel Weinreich

Bilingualism and interlanguage

As we described in the previous chapter, Lado in 1957 saw 'practical confirmation' for CA in the work of scholars in bilingualism; why this conclusion is problematical is discussed above. In the 1960s, however, I found in their work a further impetus for trying to create a new framework for what second language learners appeared to be actually doing; this framework became known as the 'IL Hypothesis'. It was also clear that we had to devise experimental procedures to test this framework. Chapter 8, concerning the proposing of IL, will pick up the former point; the experiments will be described below in the chapter on language transfer, Chapter 7. Here we will describe and discuss some of the continuing insights for SLA and IL in the work of Weinreich, for Weinreich may be the scholar whose insights have proven most important to the continuing discovery of interlanguage. For some reason, Weinreich's work is not usually featured as basic material in courses in CA, IL and SLA in general, nor is he quoted very much in this literature. For example, in James's (1980) useful book on CA, there is little mention of Weinreich (pp.9, 12). A notable exception in SLA is Odlin (1989) where concepts derived from Weinreich are integrated into extensive discussion of language transfer phenomena.

Weinreich was known primarily for his work in three fields: general linguistics, especially semantics; Yiddish studies (he was a professor at Columbia originally in Yiddish); and studies in bilingualism. It is his work in this latter area that I believe is seminal for this discussion. Along with Haugen, Hockett, Leopold, Garvin and others, he helped organize research into the immigrant languages that were still very much alive in the USA in the 1940s. The interested reader who wishes to look at only one reference may want to look at the Proceedings of a remarkable conference held at Georgetown University in 1954 as part of the 5th Round Table Meeting on Linguistics Studies (Mueller 1954). It was a *Who's Who* of linguistic scholars of the day, focusing on the problems of bilingualism. The summary comment by Weinreich is worthy of note:

> The ideal would be a central institution from which comparative research could proceed. A university with a linguistics curriculum which would be given the means to attract qualified students (perhaps themselves of immigrant backgrounds) and to apportion the field among them would, I think, be the best way of launching such a program.
>
> (Weinreich 1954, pp.48–9)

If the above could not be worked out, Weinreich suggested that specialists should work out a research programme and pilot test it, 'specifying the information we need about every language'. He stressed the 'fullest cumulative value', even if the researchers remained scattered. Weinreich's broad scope and the comparative approach is especially of note. This was an ambitious project and I gather it never really got off the ground. But the effects of these early efforts are with us, for comparative research on ILs is now being done (cf. e.g. Perdue 1984, 1991 for European work; Basham 1989, Beck *et al.* 1989, Beck and Foster 1989 for studies of Eskimo–English and Navajo–English).

The literature on bilingualism is rich – Weinreich (1953) has over 650 items listed in his references; much of it, however, appears to be not immediately relevant to those concerned with SLA and IL studies. As was pointed out in the last chapter, one needs to show empirically in what ways the study of established bilinguals (i.e. speakers of two or more languages from birth) is in fact the same domain of inquiry as learners of an L2 who are in the process of creating an IL. But Weinreich does not restrict himself to studying established bilinguals, since 'developing bilinguals' are also of immediate concern; such speakers at times may be in the mode of IL creation.

Weinreich's work can be seen to be seminal for us if we use Talmudic logic and the criterion of 'continual discovery' as discussed in the Introduction to this volume. Namely, does work on IL and IL learning continually gain from a re-examination of Weinreich's book? I maintain that it does and begin with two brief examples: in my view, two of the concepts in the SLA literature that continue to be of value are 'permeability' (Adjemian 1976; Adjemian and Liceras 1984) and 'transferability' (Kellerman 1977, 1983; Kellerman and Sharwood Smith 1986, *passim*). Both these concepts, to be discussed in later chapters, are foreshadowed in an insightful way in Weinreich.

Additionally, it turns out that phenomena which we now call 'fossilized' were pointed out by Weinreich; these developments are discussed below.

In the Preface to Weinreich's book, Martinet, Weinreich's teacher at Columbia, points out that 'all sorts of intermediate cases' exist between (a) the 'ideal bilingual situation', where an individual can leave aside one totally homogeneous system and shift off to another totally homogeneous system, and (b) the situation 'in the overwhelming majority of cases' where 'some traces at least of structural merger' exist. Martinet's perspective leads directly into Weinreich's, and this can be seen by the fact that the title to Weinreich's book was originally the title to a course on bilingualism given at Columbia by Martinet. Martinet raises for our consideration the concept which 'dialectologists have posited' of 'the permeability of linguistic cells', relating that notion to all sorts of linguistic diversity. As discussed in Chapter 1, Weinreich is clearly puzzled by the synchronic violation by bilinguals of the constraints of linguistic systems, systems that linguistics has to assume to be self-contained (the basic Saussurean position). (Though, as Ferguson (1989) points out, there are problems with this assumption.) Ard (1984, 1989), for example, presents evidence that redundant NL features are used across languages in phonological acquisition. How can it be that a phoneme or a grammatical category, which can gain linguistic 'value' only by its place in a system, have its constraints violated by bilinguals in contact situations? We move to that issue and Weinreich's important suggestions for understanding the phenomena brought about by considerations of permeability.

Interlingual identifications

On p.7, Weinreich (1953) presents *the* concept that led me to an initial understanding of language transfer (Selinker 1966, 1969): *viz* 'interlingual identifications'. We will spend some time on its discussion, believing still that it is a fundamentally correct notion and may even be *the* basic learning strategy in SLA. This concept has also led directly to a reconsideration of 'latent' structures in SLA. A rereading of Palmer's (1921) classic, where 'spontaneous powers' we have in a 'latent state' (p.11) 'are also available for one or more languages' in addition to NL, foreshadows the continuing discussion on the place of universals in SLA. One argument from Palmer's discussion of latent capacity is that 'that capacity never falls into disuse, but continues as a force for the realization of what Halliday

[1973, 1979] calls "meaning potential" of language' (Widdowson 1983, p.27).

Weinreich begins his discussion of 'interlingual identifications' (p.7) by pointing out that the Russian phoneme /p/, in terms of distinctive features, 'cannot be "the same"' as the English phoneme /p/. Yet it is known that one is influenced by the other in language contact situations. Like Lado (see Chapter 1 above), Weinreich (p.3) knows that in comparing structural systems of two languages and having 'their differences . . . delineated', the researcher gains 'a list of the potential forms of interference in the given contact situation'. If we substitute the more neutral term 'language transfer' for 'interference', we see a very current position: 'not all potential forms of interference actually materialize'. Weinreich (pp.3–4) lists twelve sets of 'non-structural factors' that relate to 'the precise effect of bilingualism on a person's speech', stating that it 'varies' with a great many factors. Such factors, continually discussed in the SLA literature, are carefully presented on pp.3–4 and in his chapter entitled 'The Socio-Cultural Setting of Language Contact'.

Weinreich points out (p.7) that what 'cannot be the same' becomes in terms of interlingual identifications 'the same', in the phonological case because 'physical resemblance' of phonetic [p] 'in certain renditions of both phonemes in speech . . . tempts the bilingual to identify the two phonemes astride the limits of the languages'. His example is Russian /t'ip/ 'type' and English /tip/ 'tip', 'both pronounced with similar [p]'. There are several points we can make here: (a) the linguistic notion of 'system', so important to generations of linguists, is somehow 'broken' by the bilingual and by the IL speaker, at least in the learning stage; (b) this breaking of NL and TL systems is done by identifying two items across languages as 'same' (Lado would have used 'similar' here, I believe); (c) in phonology it has something to do with phonetic or physical resemblance; (d) that resemblance in some way 'tempts' the speaker. Weinreich uses the metaphor 'tempt' here to get at the ultimate question of 'why' one would break the constraints of NL and TL to identify something as 'same' or 'similar' in two different systems. Haugen (1954, p.10) points out that whether or not researchers accept the formulation of 'tempting', Weinreich's analysis 'points up the importance of allophonic and distributional data in the making of a bilingual description'. This is a very current position and is correct, I believe, for IL as well. Lado (Chapter 1) was on the right track here, too. One has to ask: Why do allophonic and distributional data appear to mean more to L2 learners than particular language-bound phonemic contrasts? Part of the answer relates to the question of the nature of the linguistic units of IL, to which we return below.

Weinreich continues – and this is where he helped lead me to IL – with more theorizing and other examples, the most important being the following: 'Interlingual identifications can also be made between grammatical relationships ... such as word order.' An English–Russian bilingual, '... comparing English and Russian sentences of the order SUBJECT+VERB+OBJECT ... may identify the English order with the Russian ...' (p.52), even though the functions of these structures in the two languages are different. (Notice the hedging word 'may' that was discussed regarding Lado's claims in Chapter 1.) Importantly, the example Weinreich uses in two places (pp.30, 37) – 'He comes tomorrow home' – relating German word order to the German speaker attempting to speak English, seemed to me to match sentences I regularly heard Israelis produce in their attempted English:

I lived	five years ago	in Tel Aviv.
I bought	downtown	the postcard.
I like	very much	cats.

Initially, the only evidence that Israelis regularly produce sentences such as these was anecdotal. Experimentation (see Chapter 7 on Language Transfer) showed that this sort of thing was both right and wrong, the facts being more subtle than anecdotal evidence could produce.

Weinreich (p.37) uses the sentence 'He comes tomorrow home' as: 'an example of the application of a grammatical relation of word order from one language (German) to morphemes of another (English)'. Two important sorts of evidence are needed to augment Weinreich's account. He presents no evidence to show that this sentence is indeed deviant from American English and that the norm, presumably, is: 'He comes home tomorrow.' Nor, importantly, does he present evidence to show that speakers of other languages whose word order is like English do not also produce utterances of the supposedly deviant type. To show that deviance does exist, it is necessary that parallel NL data be collected; in the 'Language Transfer' chapter below, one way of collecting such parallel data is demonstrated. Wode (1977, 1978, for example) was among the first to show that speakers of NLs whose structure does not match the TL can also produce what seem to be transfer data, which makes unambiguous demonstration of language transfer quite difficult. Wode's data for children raise the thorny problem of the 'cutoff point' between primary and non-primary language acquisition, Zobl (1983) making the suggestion that a 'steady state' in terms of processing heuristics must be attained before one can reasonably differentiate the two types of acquisition.

Such differentiation is important to the Weinreich discussion because, as was pointed out in the last chapter, at least two distinct types of individuals are being studied in the bilingual literature: established bilinguals, with two or more languages from birth or early childhood, and second language learners who become IL speakers. Researchers in bilingual studies have tried to resolve this discrepancy by stating that there is some sort of 'continuum of bilingualism'; the key question then becomes: When does bilingualism begin? I have the feeling that in the IL framework we avoid that question since, it is hypothesized, interlanguage begins at the beginning whenever one attempts to express meaning in the target language (cf. Selinker 1972).

One set of examples that appears in Weinreich (1953, *passim*) makes it clear that at times Weinreich's subject matter is indeed very close to ours. This involves the case of 'Yiddish-speaking immigrants in the United States', something with which he was personally familiar; from my own personal experience, these are IL speakers if there ever were such. On p.7 he discusses immigrants who 'occasionally equated' whole words by their ' "identical" or "similar" phonemic shapes', an example being where the English word 'cold' and the 'dialectal Yiddish /kolt/ "cold"' become phonemically 'the same word'. Given the right NL and TL, it seems to me not unreasonable to assume that this phenomenon might occur in ILs in a fairly widespread fashion. This, of course, would involve a study in the area of the acquisition of IL lexicon, an area of study clearly taking shape (cf. for example Adjemian 1983, Meara 1984 and the papers in Gass 1987). More examples from Yiddish speakers will be brought up below.

On p.39 Weinreich points out that if a bilingual speaker identifies a morpheme or grammatical category of one language (A) with one in another language (B), 'he may apply the B form in grammatical functions which he derives from the system of A'. This would be CLI par excellence. The example presented concerns the American Yiddish speaker who, equating an item in A and B in terms of 'formal similarity', creates a process which enables him, for example, 'to identify /op/ "off" with English up', leading to innovations in American Yiddish, the NL. This would be some sort of 'reverse transfer' from an IL, in this case Yiddish–English, to the NL; this phenomenon has been noted before (e.g. Selinker 1969, 1972); Jakobovits (1970, p.88) called it 'backlash interference'. The effect on NLs of the result of IL learning is almost certainly an important cause of language change and is being investigated in its own right (Trudgill 1986 and references cited there).

Whichever way the contact influence, Weinreich states categorically (p.30) that 'formal similarity or a similarity in pre-existing functions' is what leads the bilingual to establish interlingual equivalence of the morpheme categories. Whether, in current terms, we can state that the CLI is from NL to IL, from IL to NL, from TL to IL, from previous IL to current IL, 'formal similarity and pre-existing functions' appear to be central factors (Gass and Selinker 1983a, *passim*) in the process of interlingual identifications, central enough to be investigated seriously. From the work done on IL as it developed out of these considerations of Weinreich, plus material discussed in Chapter 1, I originally tried to transform these thoughts into a series of (overlapping) general research questions (Selinker 1966, 1969, 1972):

– What does language transfer consist of?
– What actually is transferred?
– How does language occur?
– What types of language transfer occur?
– What leads a learner to establish interlingual equivalence in an IL?
– When does this onset?
– How long does it persist?
– Is the particular influence context-bound in any way?

Gass (1979) adds an important dimension to this series of questions:
– What is the relationship of language transfer to language universals?

Flowing through all these concerns appears one of the central problems of CA:
– What is 'the same' across linguistic systems?

And for this discussion:
– What do L2 learners 'make equivalent' across linguistic systems by the constant comparison that such learners often seem to do?

In my view these latter two questions are epistemologically different questions and not part of the original work in CA. Later we will look at these sorts of questions and see various possible solutions in the CA literature (Chapter 4), investigating whether and how the various analytical solutions relate to L2 learners when they compare what they already 'know' to some sort of internally generated 'target'. For now, we will simply assume that a learner makes these equivalences and try to justify this assumption later.

Reflecting on the relationship of Weinreich (1953) to such questions as why language transfer and the underlying interlingual identifications occur, it was pointed out (Selinker 1972) that Weinreich leaves open the psychological (or psycholinguistic) structure within which interlingual identifications exist. It was postulated there that such a psychological structure must be latent in the brain, becoming activated when a learner attempts to express meanings in a TL and to interact with speakers of the TL. It seemed to me then (and still seems so to me) that it is necessary to postulate this latent psychological structure (LPS), primarily because *no matter what learners do*, they fossilize some part of an IL, often far from TL norms. This fact is reaffirmed in the *Field Manual* (Perdue 1984) of the Second Language Acquisition by Adult Immigrants Project sponsored by the European Science Foundation, where it was concluded, concerning 'guest-workers', that: 'In their daily lives, foreign workers acquire what is most urgently needed, and some even attain a certain fluency. But normally, their acquisition slows down and even stops at a level that is far removed from the language of the world they have to live in' (Perdue 1984, p.19). In Ellis (1982) it was pointed out that Selinker (1972) provides little detail about this latent psychological structure, but this was remedied (at least in part) in neurofunctional terms in Selinker and Lamendella (1978). In any case, if all, or even most IL speakers fossilize, then it is clear that we must assume that they are pre-programmed to do so and this can be explained, as far as I can tell, only by assuming a latent structure of some sort; the working out of this structure is (or should be) a priority for SLA theory. (One valuable attempt based on processing constraints in the literature relates to 'general stages of acquisition' proposed by Pienemann and colleagues. There are several hypotheses in this approach that are congruent to the perspective being developed in this volume, a central one being that 'every learner builds up his or her own grammar'. The interested reader should see, for example, Clahsen 1980; Meisel, Clahsen and Pienemann 1981; Clahsen, Meisel and Pienemann 1983; Pienemann and Johnson 1986; this material is summarized in Pienemann 1989.)

From Weinreich's notion of interlingual identifications and speculations about the existence of a 'latent psychological structure', Ellis correctly points out that this latter notion relates to the debate on the learner's 'initial hypothesis' in IL, i.e. on how the L2 learner 'gets started'. The classical CA (and bilingualism) position, that of Fries/Lado/Weinreich, is that the NL is the starting point. There is speculation throughout the literature on this matter, with Corder (1983) holding that: (a) there is a difference between phonological and syntactic IL learning; (b) for the acquisition of IL phonology, there is 'successive restructuring' from the NL; and (c) for the acquisition of IL syntax, the starting point is not the NL but rather a 'universal' starting point which is something like a 'universal core' (see Chapter 6). My current position is that within this latent psychological structure, the NL both *is* and *is not* the starting point for IL learning. My hypothesis is that the NL is part of where the L2 learner has to be on day one of exposure to input from the TL, because of the pervasive reality of language transfer and, therefore, interlingual identifications. But it cannot be the entire starting point because of the reality of early fossilization of non-L1-like structures (cf. Perdue 1984).

Weinreich's concerns, data and speculation lead us to ponder deeply one question posed above: When do interlingual identifications begin? It seems that it could be as young as three. What is clearly different now from the original IL formulation (and I believe that Merrill Swain should gain the credit for this original observation) is that ILs – under certain sociolinguistic conditions – can begin with children as young as five, the insight being that puberty is not the absolute cutoff point it was suggested to be in Selinker (1972). (Cf. Scovel 1988 for a discussion of this position.) Some children have now been studied for over ten years (see e.g. Harley 1984; Harley and Swain 1984, though, specifically, no 'positive evidence' is reported) and they do appear to fossilize, thus having an IL. These conclusions relate to Toronto French-immersion data. Also, it has been reported (Prahlad, pc) that in certain Indian situations, for example as in the Central Institute for English and Foreign Languages where the mother might speak Hindi, the father Tamil, the maid a local language and the children in the community English outside the home, that ILs can form as young as three. A month's observation informed me that this is indeed a serious hypothesis to investigate.

Another point suggested by reflecting on SLA in terms of Weinreich's notion of interlingual identifications includes consideration of some of the seemingly bizarre interlingual identifications that learners can in fact make. For example, phonetic features that are sometimes identified as 'same' across language can be far from 'similar' across linguistic systems. An anecdote might help here. At the University of Washington, Tarone and I knew a Thai student who regularly, in rapid Thai–English IL speech, said that his field of study was [kwə-la-so-kwi], 'philosophy'. He did this over and over, even when told and told that it was wrong. We were puzzled of course, and investigating, discovered that his NL dialect had [kw] and [f] as variants of the same phoneme. Interestingly, this student could, in slow, careful speech (and with a smile on his face), produce [fi-la-so-fi], attention or monitoring or some such being a key variable.

Weinreich's speculations on interlingual identifications and (as we shall see below) other concepts as well are backed up by an empirical methodology: 'the recorded speech of bilinguals in guided conversations' (p.3); this methodology is akin to what many SLA researchers use today. Importantly, and I find no counter evidence, Weinreich believes that this methodology was used 'apparently for the first time' in his dissertation (Weinreich 1951). He presents (1953) three subsections, which are masterful case studies of linguistic detail in the areas of 'phonic interference', 'grammatical interference' and 'lexical interference' (Sections 2.2, 2.3, 2.4 respectively). My recommendation is a careful study of these matters by colleagues interested in empirical attempts at understanding SLA and bilingualism in one framework. Here we will of course concentrate on the SLA material, but a word of caution should be repeated: Weinreich docs not distinguish, as carefully as we might like, between 'established bilinguals' (as in the Romansch/Swiss–German case in his data) and 'developing bilinguals' (i.e. the IL case, e.g. Yiddish–English speakers or adult English speakers learning Russian). The interested reader just has to work out this distinction for him/herself, example by example, in Weinreich. (Andersen (1983) has done some of this, providing us with reinterpretations of some of Weinreich in his 'transfer-to-somewhere' hypothesis.)

✗A useful concept for IL learning provided by Weinreich (p.18) is that of 'under-differentiation' vs 'over-differentiation' of phonemes. The former occurs 'when the sounds of the secondary system whose counterparts are not distinguished in the primary system are confused'. The latter involves 'the imposition of phonemic distinctions from the primary system on the sounds of the secondary system when they are not required'. Weinreich points out (p.21) that over-differentiation, the substitution of 'a single phoneme for two phonemes ... invariably leads to a unilingual listener's disorientation'. The extremeness of the 'invariably' phrase aside, Weinreich is talking here about what we would now call NN/N interaction and provides a testable area for language transfer studies. This distinction is much quoted in the CA and early SLA literature and is particularly shown to have relevance to IL by Levenston (1971).

Weinreich provides what is clearly an IL example of CLI (p.22) when he discusses the transfer of the phonetic NL Yiddish rule of placing [h] as a 'non-phonemic glide between any two vowels' into American English. Accordingly, the production of English 'his arms' and 'two heads' '. . . will be rendered correctly', whereas 'two arms' '. . . will sound [tu harmz] . . .' while 'his head' will appear as [hiz ed]. Weinreich concludes that: 'In both examples, the bilinguals' under-differentiation is noticed but his phoneme substitution is incorrectly classified.'

In a section (p.20) that is purely about SLA, Weinreich quotes with approval the early CA work of Reed, Lado and Shen (1948) – a precursor to Lado 1957, discussed in Chapter 1 – comparing Spanish, Chinese and Portuguese sound systems with English as the TL. But he wisely points out, with foresight, that 'the many unsolved problems in this domain cry for structural solutions'. Weinreich presents the interesting case of neither French nor Russian having /ð,θ/ phonemes, 'but in contact with English', French speakers 'tend to render English /ð,θ/ as [z,s], while Russian speakers generally pronounce [d,t]'. I would like to make two points: (a) once again we have the hedged statements 'tend to' and 'generally' which signify that not all French or Russians do this, and without empirical evidence, this is correctly stated; and (b) given (a) where not all speakers do this, it is clear that what is predicted by abstract linguistic structure alone is clearly not powerful enough to account for all IL facts. Importantly, Weinreich attempts a 'structural explanation' in terms of 'continuance' vs 'mellowness' of phonetic features, which does not seem particularly enlightening in retrospect. However, the setting up of the problem from applied CA 'for theoretical purposes' provides one of the first 'residues' mentioned in Chapter 1, namely facts unaccountable by classical CA theory.

The 'phonic treatment of transferred morphemes' is presented in a useful subsection (Section 2.25). Speakers often appear to have choices here, as, for example, the Yiddish speaker who was able to choose to integrate into his NL Yiddish utterances his English pronunciation of 'Washington' either as /vasington/ or by making an 'effort to retain as much as possible the English sounds'. In a parallel IL situation, one place I have had trouble in Hebrew rapid speech (and I gather I am not unique here) is in overcoming my NL stress patterns and accompanying reduced vowels in borrowed words. One such example would be 'minister' which in TL terms should come out something like [minister], high-front vowels, the final vowel not reduced at all and the final consonant a voiced uvular fricative and with stress on the final syllable (given my native dialect, I 'should not' have this final consonant at all). Strangely enough, though, my NL English spelling has in fact been helped by referring to Hebrew pronunciation of a borrowed word, where an English vowel reduction is involved, e.g. [komparativi], [demokracia], [administracia] (comparative, democracy, administration). It is of interest to speculate how much of language is 'choice', especially regarding IL and interlingual identifications; such choice is a peculiarly neglected IL research area.

Weinreich's introductory paragraphs on grammatical interference (Section 2.31) are of particular importance to SLA and IL learning. He attempts to solve the deep disagreement among linguists at the time as to whether there exists a 'possibility of grammatical influence' across languages and, if so, its importance. This debate mirrors a more recent debate in SLA which is summarized in the Introduction to Gass and Selinker (1983a). Weinreich's summary of the argument is worth reading for historical interest as well as for the light shed on the phenomenon of language transfer itself. He suggests that one should treat the particular distinctions argued about 'for comparative purposes as matters of degree' (p.29). An example would be the 'degree of boundedness' of morphemes in a language for bilingual purposes. This degree of boundedness: '. . . is easily handled as a variable. The main requirement is that in a given contact situation, both languages be described in the same terms.' I cannot recall where, in the large SLA literature on morpheme acquisition, degree of boundedness of morphemes is integrated into the discussion. As we rethink that literature in terms of more current SLA thought, we should be sure to consider carefully Weinreich's suggestions in this regard. One place to start would be to reframe the data in the several studies on bound morphemes discussed in Odlin (1989) in continuum terms.

Weinreich's solutions to descriptive problems foreshadow and inform many of today's solutions to such problems, e.g. his noting (p.29) that 'grammatical functions which are performed in one language by morphemes may be identified' by bilinguals with 'relations of another language'. This, in my view, is one of the beginnings of the attempt, undertaken by many current scholars, to constrain a theory of language transfer (see e.g. Gass and Selinker 1983a, especially Part III and Afterword; Kellerman and Sharwood Smith 1986, *passim*). Weinreich uses the observation just quoted to set up an 'absolute' distinction: 'morphemes' vs 'grammatical relations', on which a large portion of the SLA literature, in the 1970s especially, has concentrated, either on the acquisition of morphemes or grammatical relations such as subject, object or criteria related to word order in ILs.

Transferability

Weinreich also foreshadows a continuing dilemma: transfer vs borrowing (see e.g. Corder 1983; Adjemian 1983; Sharwood Smith 1983). He points out (p.30) that 'morphemes and grammatical relations belonging to one language can occur in the speech of another language as "borrowings"', and that these are also 'subject to interlingual identifications in the sense defined' above. Corder (1983) points out the theoretical need to keep these transfers and borrowings separate, but admits that in practice this is often quite difficult. One can relate this issue to others raised above: What exactly is transferred and when and to what extent is language transfer predictable? As I understand Corder's position, he relegates borrowing to an unpredictable performance category, with Adjemian (1983) apparently agreeing and setting up the permeability issue as one of performance as well (cf. also Adjemian and Liceras 1984). Issues related to what is transferred are discussed in the empirical chapter on language transfer (Chapter 7).

Weinreich, again in a current vein, handles the predictability question (31ff) as 'the likelihood of transfer', raising two research questions we are still pondering: (a) Are forms belonging to some classes 'more subject to transfer than others'?   (b) How are the 'transferred morphemes . . . integrated with the recipient grammar'? (The notion 'recipient' and its counterpart 'source' will be discussed in the next chapter.) The following sentence foreshadows, it seems to me, Kellerman's view (1983) that transferability (i.e. the likelihood of transfer) of items is affected by the learner's 'psychotypology', i.e. the amount of closeness the learner feels the TL is from the NL in particular domains. Weinreich writes: 'The transferability of a class of morphemes is a function of both systems in contact, not just one' (p.34). On this and the next few pages, Weinreich provides a series of predictions as to which grammatical/functional classes are 'less likely to be transferred', 'less transferable', and whether or not the transfer of a class 'may be facilitated'. Weinreich (p.35) relates the notion 'likelihood of transfer' to a 'scale of adoptability' discussed by Haugen (1953) (and ultimately credited to Whitney (1881)), pointing out 'its still hypothetical nature as far as bilinguals' speech is concerned'. The hypotheticalness of 'likelihood of transfer' or 'transferability' is still under investigation.

Weinreich (p.36) attributes the origin of the notion of 'transferability' to Haugen in a section that shows how difficult it is to do word class statistics in the bilingual domain and come up with unambiguous results. In a further discussion of word order (p.38), Weinreich shows the richness of his approach in moving from Swiss–German bilingual children in Romansch to examples from 'idiomatic Yaqui' (p.38). His discussion here, where he points out that 'examples of interference in word order are plentiful', foreshadow and make more believable some of the sentences which appeared in the early French-immersion data (Selinker, Swain and Dumas 1975; Tarone, Frauenfelder and Selinker 1976). Sentences such as the following (gathered from spontaneous conversations, word games and picture description tasks), backed up by ones in Romansch (produced on the Swiss–German pattern), make their IL existence more believable as fact:

French immersion sentence:	*Gloss discernible from context:*
Il veut moi de dire français à il.	He wants me to speak French to him.
Un chalet où on va aller à.	A cottage that we're gonna go to.

Weinreich presents an example of the latter type of sentence in a Romansch sentence produced 'on the Schwytzerdutsch pattern in which adverbial complements come last in the main clause'. Weinreich, like Lado as discussed above, predicts for us the *possible* shape of IL data which more careful studies, with more stringent empirical controls, could seek to validate.

Weinreich (p.44) summarizes that the transfer of individual morphemes is possible under favourable structural conditions, 'such as a pre-existing similarity in patterns' and some other more minor conditions he lists. Yet, as he also concludes: '. . . not every conjuncture of favorable structural conditions results in *permanent grammatical interference* of the type one might predict' (Weinreich 1953, p.44, italics added). In some crucial sense, despite all the progress made in SLA and IL studies, this is where we still are today: (a) certain structural conditions, in a comparative sense, seem necessary for language transfer to occur; (b) even with these 'favorable structural conditions', transfer might not occur; (c) 'permanent' grammatical influence (i.e. part of what we would call fossilization today) exists and is to be expected as normally occurring; (d) the particular structural features chosen by learners to be made salient in CLI cannot, by looking at the NL and TL features alone, be predicted (whether they can ever totally predicted is still open to question; for some evidence of randomness in IL phonology, see Ard 1984).

Thus, the central and still intriguing questions persist and Weinreich helps us to comprehend them, for example as by his prescient claim that no one transfers his entire NL morphology system to the IL.

– What is and is not transferred?
– When is language transfer produced and when not?
– How long will transfer persist?
– Are we equally sure in every case of 'discovered' transfer that we actually have CLI at work?

Weinreich helps us to research these questions by concluding that 'there is a selection of phenomena and a complex resistance to interference'. This also foreshadows a consensus position – that language transfer is a 'selection' phenomenon (see e.g. Gass 1984). Finally, he lists possible influences, both psychological and socio-cultural, which we need to consider today, if it is the case that 'identity' is important to all of this, as Preston (1989) especially argues. If so, a careful rereading of the comprehensive discussion in Weinreich (1953) for current insight is in order.

We end this brief look at some continuing influential portions of Weinreich by quoting the following plea: 'For an analysis that can do justice to the complexity of linguistic facts, the data must be obtained, first and foremost, from the flowing speech of bilinguals in the natural setting of language contact' (Weinreich 1953, p.44). Progress is clear here, for the normal state of affairs now in SLA and IL studies is to gather such data. We owe much to Weinreich (and, as we shall see, to his student, Labov) for pointing us in this direction.

We now move to a central question of 'interlingual identifications': What do learners identify as 'same' across linguistic systems? What are the logical and empirical possibilities from which learners can draw? We approach our study initially in terms of the classical CA question: What is comparable across linguistic systems? We do so with a detailed examination, in the next few chapters, of various types of data and approaches, beginning with Lattey's question: 'What is the "same thing" in interlinguistic comparison?'

Points for discussion

(1) Consider Weinreich's concept of interlingual identifications, i.e. that the learner makes the same what 'cannot' be the same across linguistic systems. Do you agree that interlingual

identifications are necessary for language transfer to occur? It was also concluded from Weinreich that for language transfer to occur, certain structural conditions, in a comparative sense, are necessary. Choose two examples from this chapter and discuss them in light of Weinreich's conclusion that language transfer is a 'selection phenomenon'. Then find an example from your own language learning to match against the ones presented. Repeat with two examples from the previous chapter.

(2) We also concluded from Weinreich that what he calls 'permanent' grammatical influence is in large measure what we would call today 'fossilization'. Relate fossilization to the language transfer examples you discussed in (1). Relate fossilization to language transfer concerns in general. Specifically, for fossilization to occur is language transfer (always) necessary? How do you know?

(3) Consider Haugen's statement about Weinreich's analysis as developed in this chapter. Haugen states that Weinreich's analysis 'points up the importance of allophonic and distributional data in the making of a bilingual description'. The implication here is that 'allophonic and distributional' information may be *more* important to L2 learners than to native speakers involved in language-bound phonemic constraints. Evaluate this point in terms of the 'breaking up' of linguistic units as discussed in this and the previous chapter.

(4) Consider Lado's 'techniques of comparison' discussed in the last chapter. The point in (3) also seems to imply that for L2 learners such information may be *more* important than the phonemic information emphasized by Lado. How would you empirically try to determine the factual status of this claim?

(5) Consider the concept of 'linguistic value', the idea that phonological and grammatical items gain linguistic value only by their place in a native language system. Do you agree that language learners and bilinguals regularly violate the phonological and grammatical categories of their native language? That in trying to learn another language, they pull apart these native language categories? In the final analysis, why do you think that the constraints of native language are violated in language contact situations?

(6) Weinreich discusses sentences of the type 'He comes tomorrow home,' sentences that Germans regularly produce in their English (i.e. a time–place word order after the verb), but he does not give empirical evidence to back up his claim for the

occurrence of such sentences. Design a study that will produce
evidence that bears on this claim. Try to be very clear as to the
rationale you give linking your study to the general claim. You
might want to link your study to the proposed 'general stages of
acquisition' based on processing constraints proposed by
Pienemann and colleagues and mentioned in the chapter with
regard to latent structures and fossilization. If you do, then use
the original sources referenced in the chapter by Clahsen,
Meisel, and Pienemann and Johnson.

(7) Weinreich attributes such sentences as those in (6) as deriving
from the application to their English of native language German
word order. Expand the design of your study in (6) to include
this important set of variables.

(8) In this chapter there is a discussion of sentences produced by
Israelis in their English similar to that described in (6), e.g. 'I
lived five years ago in Tel Aviv,' where after the verb one also
sees a time–place word order. Ask yourself: How can it be that
speakers of a Germanic language, German, and speakers of a
Semitic language, Hebrew, can both produce sentences of the
same structure in their English?

(9) Choose a more current reference that is mentioned in the
chapter, one that is presaged by Weinreich's or Martinet's work
– for example Adjemian on 'permeability', Kellerman on
'transferability' or Gass on language transfer as a 'selection'
process – and compare the more current account with the
original as described here. Go to Weinreich (1953) and
compare and contrast the original with the two others.

(10) Both Weinreich, in this chapter, and Lado, in Chapter 1, use
such phrases as the speaker 'tends to transfer', 'may identify the
English word order with the Russian'; or that such and such
'might cause difficulty'. Discuss theoretical, practical and
methodological implications of creating general statements
about learners which use in them hedging words such as 'tend',
'may' and 'might'. Look up three references provided by the
bibliography at the end of this volume. Take a general statement
about L2 learners from these sources and insert one of these
hedging words if not already there. Evaluate the factual status of
the statement and suggest a way out of any difficulties that such
a statement provides.

3   Units and equivalence across linguistic systems: Some bilingual data

Equivalence in interlinguistic comparison

In the title to her 1982 paper, Lattey succinctly puts one of the themes that runs throughout these pages: 'What is the "same thing" in interlinguistic comparison?' (Lattey 1982, p.131). It is a theme that runs throughout the volume in which Lattey's paper appears – the proceedings of a conference on the contrastive grammar of English and German (Lohnes and Hopkins 1982). In the context of this discussion, the question is broadened to include not only the analyst's perspective but also the learner's and language user's perspective. (Cf. Widdowson 1983 for extensive discussion on analyst perspective vs the learner/user perspective.) Now we are at the heart of one of the most puzzling aspects of IL and IL learning. We discussed this issue in the last chapter in terms of the domain of research in bilingualism. Weinreich, and other scholars of that generation, speculated long and hard on what they saw as a paradox. Units of linguistic structure have linguistic 'value' only in terms of the place of these units within a linguistic system and the constraints of such units within that system, while at the same time individuals in a language contact situation clearly violate, on a regular basis, such constraints. Lado, as pointed out in Chapter 1, had little problem in general dealing with this issue since he accepted the units given by structural linguistics of his day, especially the 'taxonomic phoneme', which was his unit of phonological comparison. As will be discussed at the end of this chapter, and in other places in this volume, there is reason to believe that regarding IL, the picture is more complex than accepting a structural linguistic unit. Weinreich, on the other hand, has a clear and cogent answer to this question, one which I feel is essentially correct and which is discussed in detail in Chapter 2: units become 'the same' for the learner across linguistic systems in contact by means of 'interlingual identifications'; the research task then becomes to work out the facts of such identifications and underlying reasons for things being the way they are. These pages should help give substance to this view.

Applied linguists trained in the 1950s and 1960s were usually provided with the opportunity to gain a solid introduction to the literature of bilingualism, as well as to the carrying out of bilingual studies. In this spirit, I would now like to describe in some detail a bilingual study revised here in light of more current insights into IL. (This study originally appeared as Selinker 1967.) In retrospect, it seems that we were struggling to derive analytical tools for the empirical study of bilingualism related to some of the research questions discussed in the previous chapter. The most important were: exactly what gets transferred, and how does language transfer work? These concerns led eventually to the extended discussion of units of IL learning which appeared in the 'Interlanguage' paper in 1972.

Specifically, in this chapter, we report on the results of a bilingual study of some elements in Israeli Hebrew (IH) which historically came about as a result of several languages in contact. As it applies to the questions raised at the beginning of this chapter, this study is backed up by some insights drawn from a second study on IH (Selinker 1970). The purpose of this latter study was to try to establish the basic clausal units of IH. A final theoretical discussion here looks at the status of studies in bilingualism generally, presenting a surprising comparison with studies in IL in SLA.

Historically, the proposing of the IL concept (Chapter 8) fits in with the study of bilingualism in that as a result of the studies reported in this chapter, I began to see many similarities with what Israelis are doing in English and began to wonder how to study that empirically; some of this material is reported in the previous chapter and more later (see especially the empirical chapter on language transfer, Chapter 7).

We begin the discussion by presenting some general background information on studies in bilingualism, focusing initially on semantic, especially lexical, phenomena. First, however, two important definitions, standard to bilingualism studies. 'Recipient' language or culture refers to the 'borrower' language or culture. 'Donor' language or culture refers to the 'source' language or culture which is borrowed from. (Sometimes the more transparent terms 'borrower' and 'source' are used respectively.) In general, when a recipient culture borrows a new item or a new concept, its language often borrows the name of the item or the description of the concept from the donor language, often called a 'loanword'. However, most interestingly, this type of clear linguistic borrowing in no way accounts for all of the possibilities. Haugen (1953, Ch. 18) devotes one chapter of his massive work to lexical problems other than loanwords, discussing in that chapter 'loanblends', 'loanshifts', and their combinations in compounds. Hockett (1958, Ch.48) follows Haugen, but does not discuss the combination compounds of loanblends and loanshifts. Both Haugen and Hockett owe their initial inspiration to Bloomfield (1933, Ch.25), who describes, but does not label, many of the phenomena. Weinreich (1953, Section 2.4) differentiates between 'simple words' and 'compound words and phrases', mentioning the types of 'interference' possible under each subcategory. In a later paper (1954, p.45) he describes the mechanisms of non-loanword lexical influence as being 'loan translations' and a blending of loan translations and loanwords. Di Pietro (1961, p.1) sets up the following three categories of lexical change due to language contact: replacive (former term disappears), additive (both terms remain in use) and expansive (a new term comes into use where none existed before). In a subsection entitled 'European categorization in Israeli Hebrew', Rosén (1955 pp.80–1) briefly mentions, in addition to loanwords, loan translations and 'extensions' of ancient Hebrew words. Thus, even this cursory review of some of the relevant literature shows that these various classifications overlap and perhaps are not even all-inclusive. We may need our own categorization. (Cf. Romaine 1989, which provides a different classification.)

In what follows, we present the results of an application of linguistic analytical tools to a particular aspect of a particular situation of language contact, struggling for an understanding of the problem of units and equivalence across the particular systems in contact. The language contact situation under study involves the most influential languages – i.e. Arabic, English, French, German, Polish, Russian and Yiddish – that have come into contact with Modern Hebrew (MH) since its inception as a spoken language in the latter part of the nineteenth century. Important to bilingualism theory (and relevant to the discussion at the end of this chapter), the result of this contact, added to the 'natural drift' of any living language (Sapir 1927), would be the language of today. That is, in this case, the result of this contact added to the natural drift of MH founded on classical literary sources is the IH of today. The data presented here, starting with simple loanwords, call attention to some of the complexity for the selection of one item and the rejection of another in linguistic influence in language contact situations (cf. Weinreich 1953, Section

2.43). The data are presented in terms of six semantic, especially lexical, categories: (1) expansive; (2) additive; (3) replacive; (4) loanshift; (5) loan translation; (6) loanblend. This categorization, which leads us to a discussion of units and equivalence in terms addressed above, reveals that each category has both a formal and a semantic aspect with the exception of (4), loanshift, for which no new forms are found in this study.

For the concerns raised in this discussion, the exact donor language of each example need not concern us here overmuch. In fact, scholars working in this area do not seem in agreement among themselves as to which language in some cases is the exact donor language and even which has been the most frequent donor language to MH. Rosén believes that 'English, German, French and Arabic', in that order, have been most influential (1955, p.36). Blanc has alternated between several different opinions. At one point he specifically disagreed with Rosén, stating that 'Yiddish ... indubitably ranks first and foremost in the non-Hebraic sub-stream of Israeli Hebrew' (1956, p.759). In 1957 he listed the primary source as 'Standard Average European' (SAE), i.e. 'the many lexical and phraseological features which European culture holds in common' (Blanc 1957, p.400). Rosén also discusses a general substratum, but one consisting of common elements 'that crystallize and disappear, of the world wide language of the educated' (Rosén, 1955, p.36). Relevantly, in terms of IL learning, I do not believe that the interesting possibility of some sort of IL substratum has been investigated for particular ILs, i.e. features which might be resultant in IL from some sort of widespread though not universal source. It seems to me to be very possible that such phenomena exist in language transfer, even in some of the data collected to date.

The information we will use in this chapter on MH and IH derives from three general sources. Much more could have been added, of course, but the purpose of this data is not to be exhaustive about IH but to understand the issues involved in equivalence across linguistic systems and the ongoing process of comparison in SLA. The first source of information involves the works of those authors interested in issues of 'better style' in MH (e.g. W. Chomsky 1957; Frank 1961; Gruber 1950). The second general source involves structurally oriented linguists, usually opposed to those in the first group on matters of data as well as theory (e.g. Bar Adon 1959; Blanc 1953, 1954, 1956, 1957, 1960; Morag 1959; Rosén 1955, 1962; Weiman 1950). The third source is the present author's intuitions about IH (in doubtful cases checked by native-speaking Israeli linguists) after over a quarter of a century's experience with the language. The reader may know that the lack of agreement on just what IH is could be a serious problem if this chapter were in fact about IH. In describing the changes in MH due to language contact, the various systems of transcription have been standardized to accord with Blanc (1960, p.8).

Category 1: expansive

The first bilingualism category we will look at occurs when the recipient language borrows the name of an item or the labelling of a concept along with the importation of that item or concept. This is an easy category to spot in IH; examples abound and are immediately transparent: /kategoria/ 'category', /televizia/ 'television', /stratosfera/ 'stratosphere', /metafizika/ 'metaphysics', etc. Such forms are usually 'reshaped' to the phonemic patterns of the recipient language. As was pointed out in Chapter 2, it seems difficult for some English speakers in their English–Hebrew IL to gain a TL approximation of these forms in conversational NN/N interaction. This suggests that in IL 'coexistent phonemic systems' exist as Fries and Pike (1949) suggested in a related case many years ago, what we might today call IL lect-switching (cf. Preston 1989 for discussion of the advantages and disadvantages of the notion 'lect' in SLA). Reshaping into IH appears to be the case with two interesting exceptions:

(a) The IH phonemes /tč/, /dʒ/ and /ž/ do not occur in classical Hebrew. Some linguists who wish to recognize them as phonemic in IH by standard tests are sure they have come into the language as the result of borrowings (though the source is not always agreed on), e.g. /tčips/ 'French-fried potatoes', or 'chips' in British English; /dʒip/ 'a jeep'; and /ʒaket/ 'a jacket' (Blanc 1960, p.18). In fact, the consonantal writing system of IL has been modified slightly to accept these new 'letters'.

(b) After borrowing, stress is usually retained on the syllable where it occurred in the donor language, even when inflectional suffixes, which take the stress in IH, are added (Bar Adon 1959, p.37; Blanc 1960, p.31), e.g. /atóm/ 'atom' (from French); /atómim/ 'atoms'; /atómi/ 'atomic'. In terms of equivalence across systems in this case, one can say that atomic, as a 'word', is borrowed into IH since its original stress patterns are retained.

The reason this first category is called 'expansive' is that the name is intended to convey the fact that 'semantic shifts' can occur after borrowing, with the new word (or more probably the 'root'

morpheme) taking on a meaning in the recipient language that it did
not have in the donor language. My favourite example concerns the
English word 'puncture', which has been 'phonemically reshaped' as
/pantčer/. The meaning of the IH word is not 'pierce with a pointed
instrument' but 'something that has gone wrong', which is, of course,
what happens when a tyre is punctured. The word /kvaker/ does not
mean 'Quaker oats' for some speakers, but 'any cereal'; /finjan/,
which means 'a coffee cup' in Jerusalem Arabic, has come to mean
'an Arabic coffee pot' in IH. There are indeed many such semantic
shifts in IH which Blanc, Bar Adon and others detail. These surely
must exist in IL, though no studies here come to mind.

Category 2: additive

The second category concerns a new form and an old form existing
side by side for a while, usually with no apparent differentiation in
meaning. Words coming into 'competition' in the language contact
situation has been discussed by Weinreich (1953, pp.54–6; 1954,
p.45) and Diebold (1961, p.108) discusses this question in detail with
regard to Spanish interference on the Huave semantic system. (The
notion of such 'competition' may prove important in the long run as
regards the relationship of IL behaviour to abstract linguistic
categories. Cf. Gass (1988), who points out that SLA is where one
can study competing linguistic systems, proving its importance to
linguistic theory.) In IH, the loanword /telegrama/ 'telegram' was
introduced into MH several generations ago. To some speakers this
word 'sounded foreign' and a new word, /mivrak/, based on the
biblical root /b-r-k/ 'lightning', was invented and introduced into the
language. Interestingly, in this case the more native Hebrew word
seems to be winning out. However, to this observer (and there will be
dissenters), at the present time there appears to be free variation, for
some speakers at least, between another pair: /administracia:hanhala/
'administration'.

A related phenomenon occurs when certain European loanwords
'have not preserved their original meanings in full' (Morag 1959,
p.260; cf. Blanc 1954, p.388). For example, these sources point out
that /energia/ in IH means 'energy', but usually only in the scientific
sense. For other semantic aspects of 'energy', as used in SAE, IH
uses the original NL term /merec/. The IH form /reakcia/ means
'an historical reaction', while /tguva/ means 'a personal reaction' or
'a chemical reaction'. The term /sociali/ means 'social' as regards
social work, but for most other meanings of 'social' from SAE, the

ancient Hebrew term /xevrati/ is used. This latter term would also involve an 'extension of meaning' from its use as an abstract noun meaning 'association' or 'company' in its biblical sense (Job, 34:8).

The semantic limits of terms such as these do not always seem clear and surely lead to IL confusion. That is, in such cases of competing forms, alternations from native speaker to native speaker, and sometimes within the usage of the same speaker, may occur. It has been impossible for this writer, an IL though fluent speaker of Hebrew, to discern, for example, even after asking many NSs, a clear demarcation of the semantic ranges of such overlapping terms as /oto/, /mxonit/, /teksi/, /monit/, /prayvit ka/ – all of which appear to refer to cars, automobiles and taxis. The sources (both printed and pc) just do not agree.

Category 3: replacive

In languages in contact, a new term may replace a former term, with the latter either disappearing entirely from the language or being used infrequently in special situations, e.g. formal literary style. This does not appear to have happened very extensively in IH, but there are some examples. The form /universita/ 'university' is now universally heard replacing an earlier form /mixlala/. The word /hatiz/ 'splash' has just about been replaced by /špric/, a Yiddish word of similar meaning. The latter has completely assimilated to the IH verb conjugation, with the initial consonant cluster functioning as a single consonant of the usual tri-consonantal root (e.g. /šp-r-c/ vs /d-l-k/ as in /maspric/ 'splash' (sing. present tense); /madlik/ 'light' (sing. present tense); /hišpracti/ 'I splashed'; /hidlakti/ 'I lit', etc.). Another example of this highly adaptive phenomenon is the common replacement of /hezia/ 'sweat' by the Yiddish word /švic/. In this latter example, since there already is a 'tri-consonantal root', there is no structural need in the verb conjugation to have a consonant cluster function as a single consonant. So, what appears to have happened historically in these sorts of cases is that first a noun is borrowed, then an already existing form is replaced, then there is a 'need' to use this noun as a verb. This is no trouble if the borrowed noun has three consonants, which allows the recipient language to accommodate it easily into the verbal declensions. If, on the other hand, there are four consonants in the borrowed noun, a strange thing happens: two consonants are identified interlingually as one, I hypothesize, and the usual verbal declensions then occur.

Category 4: loanshift

In terms of lexical change, a new item or concept may be borrowed without its original name and the individual borrower 'may somehow adapt material already in his own language' (Hockett 1958, p.411) by making 'morphemic substitution without importation [i.e. by] changes in the usage of native words' (Haugen 1950, pp.215, 219). If 'native' here were to be substituted with 'present state of IL', I would think that IL learners would regularly use this strategy. Usually this phenomenon involves an 'extension of meaning' given to an already existing term in the recipient language. This is a widespread phenomenon in language contact situations:

Term	Biblical meaning	Extension of meaning due to language contact
zerem	'stream'	'stream (of history)'
	'current'	'(electrical) current'
nešef	'evening'	'soirée, social gathering'
sviva	'surroundings'	'cultural environment, milieu'

(adapted from Weiman 1950, Ch. 6)

The recipient language identifies a semantic or conceptual feature as 'the same' across languages and 'extends' an already existing word through this usage. IL learners surely do this as well, though data appear to be lacking.

Sometimes an MH word will sound like an SAE word and may then acquire an extension of meaning in that way. Weiman (1950) states that /mxona/, whose original meaning was 'fixed place, base, stand, etc', received its new meaning 'machine' on the basis of words like German Maschine, Mechanik, etc. and similar words in other European languages. He also cites /mapa/ 'map', which originally meant only 'cloth or napkin', and /masexa/ 'mask', which originally meant 'moulten image'. Is there an IL point here as well? Most of the earliest speakers of IH (end of the nineteenth and beginning of the twentieth century) were clearly IL speakers of MH. Weinreich does talk about similar cases (see Chapter 2), noting that 'phonetic similarity . . . tempts' the bilingual to identify items across languages as the same.

Category 5: loan translation

A loan translation involves a new item or concept which is imported from a donor to a recipient culture and is translated literally. This area of bilingualism studies is particularly important to us because it touches on the CA/IL concept of language transfer. Often it is not known if the source of an IL form is transfer or translation. This is particularly true of syntactic processes; the problem is discussed in Tarone *et al.* (1976, 113ff). In IH, translation of NN concepts is quite frequent and may involve morphological or syntactic constructions.

(a) Morphological constructions are often built quite consciously on a foreign model. The word /iton/ 'newspaper' is an example of this process:

German	Hebrew	Gloss
Zcit	et	'time'
Zeitung	iton	'newspaper'

(The shift of the initial /eˑi/ in /iton/ is due to a morphophonemic change that need not concern us here.) In terms of assimilation to the recipient language, many new morphemes enter IH as abbreviations of translations. Blanc (1956, p.779) cites the following three examples:

/makab/	‹	/mikla beynoni/	'medium machine gun'
/xarap/	‹	/xeyl refua/	'Medical Corps'
/lap/	‹	/loxma psixologit/	'psychological warfare'

The assimilation occurs since abbreviations on this pattern are not limited to loan translations but are a common process in Hebrew.

(b) Syntactic constructions begin to take us away from purely lexical concerns to other areas involving semantic effects on language constructions. For IH, Blanc (1954, pp.388–9) provides some examples: /mxonat ktiva/ 'a typewriter' (literally 'a writing machine' assimilated to IH morphosyntactic processes) may have come from the French machine à écrire or from the German Schreibmaschine. The form /gan yeladim/ 'kindergarten' (literally 'garden (of) children', assimilated to IH in almost the same way as 'a writing machine') is, Blanc claims, a translation of its German counterpart. The form /paxot o yoter/ 'more or less' has unclear origins, but Blanc believes that the word order (i.e. 'less or more') 'seems to indicate a Polish prototype'. Translation of whole sentences or phrases reminds us of some of the language transfer data, and is extremely common in IH. The sentence /hi nora yafa/ 'She's awfully pretty', instead of the 'more correct' (W. Chomsky 1958, p.193) /hi yafa meod/ 'She's very pretty' (literally 'she pretty very', copula deleted), could have come from either Yiddish or English, or perhaps one could have reinforced the other as we have seen in language transfer data (Gass and Selinker 1983a, *passim*). Yaacov Danzig (pc) provides an interesting potential source for phrases such as /hi nora yafa/ and /sidarti oto/ 'I fixed him'; his supposition is that they 'entered the language through literal translations of Damon Runyon who was and is still widely read'. This may be, and in my experience, material from written TL sources seems to enter not only the written IL of NN speakers but their spoken IL as well. I know of no IL studies of this phenomenon.

Category 6: loanblend

Hockett (1958, p.413) defines a loanblend as a case in which 'the borrower imports part of the model and replaces part of it by something already in his own language'. This is something I am sure that IL learners do, especially if the phrase 'his own language' means not only the NL, but the current state of the IL. For the purposes of the bilingual data being presented here, I would like to expand Hockett's definition to include a blending in the recipient language of two or more items derived either from one language source – even though the particular combination may not have occurred in the donor language – or from several language sources. This happens to be a productive category in IH and one where the Hebrew IL speaker has clearly been of influence in terms of language change. In this case the NN speaker of IH will take some item from a linguistic source s/he knows well (usually the NL) and use it either to fill a need (i.e. a communication strategy), or sometimes 'salt' one's speech. Many of these creations have become a part of the language of monolingual IH speakers. A common curse formula, for example, begins with the Hebrew /lex/ 'go' and ends, as Blanc (1957, p.404) puts it, 'with some more or less adulterated Russian words, which, in the original, send the hearer to his mother in highly unprintable terms'. A common device in IH is to add borrowed affixes to IH stems, e.g. pro- in /pro maaravi/ 'pro-Western' and /-le/ (a term of endearment in Yiddish) as in /imale/ 'dear mother'. Many other instances of this type exist. On the other hand, IH affixes may be added to borrowed stems, e.g. /eleganti/ 'elegant' and /elegantiut/ 'elegance', where IH /-i/ forms adjectives and /-ut/ forms abstract nouns. Finally, a melange may occur where a blending of both borrowed stem and borrowed affix are joined with the pieces derived, first of all, from one donor language, even if the combination did not exist in that language. My favourite example here is the IH word /trempist/ 'a hitchhiker', both pieces, it is widely claimed, being from English (Blanc 1954, p.78) (Though perhaps the stem is from German 'trampen', 'hitchhiking'; Chris Candlin, pc. Note that the source might be *both* languages, each reinforcing the other, a situation common in second language research.) However, note that in the IL /trempist/ both pieces in do not occur in that combination in the donor language: /tremp/ from tramp – with an accompanying semantic shift – and /-ist/ the suffix in bigamist, communist, etc. (Do IL speakers do this sort of thing, one wonders.) There are also IH formulations where the pieces are derived from several donor languages. In /švicer/ 'a showoff', for example, the first part /švic-/ 'sweat' (see above) comes from Yiddish and the part /-er/ 'one who does' comes from either (or both) English or German. Note in these examples the pieces that are identified as same across linguistic systems *before* some blending and/or extension occurs.

In concluding the presentation of this sampling of bilingual data, I would like to call attention to the apparent complexity of choice in (as Weinreich puts it, 1953 Section 2.43) the 'selection' of one item and the rejection of another in linguistic borrowings. IL speakers, as pointed out in the previous chapter, are involved in such selection processes as well. An illustration of this complexity in IH is provided by an example taken from W. Chomsky (1957, pp.194–5). To indicate 'belongingness', IH usually adds the suffix /-i/ (masc.) and /-it/ (fem.) to the stem, as in /cioni/, /cionit/ 'a Zionist' (masc. and fem. respectively). Certain stems, however, do not occur with the masculine suffix /-i/ but with the suffix /-nik/ (same meaning) borrowed from Russian. Such blends as /kibucnik/ 'member of a /kibuc/' and /mapamnik/ 'a member of the Mapam party' occur. However, there is no form in IH comparable to the Russian /-nica/, feminine of /-nik/. In IH, the suffix /-nik/ is added to the stem to form a new stem with /-it/ added to that, 'thus yielding the feminine forms /kibucnikit/ and /mapamnikit/ rather than /*kibucnica/ and /*mapamnica/' (W. Chomsky, *ibid.*). We could, thus, in a bilingual sense, analyse the IH form /kibuc–nik–it/ as:

(a)	(b)	(c)	Source	Class
kibuc			Hebrew	stem
	nik		Russian	affix
		it	Hebrew	affix

In examples such as these there appears to be a language contact syntax, which approximates, at least in some ways, but is not identical to the native IH syntax.

Interpretation of bilingual studies

Earlier in this chapter I promised a theoretical discussion which would look at the status of bilingual studies, including a 'surprising' comparison to studies in IL and IL learning. In general, as was pointed out in Gass and Selinker (1983a, Ch.1, with much of that discussion originally worked out in Selinker 1966), major interest in linguistically oriented bilingual studies has traditionally been twofold:

(a) 'those instances of deviation from the norms of either language, which occur in the speech of bilinguals . . . as a result of language contact . . .'
    and
(b) the impact of these deviations upon 'the norms of either language exposed to contact' (Weinreich 1953, p.1).

It has been clear to me for a long time (Selinker 1966, pp.25–7) that there are serious difficulties with this type of approach. First and most important, a reconstructed form of the source or donor language has to be 'inferred'. For example, Haugen (1953), Di Pietro (1961) and Diebold (1964) attempted empirically to discover deviations that occurred in Norwegian, Sicilian and Greek, respectively, upon contact with American English in a second language environment. Although the research methodology was not stated in every case, it was generally as follows: a comparison of the source language (Norwegian, Sicilian or Greek of, say, 1900) with the recipient language (American Norwegian, American Sicilian or American Demotic). This comparison gave the analyst a 'residue' of the recipient language which was then compared with the TL (in this case American English). What was then isolated in the Norwegian, Sicilian or Greek was said to be the result of languages in contact. This procedure, however, could not be fully carried out, since no speaker of the historically earlier source language existed for the analyst. That is, one linguistic system being compared does not at present exist, has to be inferred, and, importantly, as reconstructed, may not have existed.

A second difficulty concerning the interpretation of bilingual studies centres upon the concept of 'norm' of a language, from which deviations are to be measured. An important theoretical question is: How were these norms obtained? The answer in every case I know of

in the bilingualism literature is: They were assumed. Recall the
Weinreich example discussed in Chapter 2: 'He comes tomorrow
home.' As reported above, Weinreich claims that this sentence is 'an
example of the application of a grammatical relation of word order
from one language (German) to morphemes of another (English)'.
This may be the case, and the importance of Weinreich's views is
discussed in the previous chapter. But note that Weinreich presents
no evidence to show that this sentence is indeed deviant from
American English and that the American English norm (presumably)
is: 'He comes home tomorrow.' No matter how trivial this example
might seem, it is widely agreed, I think, that assumed norms of a
language often, in fact, hide important sources of variation. (This
point is argued most cogently in Preston 1989.) Importantly, as was
pointed out in Gass and Selinker (1983a, p.5), evidence was not
presented by Weinreich (nor in parallel cases by Haugen, Di Pietro
and Diebold) that speakers of other languages, whose word order is
not like English, do not also produce utterances of the sort: 'He
comes tomorrow home.' If they do, then this analysis would be
suspect as Wode (1978) describes concerning language transfer in
IL.

In spite of this lack of empirical control, bilingual studies,
especially those achieved through the use of the tools of CA (e.g. cf.
Chapter 1), provide us with an excellent source of hypotheses
concerning specific instances of the phenomenon of language transfer
in IL learning, hypotheses which can then be tested empirically. But
one has to ask: Are there similar problems of interpretation in IL
studies in SLA? The answer, unfortunately, is too often yes, and this
is where the surprising parallel occurs between bilingual studies and
IL studies. The first criticism raised against bilingual studies as
traditionally carried out is that a form of one of the three languages
being compared has to be inferred. Are IL studies in a similar
situation? Unfortunately, yes. If, for example, one is discussing
'errors' made by speakers of a particular NL, then one is usually
comparing the actual speech of an L2 learner with the hypothesized
speech of the TL. That is, one is comparing speech events with
inferred speech event from an inferred system. This is normal
procedure for teachers correcting oral or written errors in a
classroom situation. 'What would I have said?' is the usual question
(which is another variation on the theme: What is 'the same' across
linguistic systems?), but the 'norm' being used as the model is
hypothesized. Researchers may fare no better. Often the researcher's
data are no more and no less than the hypothesized corresponding set

of utterances which 'would have been produced' by an NS of the TL had he or she attempted to express 'the same meaning' as the learner. Thus, here too, actual speech events are being compared with hypothesized or inferred speech events. That criticism can be equally levelled at studies in language transfer IL research when actual IL speech events are compared with hypothesized NL speech events. In every case, what is called for is an empirical justification as to why language transfer is being claimed without reference to hypothesized speech events.

Concerning the related second criticism of bilingual studies, namely that 'norms' of languages are assumed, one has to admit that such norms are usually assumed in IL research as well. There is an interesting difference, though, between classical bilingual research and IL studies in SLA. In the former one is dealing with a 'dead' and thus irretrievably lost state of a language, but this is not the case in IL studies (except for historical IL studies where historical change is involved, for example the first French–Anglo-Saxon IL after Hastings). Here two theoretical concerns merge; the first being discussed involves inferred languages and assumed norms. The second is the problem discussed in Chapter 1, namely, that classical CA predictions were usually statistical in nature but were not presented with statistical controls. (See Chapter 7 for empirical discussion.)

The twin problems of assumed norms and statistical predictions can be related to a distinction made in Tarone, Frauenfelder and Selinker (1976, pp.98–9) between *Type 1* individuals, whose IL is characterized by stability, and *Type 2* individuals, who continue to 'learn' in the sense that their IL is changing over time. We can say that a Type 1 individual has stopped learning, where 'learning' is defined as instability or change in the IL system over time. A Type 1 individual has been variously described in the literature as having a 'fossilized competence' (Coulter 1968), a 'functional competence' (Jain 1969; see also Jain 1974, p.208) or a 'stable approximative system' (Nemser 1971a). A Type 2 individual, on the other hand, has an IL system characterized by its instability; it is in a constant process of change over time, with the exception of some stabilized parts. Studies by Cancino *et al.* (1974) and Hakuta (1974) describe Type 2 learners, for example, and note the difficulty involved in attempting to make empirical or theoretical statements about such learners due to their characteristic lack of stability over time, as well as their frequent lack of systematicity at a particular point in time. Adjemian (1976, p.21) describes the competence of the Type 2 learner as 'permeable',

where 'permeability' is defined as 'the property of ILs which allows
... penetration into an IL system of rules foreign to its internal
systematicity'. Toronto French-immersion children (Tarone *et al.*
1976) are Type 2 individuals. It may be that with the passage of time
they will become Type 1 individuals. Of course, whether such a
sharp dichotomy is reasonable in practice has to be empirically
worked out.

The problems of assumed norms and statistical predictions must
take into account these two types of IL individuals. The problem of
assumed norms and inferred languages should be lesser for the Type
1 IL speaker. A Type 1 IL speaker can hardly be called a 'learner'. It
is my contention that this individual will not only cease IL
development but will cease the process of comparing his current IL
production with expected TL norms. Type 2 individuals, especially in
the classroom, will be constantly reminded of expected TL norms
and will probably be constantly comparing this with their current IL
output as they try to approximate the TL. This point of TL/IL
comparison by learners has been brought up before and will be a
recurrent theme throughout these pages.

Possible phonological units

We will end this chapter with a discussion of what we have learned
about 'units' and 'equivalence' across linguistic systems by looking at
the set of bilingual data presented in this chapter. We will start with
the phonological case. Does the study described in this chapter show
that the structural unit, the phoneme, is the one that is operating in
the contact situation? Yes, at times. New phonemes (/tč/, /ǰ/, /ž/)
were added to IH through bilingual experience. But the example of
[pəŋkčər] turning to [pančer] (i.e. English 'puncture' with semantic
changes) shows the possibility of an n/ŋk equivalence. To complicate
things, [baeŋk] 'bank' does not come out as [ban] but [bank], with [n]
being identified interlingually with [ŋ]. Two consonants interlingually
identified with one does show up in the /špric/ example with NL
structural reasons being dominant, as Weinreich might have
predicted. The change of /æ/ to /e/, 'tramp' to /tremp/, supports
the phonemic perspective in the bilingual domain, since /æ/ is not in
the recipient language, the borrower choosing its 'nearest' phoneme
/e/. Stress is retained in the recipient language, after borrowing, on
the syllable where it occurred in the donor language (the /atóm/,
/atómi/ examples), even when inflectional suffixes which ordinarily
take the stress are added; this argues for the importance of syllables

being identified across linguistic systems. Weinreich's case for 'phonetic similarity' as being important in 'interlingual identifications' is strengthened by /mexona/ and /mapa/ examples discussed above. The case of /kvaker/ as [kfaker] from Quaker when looked at phonetically is instructive. There is disagreement, but here is what this observer believes happened and happens. In words of this type /w/ is not brought into IH; there is no /w/ and no new phoneme has been created in this case. As in the /æ/ to /e/ case, the 'nearest' recipient phoneme /v/ replaces the /w/. But what I have heard some Israelis say is [kfaker]. This devoicing fits in nicely with IH rules, where the word /kvar/ 'already' in rapid speech can appear as [kfar]. (Rules of (de)voicing in IH are quite complicated and are described by Blanc 1960, vol.1 in much detail and with abundant examples.) How one gets from /w/ to /f/ is explainable as a series of steps, with interlingual identification the first one.

What does the voicing/devoicing – widely applying phonological rules – lead us to regarding IL speakers of Hebrew? Some IH voicing changes appear more 'salient' than others, e.g. /zoxer/ 'remember' (sing.) – which follows the root /z/ – but /lizkor/ becomes [liskor] due to devoicing rules. What do IL speakers do in these and similar cases? How are general IL principles constrained? I am not sure. One has need of careful IL descriptive studies in the area of widely applying IL phonological rules.

The case of widely applying phonological rules is of interest here since they may very well affect intelligibility (see e.g. Candlin 1966) and certainly relate to the determination of insider/outsider status, which is important in terms of 'identity' questions (see Chapter 1 for a discussion of gender rules in this regard). Such widely applying rules have called into question in linguistics the psychological reality of the taxonomic phoneme. This issue should be important to us since it looks as if the taxonomic phoneme is, at least at times, *the* phonological unit of linguistic borrowing and of IL transfer. One recalls the extended (and, unfortunately, often overheated) argument between Halle and Ferguson, among others, in the early 1960s, for example over 'the Russian devoicing rule' (Halle 1963a, 1963b), a rule that applies uniformly across the language. In some cases its result is the taxonomic phoneme and in other cases an allophone. This fact led Halle to argue strongly against the taxonomic phoneme and for generative phonology, where this rule can apply uniformly across the language. In this theory, the necessity for the distinction phoneme/ allophone is obviated. Ferguson (pc), on the other hand, argued that these 'marginal cases' (there are examples in English) are peripheral to a phonological system and should not be used to knock down by themselves the edifice of classical phonemics which had stood its ground for close to a century. For CA and IL studies these are not arcane and irrelevant arguments but can reveal some of the perplexity we face in trying to understand equivalences in terms of interlingual identifications and units of IL phonology.

The case of Hebrew (de)voicing is interesting here. Take the following example, which mirrors the Ferguson/Halle debate: /codek/ 'I, you [masc.], he is right', /hicdik/ 'he was right', [hiždik] by a voicing rule. The segment /c/ or segments [ts] are known to English monolingual speakers, e.g. [kæts] 'cats', but [dž] is not. Some English speakers do nevertheless voice in IL cases like this, while others do not. Observationally, English speakers mostly appear to devoice [z] to [s] in the [liskor] example, but not with /sovel/ 'I, you [masc.], he suffers', /lisbol/ 'to suffer' to [lizbol] and not [t] to [d], as in /ιguva/ 'reaction' to [dguva]. Why should L2 learners not (de)voice uniformly across an IL? Are 'coexistent phonemic systems' mentioned above possible in IL, or are constraints of CLI involved?

In these cases, [s] to [z] are both English phonemes which seem most 'salient' in [sk], a permissible English consonant cluster in syllable initial position, they seem less salient in an impermissible English consonant cluster [zb}; and [t] and [d] are at the same level of salience regarding the cluster [dg]. Even further down a potential hierarchy of interlingual salience, lies the example of [c] to [dž], with the latter being an impermissible English phonemic unit. So, unlike native (N) dialects of IH, non-native (NN) dialects may operate on different partially independent (i.e. NL/TL independent) IL rules, many obviously not yet known. Such reflections lead us to believe that partially independent units and rules should be empirically studied. Note that an example such as this leads us to suspect that such discredited linguistic units as the taxonomic phoneme might be operating in the language contact situation, at least at times.

Possible lexical units

We continue here our attempt to understand units of IL and IL learning in SLA, expecially how equivalences across languages relate to such units. We know from the discussion above that 'words' are very good candidates for units of equivalence in language contact situations, with 'loanwords' being rather a transparent category. We also know that some sorts of semantic features are good candidates for units of equivalence in such situations (cf. /zerem, nefeš, sviva/

examples above), with 'extensions of meanings' according to some such feature analysis being reasonable. We know that affixes of all three kinds (prefixes, infixes and suffixes) are good candidates for interlingual units, since we have seen all three (pro-, -nik-, -ist) in morphological melanges of various types. We know that there exist word-order units which are good interlingual candidates: adverb–adjective vs adjective–adverb, as in the examples translated above as 'She is awfully pretty' vs 'She is very pretty.' As was pointed out in Chapter 2, the following is also a good candidate: time–place vs place–time as in the Weinreich example 'He comes tomorrow home' and the Israeli–Hebrew English IL example quoted there (please see how this is developed in Chapter 7). We surely should know, after going through the data presented in Chapters 2 and 3, that 'pieces across languages' can be mixed in ways that are often not predictable from just a source language/recipient language comparison. We are bound to ask if this is not the same lesson learned in Chapter 1 concerning an NL/TL comparison (cf. Chapter 7 for Nemser's puzzlement over this question).

Possible syntactic units

Earlier in this chapter it was suggested on the basis of bilingual data that it is possible there exists a 'language contact syntax' which, at least in some ways, approximates but is not identical to the syntax of the recipient language. I find here one of the strands which led to the notion of IL, a linguistic system that is at least partially separate from NL and TL (see Selinker 1966, pp.24–30). In Chapter 2 I argued for an openness to the suggestion that there exists a 'latent psychological structure' (LPS) within which units of interlingual identification exist. We are here slowly moving towards a discussion of the relevant units of this hypothesized LPS, which in essence allows for the L2 learner to set up equivalences across *three* linguistic systems: the NL, the developing IL, and the learner's view (imperfect though it may be) of the TL.

How do units of cross-linguistic experience – either bilingual or IL – relate to formal principles of language organization? In Selinker (1972, p.225) I argued that: '. . . no unit of linguistic theory, as these units are currently conceived, could fit [the criterion] of a unit identified interlingually across three linguistic systems (NL, TL and IL) by means of fossilization . . .' or by strategies of learning and communication described there for IL. The evidence presented here for mixing and merging of systems in language contact situations strengthens the case for units of monolingual linguistics, i.e. of linguistic theory as mostly practised, not being the units of interlingual identifications. Long and Sato (1984) also provide a review of several studies which claim that the units of linguistic theory related to monolingual systems are not the units of SLA and thus of IL. This point is summarized in that same volume in Selinker 1984, Issue 6.

Evidence for relevant units of surface syntactic IL structure and phonological IL structure are presented in Selinker 1972, (pp.227–8) and we concluded there that:

> If these units in the domain of interlingual identifications are not necessarily the same units as those in the native-speaker domain, then where do they come from? An interesting bit of speculation about native-speaker performance units is provided by Haggard (1967, p.335) who states that searching for 'the unit' in native-speaker speech-perception is a waste of time. Alternative units may be available to native speakers, for example under noise conditions. While other explanations are surely possible for the well known fact that noise conditions affect performance in a second language, and sometimes drastically, we cannot ignore the possible relevance of Haggard's intriguing suggestion: That alternative language units are available to individuals and that these units are activated under certain conditions. It fits in very well with the perspective outlined in this paper to postulate a new type of psycholinguistic unit, available to an individual whenever he attempts to produce sentences in a second language. This interlingual unit stretches, we hypothesize, across three linguistic systems: NL, IL, and TL, and becomes available to the idealized second-language learner who will not achieve native-speaker competence in the TL, whenever he attempts to produce a TL norm. These units become available to the learner only after he has switched his psychic set or state from the native-speaker domain to the new domain of interlingual identifications. I would like to postulate further that these relevant units of interlingual identifications do not come from anywhere; they are latent in the brain in a latent psychological structure, available to an individual whenever he wishes to attempt to produce the norm of any TL.

I believe that empirical evidence gained over the last two decades shows that this is still an essentially correct position. Indeed, it was pointed out in that paper (p.225) that 'the linguistic status of ILs has still to be determined'. This is still true, given the lack of IL description hinted at over and over so far in the discussion. It is still early days.

Summary

In this chapter we have looked at bilingual data, gaining some insight into possible cross-linguistic equivalences on several levels. We have argued that to undertake SLA we have to attempt comparisons of various types. We now ask: How do we then progress in our attempt to understand exactly what learners make equivalent across languages? Are we clear yet on problems of comparison that we must confront to understand such matters? I think not, and in justification propose we now move to a discussion of selected works in CA which have attempted to address some of the comparative questions necessary to understand the relationships involved in creating IL.

Points for discussion

(1) There are numerous comparisons between bilingual and IL speakers in this chapter – for example, whether an IL learner creates 'loanblends'. Do you think the IL learner does? Explain your rationale. Choose two other examples and repeat the exercise.

(2) It is argued above that the bilingual data discussed here back up a reformulation of Lado's position concerning language transfer discussed in Chapter 1, specifically that the L2 learner sets up equivalences across *three* linguistic systems: the NL, the developing IL, and the learner's view of the TL. How might this actually work if the learner's view of the TL is *imperfect* from the point of view of the TL as set up by textbooks and, perhaps, by the teacher?

(3) In the previous chapter we discussed in some detail Weinreich's conclusion that learners 'make the same what cannot be the same'. Consider examples in this chapter at the vocabulary or lexical level. Words are very good candidates for units of equivalence in language contact situations. Do the examples in this chapter justify that conclusion? If so, how do learners create such cross-linguistic interlingual identifications?

(4) Discuss several of the phonological examples in this chapter in terms of the questions in (3). Then, consider in general Weinreich's discussion of phonological features and extend it to semantic features, relating your discussion to the six categories

of examples presented in this chapter: expansive, additive, replacive, loanshift, loan translation and loanblend.

(5) In this chapter it was suggested that there exists a 'language contact syntax' which approximates but is not identical to the syntax of the source and recipient languages. Evaluate this statement based on some bilingual data you collect.

(6) Consider once again Weinreich's notion of interlingual identifications. What do you think of the idea discussed here of the existence of a 'latent psychological structure', the cognitive structure within which units of interlingual identification exist? How would you begin to evaluate such a notion empirically?

(7) Consider the notion of 'errors' as discussed in the first three chapters. How empirically reasonable is the concept? Specifically, where do Fries, Lado and Weinreich stand on this question?

(8) Now broaden your concern in (5) to the bilingualism data presented in this chapter and the discussion above about 'hypothesized norms'. Then see if you agree with the statement that when one is discussing errors made by speakers of a particular NL, one is comparing two unequal things: the actual speech of an L2 learner with the hypothesized or inferred speech of the TL. Now consider where this puts the language teacher when correcting oral or written errors in a classroom situation.

(9) Now consider whether you agree that the concern with the concept error as presented in (5) and (6) is another variation on the theme: What is 'the same' across linguistic systems? How does the following quote from the chapter affect your concept of research in SLA?

> Researchers may fare no better. Often the researcher's data are no more and no less than the hypothesized corresponding set of utterances which 'would have been produced' by an NS of the TL had he or she attempted to express 'the same meaning' as the learner. Thus, here too, actual speech events are being compared with hypothesized or inferred speech events.

How might this statement 'demystify' research? Is this a good or bad result?

(10) If you have studied linguistics, relate your experiences to the statement in this chapter that no unit of linguistic theory, as these units are currently conceived, could fit the criterion of a

unit identified interlingually across three linguistic systems: NL, TL and IL. How then might units of cross-linguistic experience – either bilingual or IL – relate in the final analysis to formal principles of language organization?

4 Some problems of comparison: The CA literature

CA and linguistic theory

Let us now consider some problems of comparing linguistic items across languages. We begin by discussing the relationships possible between CA and a linguistic theory that is in a constant state of flux. We do this to try to clear the air since a linguistic theory of some type must be involved in understanding comparisons across linguistic systems, an endeavour basic to understanding IL. Our hope is that linguistic theory can leave its traditional over-emphasis on mono-lingual concerns and relate reasonably to a world that is far from monolingual. Linguistics should incorporate into its concerns CA problems of language transfer where in IL some predicted structures occur, but not others, and at times the reasons may be linguistic, as in the allophonic cases described above.

In this chapter we first describe an attempt in 1971 to address this issue (Selinker 1971) and then struggle back through some of our CA roots with the aim of looking at current SLA in terms of this earlier work. As before, this discussion is not to be considered a history per se, but an attempt to understand issues raised in this book about the continual discovery of IL.

Concerning the linguistic theory/CA relationship there are, it seems, two major views. *View 1:* a particular theoretical model is first chosen by the CA analyst and two comparable structures are then compared and contrasted; problems with the theory are considered irrelevant to this task and (as shown with the work of Lado in Chapter 1) the problem of equivalence does not come up, since units provided by the theory are accepted as given. As pointed out, this view is problematical for IL because of the paradox discussed at the beginning of Chapter 3. *View 2:* a CA is undertaken in order to shed light on a particular theoretical issue by gathering relevant data in a contrastive framework. Here the central problem of equivalence or comparability across linguistic systems cannot be ignored.

In the first view, there are important insights. For example, let us look at a relatively clear case provided by Sauer (1970). Consider these four sentences from English and Spanish:

(1)

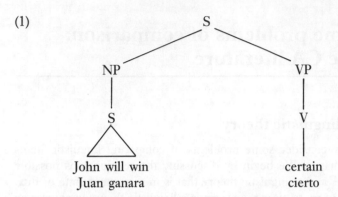

(2) That John will win is certain.   Que Juan ganara es cierto.
(3) It is certain that John will win.   Es cierto que Juan ganara.
(4) John is certain to win.   *Juan es cierto ganar.
      (likely, unlikely)

Let us agree that sentence (1) shows a basic semantic structure which is common to the two languages. Sentences (2) and (3) show that each language has identical transformations (in one generative view of things) up to this point. It surely shows that up to this point there are equivalent sentence structures (ignoring the dummy 'It'). Sentence (4), on the other hand, shows a distinct difference in structures possible, and a difference in the transformations possible in the two languages. In one analysis, 'subject raising', i.e. taking 'John' out of the embedded sentence and making it the subject of the main sentence, produces a commonly occurring structure in English but a rare one in Spanish. Some sort of language learning confusion often occurs right at this point for the English learner of Spanish in his English–Spanish IL. This is also true for other interlingual situations, e.g. English–French and English–Hebrew since their non-grammatical equivalents –

   *Il est certain gagner   and /*hu batuax lenaceax/
   (English–French and English–Hebrew respectively)

– appear to occur. This example presents the very real possibility of some sort of 'deep-structure grammatical transfer', if it can be established empirically beyond doubt that sentences such as (4) regularly occur in English–Spanish and the other ILs. The problem is: Is deep-structure grammatical transfer a reasonable analysis? This has been discussed extensively in the literature in various forms; see for example discussion in Selinker *et al.* (1975) Tarone *et al.* (1976, especially pp.113–24) and *passim* in Gass and Selinker (1983a), in Eckman *et al.* (1984), Davies *et al.* (1984), Rutherford (1984b) and Gass and J. Schachter (1989). If we can show the reasonableness of deep-structure grammatical transfer, then this would become another case where IL behaviour matches abstract linguistic categories, involving a different sort of interlingual identification than reported in this discussion to date. For this reason, among others we need to develop a strong interlingual linguistics.

View 1

There is no question that Lado (1957) fits into the first view of doing CA. On p.67, for example, he tells analysts to get the best matching description they can find of two languages and compare and contrast them in terms of the specific procedures described in Chapter 1 above. One difficulty with carrying out this research programme is that at times the *size* of the structure to be compared must be left vague. For example, can one study 'questions' in two languages (Langacker 1969) or only 'primary questions' in two languages (Armagost 1970)? Is this an IL learner's problem as well? The purpose of the CA is clearly relevant here. Lattey (1982) provides evidence that there is a problem with the very concept of 'name' of a structure in the CA framework.

> [CA] has traditionally been carried out with respect to particular structures in two languages [which] has led in some cases to the comparison across languages of things with the same name, without considerations of whether these things *are* in fact the same. (Lattey 1982, p.131, emphasis in the original)

This may be another important IL learner problem.

Interestingly, Lattey, despite the sophistication of the question referred to at the beginning of Chapter 3 above ('What is the "same thing" in interlinguistic comparison?') and her pointing out the problem of 'things with the same name' across languages, fits in with View 1. She chooses a particular theoretical model and, as far as I can tell, considers problems with this theory irrelevant. She chooses the model, ascribed originally to Diver, which is called 'Form–Content analysis' (Lattey 1982, p.137). She lists advantages to this approach in which 'semantic analysis' is 'used as a basis for comparison' (*ibid*, p.141) and presents several interesting examples that could be tested in an IL framework.

A fairly widespread instance of View 1 is the case in which CA studies present the ASPECTS model (Chomsky 1965), contrasting English with some other language with little questioning of the basic framework (e.g. Fox 1968), even though the model was in flux even before it was off the presses.

View 2

View 2 considers one of the major purposes of CA as being to shed light on theoretical issues by gathering relevant data in a CA framework. Some researchers in CA (e.g. Fisiak 1980) have claimed that purely descriptive CAs (i.e. with no systematized behavioural evidence) should be on an equal footing with other types of linguistic descriptions. (Some nomenclature distinctions such as CA vs applied CA vs contrastive linguistics are ignored for the present discussion.) He defined contrastive linguistics as a 'subdiscipline' of linguistics concerned with: '... the comparison of two or more languages (or subsystems of languages) in order to determine both the differences and similarities that hold between them' (Fisiak 1980, p.1). In addition, Nickel, when he was director of the important German–English CA project PAKS, stated that his hope was that research done in that project would yield interesting results for 'two major problems of linguistic theory', which he named as the construction '... of a theory of contrastive linguistics and the construction of a general theory of language' (Nickel 1970, p.iv). (I provide further information about the PAKS project as EA in Chapter 5.)

Given that this view is a rather common one (see Gass 1982 for discussion), it is not surprising that many CA studies (e.g. Wagner 1969) are primarily attempts to explore linguistic theory, not attempts to consider theoretical questions in a CA framework. One feels that De Geest *et al.* (1969), for example, is performing the same function, i.e. using CA to do theoretical linguistics. One wonders why; the latter is its own justification. What one would really like to know is how these and other authors would handle theoretical questions (e.g. questions of equivalence and comparability and units of CA) with theoretical data organized, as they have done, in a CA framework.

One might also think of this second view of CA as an attempt to respond positively to the problem of 'contrastive challenges', which is one of the many statements in the theoretical linguistics literature which specifically call for an examination of languages other than

English to 'follow up' a universal hypothesis. For example, Newmeyer (1969, p.25) states that: '... in *no* languages can an aspectual verb co-occur with adverbials, tense, or aspect' (his emphasis). This is a strong claim, one which I feel certain can be systematically investigated in a CA framework. Such studies could help those interested in the IL questions raised to point in this book, e.g. units across linguistic systems identified as same (e.g. NL/IL; IL/TL), related to whether things with the same name across linguistic systems are, in fact, the same. An important such unit is the notion of 'verbal tense'. In my view, in IL learners often have a domain of discourse, labelled for us by one subject as 'Grammar ... is ... was bad' (Selinker and Douglas 1989), which can help us understand in a CA framework the early IL strong appearance of adverbs in some IL genres with and without aspectual verbs (cf. Perdue 1984, Klein 1986; cf. Zuengler 1989a, b, and c for an experimental expression of the domain theory in IL).

In Selinker (1971, p.5) it was pointed out that, in the 1960s, Ross was a linguist who constantly threw out contrastive challenges. For instance, his major claim that declarative sentences are derived from a clause embedded in a higher performative verb phrase was tested against CA data from Arabic, Thai and Basque (Ross 1969, pp.4, 40–2). James (1980, pp.7–8) points out that what he calls 'pure' linguists have been doing something close to CA for a long time, and also uses Ross as an example. Ross discusses the possibility that adjectives are derived from noun phrases in deep structure, testing this claim against data from German and French. James points out that Fedorowicz-Bacz (in a paper unavailable to me) provides counter evidence to the Ross claim using data from Polish, stating that, 'What we have here is very reminiscent of CA, but Ross is doing 'pure', not 'applied' linguistics (James 1980, p.8). I find James's distinction not too useful for the kinds of questions raised in this volume concerning IL and IL learning in SLA. A clear understanding of IL is without doubt a theoretical task and Ross's concerns, with a slight reworking, could fit nicely into it. I thus find the concern of theoretical linguists with contrastive questions to be of help in focusing our conceptual attention, whatever their concerns might be.

But how might this work? We must take notice when theoretical linguists group data that are relevant to our concerns, groupings that we might not previously have noticed. As pointed out in Chapter 2, sentences such as:

(5) *Il veut moi de dire français à il.
    He wants me to speak French to him.
    (Gloss discernible from context)

occur in the English–French of Toronto French-immersion children. These and similar sentences appear to be due to transfer of NL English structures underlying sentences of the following type:

(6) He   wants   me   to speak French.
(7) I   want   you   to leave.

French does not permit such sentences as (5) and that is why the IL sentence is starred. Linguistically, what is clear is that the subjects of the two verbs, both in English (6), he/me, and in English–French (5), il/moi, are not alike in that they do not refer to the same person. This sort of underlying syntactic information is what might be being transferred. What is useful for SLA about (CA) concerns of some theoretical linguists, as pointed out by Sauer in 1970 (see above), is the bringing together of data that we might not have noticed as having relevance, i.e. 'related data'. Sentences like:

(8) He   wants   to speak French.
(9) I   want   to go.

have long been related to (6)/(7) type sentences, but (10) has not been:

(10) I tried to be arrested.

Concerning sentences like (9), there has been much discussion about the 'like-subject constraint'. This constraint refers to the often observed identity between the subject of a verb and the missing or 'deleted' subject of its infinitive complement. Perhaps it is this syntactic constraint that is being transferred when one gets such congruence of structures. (Issues concerning whether one can do a linguistics without deletion structures should not halt our discussion here at all.) In (9), presumably 'I' is the subject of both verbs. To encourage such studies, considering CA as relevant to theoretical linguistics, and thus to View 2 of CA, we can note that the much argued about like-subject constraint was first called into question on the basis of a Dutch–English CA statement. Sentence (10) shows a counter example to the constraint, since the subject of the second verb is presumably different from the subject of the first verb. Sentence (11) is the Dutch translation equivalent of (10):

(11) Ik probeerde mij te laten arresteren
      I tried   me to let   arrest
      'I tried to let myself be arrested'

These data appear in Perlmutter (1968, p.56), who argues for the constraint by postulating an intervening sentence in both the Dutch and English deep structures, since the two sentences (10) and (11) are equivalent and since, in this analysis, 'let' must be used to generate a grammatical Dutch sentence. For Perlmutter, then, the deep structure for this synonymous pair of sentences in English and Dutch are the same; the languages differ in a transformational rule of verb deletion. (But cf. Newmeyer 1969, p.47 for arguments against Perlmutter's analysis using English data only.) As we shall see, it has not been unusual in CA to take the position that deep structures are the same across languages, that transformations are different, *and* that this affects language learners. Is it deep structures that are identified as same? Maybe, since I know of no strong evidence that this is in principle impossible, and as shown above at the beginning of this chapter, there is some evidence to state that at times this is reasonable. The CA problem we face here involves this question: What are the interlingual identifications in the case where a constraint such as 'subject raising' also includes other 'related data' whose status is not clear given the IL evidence?

Concerning the examples discussed in the preceding paragraph, we in IL studies in SLA must ask some serious questions, such as:

(a) If it is the case that in English–French IL, sentences such as (5) are common and fossilizable, how are we to take this notion of 'related data', such as 8–11 above?

(b) What does 'related data' mean if we find that similar sentences in other ILs equivalent to (5) exist, e.g. the English–Hebrew IL translation equivalent of (5)?

(12) *hu roce oti ledaber corfarti.
      He wants me to speak French.

(c) Given also that interlingual identifications (of some sort) are made between structures related to sentences (5) and (6), then should the IL analyst include in the same research framework sentences such as (8) and (9), where something like the like-subject constraint also probably operates?

(d) Also, if at all, how does one bring into IL studies an argument for underlying structure with the verb 'let'?

(e) If one does, then what would this say about units of interlingual identifications, and eventually of IL?

The answers are far from clear and, in my view, have not been adequately faced by those arguing for universal grammar constraints operating on IL formation. (Interesting discussions of further unresolved questions relating universal grammar concerns to second language acquisition appear in the introductions to Flynn and O'Neil 1988 and Gass and J. Schachter 1989.)

More current linguistic theory

Given our premise at the beginning of this chapter, that to understand the formation of IL some sort of linguistics must be involved, it is interesting to contemplate in some detail more current linguistic theory, a theory still deeply 'in a state of flux'. Eubank (1989) describes one case where he argues that the 'linguistic underpinnings' of a much-discussed series of SLA experiments (Flynn 1987a and b) were 'superseded' by a more recent linguistic analysis, one which does not support the particular SLA theory being put forth. This point becomes important for both SLA and linguistic theory: if it can be shown that an L2 learner refers during learning to the particular universal principle proposed, then its existence must be assumed and language transfer effects made to accommodate the abstract model. But showing conclusively that abstract categories exist as fact is most difficult. (For further discussion, the reader is referred to Flynn 1989, Eubank (forthcoming) and Bley-Vroman and Chaudron (forthcoming). Like other approaches discussed here, it is assumed that for IL purposes, including the development of an independent theory of SLA, 'purposeful misreading' of linguistic theory is justified and may in the long run be the most fruitful.

We can begin our look at more current linguistic theory by noting that there appear to have been great strides taken in making the syntactic component of the grammar 'simpler'. One can ask here: Should this be reflected in a simpler 'core IL grammar' than that derived from Chomsky 1965? Also, one sees a healthy trend in theoretical linguistic work towards CA; i.e., the use of contrastive or comparative information to develop (and criticize) the theory is strong, see View 2 above. Earlier in the history of generative grammar, overt comparative work was a minor part of the endeavour, with Chomsky (1965) going so far as to argue that the linguist can discover significant information about universals of language by looking at one language (it always seemed to be English) 'in depth'.

This position was widely criticized. In fact, I remember a whole panel devoted to it at the 1966 LSA summer meetings at UCLA. Since then, as Rizzi (1982, p.viii) points out, there has been a 'deepening' of the grammatical model. This deepening has proceeded 'in conjunction with' renewal of interest in comparative syntax.

> Careful formal analysis of various syntactic domains, especially in the Romance and Germanic areas, have provided new types of empirical evidence for testing the general theoretical framework and have suggested significant refinements of the theory and sometimes also radical modifications of specific hypotheses.

Rizzi also points out that for the first time in generative grammar, there is now 'a sufficient empirical basis' for addressing theoretical problems concerning syntactic variation across languages. There is thus occurring the accumulation of cross-linguistic knowledge that I believe will prove important to all linguistic endeavours.

At conferences where papers in generative grammar make a strong showing, one hears an explicit attempt to describe such differences. For example, Carstens (1984), in the conclusion to her paper, explores some differences between English and Yoruba with respect to multiple interrogation. Yang (1984), in exploring several distinctions between the theoretical concepts of 'control' and 'binding', shows where possessive pronouns in English and Korean differ. He argues for the position that 'lexical and pragmatic factors may override' the syntactic condition of control differentially in both languages, but not that of binding, showing an important attempt to extend the theory beyond the rigid constraints of sentence-bound grammar. Yang presented his paper orally in an apparently fossilized IL, Korean–English, and, as noted above, such IL data are themselves being legitimized and integrated into these studies, thus extending the database upon which linguistic theory depends beyond the rigid constraints of the 'ideal' monolingual native speaker of Chomsky (1965).

Another IL prominent at such conferences is Dutch–English. Dutch, and especially its differences with English, has become important in what I regard as the CA influence on linguistic theory. As noted above with the Perlmutter (1968) case, syntactic differences between Dutch and English have for a long time had an influence on linguistic theory. One case involves the phenomenon of 'parasitic gaps' vs 'real gaps' in sentence structure, with the latter corresponding to some 'extracted' element in the derivation (Hoekstra 1984; Cowper 1984; Huybregts and van Riemsdijk 1984) and such regular gaps derived by 'movement'. It was pointed out in these papers that the distribution of parasitic gaps in Dutch is much more restricted than that found in English. This is related to noun phrase shift, a potentially important factor in IL word order not taken account of in Selinker (1966 and 1969). In noun phrase shift there is a different linear effect found in Dutch and English, the difference according to Hoekstra relating to 'heaviness' of noun phrases. Hoekstra, like Yang above, suggests that a theory of pragmatics has to account for these differences, though he is not very explicit here. (A particularly enlightened attempt to incorporate pragmatic constraints in IL and UG is presented in Rutherford 1989.) Huybregts and van Riemsdijk disagree with Hoekstra, maintaining that it is not heaviness but 'left node raising' that relates to the lack of parasitic gaps in Dutch. However the theoretical debate comes out, another CA phenomenon, one for a while in the linguistic spotlight, has been described and in an area where it seems to me that there is non-native confusion – the gapping of syntactic information.

There are now CA-type book-length studies available in the generative literature. For example, Borer (1983) explores syntactic differences in Semitic and Romance languages, focusing on an in-depth analysis of several constructions in Modern Hebrew and Romanian. In classical CA fashion (View 2), Borer's goal is to suggest modifications of some central concepts to the theory within which she is working: 'Government and Binding' of Chomsky (1981). She claims that her work confirms that some proposed concepts (e.g. government, case, binding) are central to a theory of grammar. Her section (pp.132–6) on differences in 'extraction' between Hebrew /šel/ and Romanian /pe/ is illustrative. She shows first that there is a need to posit extraction from 'clitic-doubling constructions' in each language (Section 2.3 for Hebrew and 3.3. for Romanian; this is summarized on p. 127). Then she shows that crucial differences in each language follow from different properties of case markings in each language. In the analysis of Hebrew, /šel/ is not 'available' in the base of the grammar and hence cannot be fronted with wh-elements, whereas in Romanian, /pe/ is available and can be fronted. As a fossilized learner of Hebrew I found this discussion revealing, especially in its implicit comparison with English; /šel/ constructions at times seem quite tricky.

Let us now look at examples of the vast CA literature. One way to make this literature manageable is to face the CA problem: *How many fundamentally different CA models are there?* We wish to know this because of our hypothesis (Chapter 2) that 'interlingual identifications' are perhaps *the* basic learning strategy in SLA. We create this hypothesis because of Weinreich's suggestions that interlingual identifications are the answer to the paradox described in the first paragraph of Chapter 3.

A model with 'holes' resolved

We hinted in Chapter 1 that if one follows Lado's dictum that structures are to be compared pattern by pattern, 'holes' in patterns across languages develop as a matter of principle. What we did not state there was that this may be one of the reasons for the break-up of linguistic patterns across languages as noted by Weinreich in a language contact situation, the learner searching for reasonable (to him/her) interlingual identifications. One way to demonstrate this concept of 'hole' is that if one is comparing a Semitic language with an Indo-European one and the Semitic language is the source language, the analyst will find that one of the crucial structural elements involves a root that is manipulated in all sorts of morphological ways. One way to conceptualize this is as follows:

Semitic	Indo-European
C-C-C	-
V-C-C-C	-
P-C-C-C	-

(C = consonantal root; V = vowel; P = prefix)

No equivalent structures exist in Indo-European languages, but of course other things *function* in the same way as root plus vowels do, e.g. nouns, verbs, actives, passives, causatives, etc. People working in early CA noticed such 'holes' and went back to an earlier article by Harris's important paper, for in his textbook Gleason (1955, p.207) a translation-type model in a generative framework and, historically, this is one of the earliest studies in generative grammar. Harris's point was that in a purely structural comparison of languages many constructions in one language have no parallel in another. But on a translation basis, one can find a parallel in one language to 'almost anything' in the other. That is, almost anything in one language can be translated into any other. Whatever the truth of this claim, it is clear that learners of a second language do use translation as a learning strategy and the relationship between language transfer, translation and linguistic structures is one we have raised before in this volume and is far from resolved in IL theory. But let us look at Harris's important paper, for in his textbook Gleason (1955, p.207) went so far as to equate CA with Harris's transfer grammar, showing its importance to the general debate. Harris is another source ignored in most CA treatments.

Harris was concerned with matching morpheme classes across languages. This is a reasonable activity for us to contemplate since so much SLA research has been concerned with the acquisition of morphemes. (See Chapter 8 below for some comments on this phenomenon.) Looking at Korean and English, Harris found the morpheme classes N+V matched by their distribution, but A was unmatchable structurally (where N = noun, V = verb, and A = adjective):

English	Korean
N	N
V	V
A	-

Once again, we face the problem of 'equivalence' across linguistic systems. Using 'translation-paired sentences', Harris found that English noun morphemes translated generally into Korean nouns, English verbs into Korean verbs, and English adjectives into Korean V+vn (where vn = a particular type of verbal affix). The point for Harris is that English adjective has a 'translation correspondent' in Korean, even though it does not have a morpheme class correspondent. If one were looking for initial IL hypotheses, notice that Harris is presenting an ordered hypothesis as to interlingual identifications: translation correspondents after morpheme correspondences in early IL grammar. Harris here provides another of the intellectual precursors of IL, when he comes to the problem of the detail of translation not yielding neat structural results. He talks about an 'in-between grammar' which would have 'a common part' for V+person and V+ed, i.e. in English vs Hebrew above. Then, for Harris, 'certain changes' '. . . would yield E[nglish] out of this Z, and other changes would yield H[ebrew] out of this Z. The difference between E and H would be the sum of these E – Z and H – Z changes [where Z = the in-between grammar]' (Harris 1954, p.270). Harris may be the first in the literature to talk about in-between grammars. (Harris's solution to the lack of structural correspond-ences between linguistic systems is reminiscent of a later attempt, Van Buren's (1972) 'grafting' component (cf. Chapter 6).)

Ferguson (1968) brings up the 'descriptivist's basic dilemma', the imposition of categories from outside the language. Historically this was an important principle in linguistics, namely, the struggle against the imposition of Latin categories upon English or upon American-Indian languages. It is an important problem in IL studies as well: How do we avoid imposing outside categories upon a learner's developing IL (cf. Klein 1986)? In order to contrast two linguistic structures, Ferguson points out, the linguist *must have some frame of reference* into which both structures fit. One cannot compare the noun system of one language, for example, with the noun system of another language without making it clear why the term 'noun' is given to two classes which might have been differently defined, with different relationships within each language. Ferguson's point is that linguists working on CA are being called upon to create a new universal grammar, a comprehensive theory of linguistics which has comparison as a base, something that might work for IL as well. Ferguson's examples concern relative clauses (also studied in SLA; see e.g. J. Schachter and Rutherford 1979; Gass 1979) and he concludes that comparison of structurally divergent languages yields several hypotheses about relative constructions that were *not* yielded in the literature when only isolated languages were described in a non-CA framework.

Transformational/generative influence

Chomsky's (1965) version of transformational/generative grammar presents notions that have affected CA and IL studies: deep structure/surface structure, competence/performance. As pointed out above, scholars are updating these and similar notions for SLA and also for pedagogical grammar (cf. Rutherford 1987 has the most comprehensive discussion available on the relation between grammar and SLA). Sharwood Smith and Rutherford (1984) postulate the existence of an 'IL base or core grammar'. The CA and IL point here is that the existence of some sort of deep or underlying structure greatly improves the equivalence problem, since comparable units are given by the theory. We take the position here that Chomsky has not been shown to be false for IL; its current obsolescence is based on linguistic arguments, never enough for SLA theory.

According to Chomsky, all sentences have both a deep structure and a surface structure. The deep structure is specified by a set of 'base rules' and includes all of the syntactic features (e.g. constituency relations) relevant to the meaning of a sentence. The surface structure of sentences results from the operation of another set of rules, the transformational rules, upon deep structure. The surface structure includes all of the syntactic features (e.g. order relations) that are relevant to the way sentences are produced. The important point for us is that, changes in detail notwithstanding, a central part of the underlying rules of the grammar of any language may not be specific to that language but may instead be rules of human language in general and, as a hypothesis, to IL in particular. This view has spawned a whole area of SLA, relating universal concerns of language to IL learning, under the assumption that rules of human language must be central to all types of language learning.

There is in the view of Chomsky (1965) the perspective that to account for differences that occur between languages, one has to postulate these differences on the basis of the effect of diverse sets of transformational rules operating upon essentially similar deep structures. The claim that languages are highly similar in their deep structures, if true, has important implications for CA, since CA can then concentrate its attention upon the transformational rules of languages being compared, investigating ways in which these rules operate to change similar deep structures into possibly very different surface structures. We will look at this view as it has developed in CA, noting CA problems that may have IL ramifications and also suggesting that what might become obviated in theoretical linguistics might still have relevance in the IL realm of interlingual identification.

P. Schachter (1966) carries these thoughts to their logical conclusion for CA: from the hypothesis that base rules are non-language-specific, or universal, it follows that if in any one language there is a certain deep structure that must undergo transformations, there will be corresponding deep structures in other languages that must also undergo transformations. This means that the CA analyst knows precisely which transformational rules to compare – namely, those transformational rules that apply to the corresponding deep structures in the several languages under comparison.

Let us take, as an example, relative clauses, since they keep showing up in both the theoretical linguistics literature and the SLA literature. Chomsky proposes that relative clauses represent transformations of deep-structure sentences, specifically sentences that are part of, or imbedded in, noun phrases, i.e. NP → N+S (noun phrase rewritten as noun plus sentence). The base rules of English, according to this model, include a rule to the effect that an NP may consist of, among other things, a noun plus a sentence, and the transformational rules of English include rules that, under certain circumstances, transform a sentence that is part of an NP into a relative clause. The base rules might specify an NP that includes the

N 'people' and the S 'I saw people.' The transformational rules might operate and transform the structure NP → N+S into N + Relative Clause, i.e. 'people whom I saw'. Changing details of the model aside, suppose that relative clauses in all languages represent transformations of deep structure sentences that are embedded in NPs. The English rule NP → N+S becomes not a language specific but a rule of human language in general. Then is it a rule of human ILs as well?

According to P. Schachter (1966), our task in CA is to compare transformational rules that operate in the languages we are interested in, to convert deep structures into surface structures as discussed and the learning predictions will follow. In the ASPECTS model (Chomsky 1965), transformational rules have two parts: a structural description which specifies the domain or the scope of the particular transformation, and structural changes specifying ways in which the transformed structures differ from the structures specified in the structural description.

In comparing relative clause transformations in two or more languages, structural description differences correspond to differences in the scope of relativization in the languages concerned, i.e. differences in the types of deep structures that can be relativized, and differences in the structural changes correspond to differences in the surface structure of the relative clauses themselves. P. Schachter compares the structural descriptions of the transformational rules of English and Tagalog relative clauses. In both languages the structural description also specifies certain NP structures that include an N and an S, i.e. a head noun and an embedded S, and the structural description also specifies that the embedded S must include an N that is 'identical' with the head noun; a deep-structure English head noun 'people' is relativizable with an embedded S 'I saw people.' Thus, one restriction is that the relative transformation will fail to operate if the base rules produce a deep structure NP with the head noun 'people' and the embedded S 'I saw animals' or 'John loves Mary.' Other restrictions on the structure of the embedded S are that it may not be a question and it may not be an imperative.

Tagalog relativization transformations, and presumably those in other languages, include similar restrictions, so it may not be the base alone that is universal. Here, P. Schachter superimposes translation criteria on generative criteria and, comparing translation equivalents, he finds that the most important difference in the structural descriptions of English and Tagalog relativization rules is the restrictions upon the syntactic role of the identical N within the embedded S. English generally has no restrictions. The identical N may be the object, as in the deep structure underlying 'people whom I saw', or it may be the subject, as in 'the flowers which are on the table', or it may be the object of a preposition, as in 'the table which the flowers are on'.

According to P. Schachter, the identical N in Tagalog almost always has the same syntactic role within the embedded S, that of 'topic', and although we use the 'same name' for other phenomena, this has no exact correspondence to English grammar. In Tagalog, the simple sentences generally include only one noun functioning as topic, and only this noun may serve as the identical noun specified in the structural description of the relativization transformation. For example, the Tagalog translation equivalent of the embedded S is 'The flowers are on the table' 'Nasa mesa ang bulaklak': the N 'bulaklak', 'flowers', is the topic and may serve as the identical N for the purpose of relativization, but 'mesa', 'table', is not a topic and may not serve as the identical N for the purposes of relativization. The point is that Tagalog has no structure precisely paralleling the English 'the table which the flowers are on', or 'on the table which the flowers are'. But in a translation equivalence sense, the 'approximate' semantic equivalents exist: 'mesa ang may bulaklak', 'table having flowers'. P. Schachter claims that this structure results from application of a relativization transformation of the deep structure NP → 'mesa' + 'May bulaklak ang mesa', where the second 'mesa' is the topic of the embedded S.

P. Schachter is trying here to account for some language learning difficulties in terms of some language differences in a particular theoretical framework (the paper was originally presented to an applied linguistic audience) and his analysis should be taken seriously. A hypothesis we can now make is that the L2 learner here might substitute Harris-type translation correspondence in an underlying sense when the structural categories do not work. Suppose some sort of deep structure *is* at work in cases like these. One would clearly love to know, for example, when creating interlingual identifications across linguistic systems of relative clause structures, whether such learners identify as same all of underlying structure defined as relevant to the analysis. Or only parts? And which parts? Or, given one of the basic tenets of the IL hypothesis, that learners create partially separate linguistic systems, do such learners create in this domain something structural that is in neither NL nor TL, and how does this relate to universals of language and of IL? And we must ask if there is a point at which IL learners impose translation criteria on structural criteria. Unless it is that there are cases where structural criteria are imposed on translation criteria.

P. Schachter argues that there are three types of changes in the relativization transformation of all languages.

(a) The first is some kind of linking, i.e. an explicit marking of the fact that the clause is syntactically connected to the head N. Here Schachter provides information from four unrelated languages, one Indo-European (English), one Malayo-Polynesian (Tagalog), one Niger Congo (Twi) and one Afro-Asiatic (Hausa). In all four, linking is accomplished by the insertion of a linking element at or near the beginning of a relative clause:

English	Tagalog	Twi	Hausa
wh-	-ng	a	da
	na		

(Ferguson 1968 has a broader set of descriptive categories in this respect: (i) attributive, no independent linking morphemic material; (ii) independent connecting morphemic material; and (iii) dependent, connecting material in main clauses, but does not mention P. Schachter's point (b).)

(b) A second kind of structural change is the alteration of N within the embedded S that is identical with the head N. For example, in English, 'people' + 'I saw people' → 'people whom I saw'. In Twi, the identical N is replaced by a personal pronoun counterpart and is like English, except that English has a special set of forms, e.g. 'whom'. In Hausa there is the deletion of the identical N in some cases, in others pronominalization of it, and in other cases Hausa allows deletion of the pronoun. Tagalog is the simplest; it deletes the identical N and uses a linker.

(c) The third type of structural change is what P. Schachter calls 'other subordinating devices', and here the four languages show the most idiosyncratic characteristics. In English there is front shifting of the pronoun replacement of the identical N, regardless of its syntactic role with the relative clause. Twi uses a special set of tone patterns that occur only in subordinate structures. Hausa has a special set of verb tense markers that occur only in subordinate structures. Tagalog uses no other subordinating material except linkage and deletion of the identical N.

CA Models

But what models are there in the CA literature to help us understand interlingual identifications and the CA problems inherent in them? How many distinct ways do we know of in which one can 'look across' linguistic systems? I have looked through the vast CA dissertation literature of the 1940s to the 1960s; I find perhaps 8–10 distinct models and now present exemplars.

(1) A structural model

An interesting CA dissertation of the 1950s (what Lado several times (pc) called one of the best) is that of Kleinjans (1958). This thesis, done at Michigan, deals with the modification of nouns in English and Japanese, compared from the point of view of Japanese learning English. It is one of the first discussions of CA problems that arise out of the ESL concerns of Fries (See Chapter 1 above). Comparison is made of the noun-head modification structure of the two languages, pattern by pattern on the basis of the differences in the three key factors set out by Lado (see Chapter 1 above): form, meaning and distribution. Kleinjans first sets out (11ff) the significant aspects of structures he will compare using Fries's grammatical theories. On p.25 he states that 'immediate constituents' will form the basis for comparison between English and Japanese, thus *accepting as same* across languages the unit of syntax posited by structural linguists. And on p.33 he sets up 'test frames' for Japanese, as Fries had done for English, to describe Japanese word classes. On p.50 he raises equivalence problems, seeing areas of non-comparability and 'holes', as described above, but provides no solutions.

This thesis, however, should be seriously studied for problems of units in language contact situations and equivalence across linguistic systems. I provide here a brief outline of useful linguistic portions for the reader and note that in several places – Selinker (1966, 1969) and Gass and Selinker (1983a Ch.1) – I have critiqued, perhaps too harshly, Kleinjans' (Ch.4) psycholinguistic attempts to superimpose on his data, *after the data are in*, the 'transfer paradigm' and 'transfer surface' model of Osgood (1953). It is interesting to note the range of topics discussed. For example, on p.53 in Kleinjans there is discussion of feasibility tests of comparison (cf. Nemser's tests in the next chapter); p.54: when there is not complete 'congruence' of structures, 'compare patterns' must equate as well as contrast; p.71ff: a key chapter on comparison and prediction; p.72ff: premodification structures and examples of grammatical meaning; p.112ff: post-modification structures; p.136ff: determiners. English structures are presented in formulaic form on the left of a table with examples, and Japanese structures are on the right. There are blanks on the right and lots of holes, but there is a wealth of data and one could form numerous IL learning hypotheses from it. This model, which provides extensive tables with NL structures clearly presented formulaically on the left and with TL structures on the right, is where I began to understand in detail how the TL can look structurally chaotic to the learner. The hypothesis follows: When trying to set up interlingual identifications, the learner looks for criteria that are more than structural. But what are they? We look at the next model.

(2) A diaform/functional model

Sebuktekin's (1964) thesis, presented at Berkeley, has the direction of contrasts from Turkish to English (so English will look 'chaotic'), and is based on available descriptions for Turkish and English. The scope is ambitious, covering morphological structures, types of morphemes, morpheme combinations, derivational and inflectional morphemes. This work teaches us much about the structure of morphemes, their combinations and so on; it is surprising that studies on morpheme acquisition in SLA do not consult this work. Sebuktekin, who like Kleinjans is aware of the problems of comparison, points out that one's emerging contrasts may be a function of one's methodology. His sources for English are the structuralist writers Francis, Sledd and Hill. He handles the equivalence problem in terms of the common definition of selected linguistic features across languages. He looks at 'plurality', for example, and notes that the functions of forms across languages are not formally analysable. He points out that one can compare forms across languages but needs to consider the semantic and functional content of one's CA labels to compare functions across linguistic systems.

Sebuktekin presents two lengthy sections on morphological processes and parts of speech in the two languages. These sections are interesting from the CA point of view of morpheme processes in a language like Turkish, since he employs translation as a tool intersecting structural criteria. He provides a unique solution for the problem of equivalence by proposing a unit of contrast he calls the 'diaform'. Diaforms for Sebuktekin (p.72) are forms which are identified consistently as same in translation and function from the source language to the target. The smallest dialinguistic unit is the 'diamorpheme' and the largest is the 'diasentence'. (Selinker and Lamendella 1978, p.172 illustrate in detail the possible shape of an 'IL diasystem' from a neurofunctional perspective.)

Sebuktekin provides micro-detail. His symbology, a slanted line placed between forms, indicates a diaform, e.g. kiz/girl; -ler/-s 'plural'. The limits of his analysis are clear – the extent of Turkish morphology. His major symbols are:

S: suffix	MM: more than one morpheme
P:prefix	FM: free morpheme
I: internal change	WO: word order
PM: portmanteau morpheme	PP: paraphrasing

I will now present for the reader a brief guide to Sebuktekin's work which provides excellent background for dealing with problems of comparison across linguistic systems. It is important to remember that Turkish is an example of an agglutinative language, whose characteristic feature is its single word constructions with as many as fourteen suffixes expressing structural meanings often marked syntactically in English. Section 4.1 discusses substantive derivational affixes – e.g. -ci is a 'professional' morpheme with its diaformic structure being S/S and S/MM; -lik is an 'associative' morpheme with its diaformic structure being either S/S,I, S/FM,PP or S/FM,MM; -li is an 'attributive' morpheme with its diaformic structure being either S/S or S/FM,MM. An example of the attributive S/S diamorpheme would be -li/-ful. We can coin a more modern term for such variation – 'diaformic variant' – and ponder how these relate to attested IL variants.

Other material the reader might wish to study includes: loan affixes (p.82); from verbal to nominal derivational suffixes (Section 4.2); from nominal to verbal derivational suffixes (Section 4.3); reflexive, reciprocal and causative 'voice' suffixes (pp.113–14); inflectional suffixes, especially nominal, e.g. plural (p.140); predicative (p.144) and past tense (p.149). An interesting feature of Section 4.5 involves matchings of 'complete correspondence', 'partial correspondence' and 'no corresponding overt form'.

The diaform unit, especially given its variable nature, is a potentially relevant one for IL theory. It appears to match the criteria for 'linguistically relevant units' of IL learning as set forth in Selinker (1972, Section 5.4), to be discussed in Chapter 8. Sebuktekin's translation-structural criteria are important, since he has empirically discovered that there exists a 'range of forms' identified as same across linguistic systems but having no correspondence in their morphological or syntactic features. This is one of the confusions that I think the IL learner is up against. I hypothesize that IL learners create a similar unit for themselves while in the process of comparing TL input and their emerging IL. This gives us yet again more detail in working through the puzzle of interlingual identifications. That Sebuktekin's work has not been discussed in the SLA literature is mystifying.

(3) A pragmatic model

We next look at the dissertation by Atai (1964), a study also done at Michigan but after Lado had moved to Georgetown. Atai looks at the 'major English question signals': word order, function words and final intonation contours, comparing them with the 'major Persian question signals': 'addition of a non-falling intonation contour, question words and other function words'. This is a pedagogically oriented study, but comparison is nicely separated from pedagogical concerns. The study handles the problems of size and units of a CA, discussed above, by accepting these structural linguistic classifications.

Atai provides two reasons why he chose to study question signals: (a) according to Fries (1952, p.51), question signals are the second most frequent sentence type, and (b) they are one of the most 'persistent problems' for Persian-speaking students learning English. (On pp.4–5 he notes fossilization without naming it.) Atai defines 'question' pragmatically in the way Fries did, namely, 'an utterance deliberately directed at getting an answer' (p.52), and a question is an utterance which is 'intended to bring forth an oral response'. (p.13). He points out that this pragmatic definition does have problems: if an 'utterance' is a stretch of speech between pauses (a Fries idea), this is a definition widely attacked in the literature. Also, as Atai points out, there are other things one wants to call questions that are not intended to bring forth an oral response. On pp.28–43 Atai presents a statement of the structural facts of four types of questions in English, providing useful charts.

Atai solves the problem of equivalence by defining the notion 'question' the same in both languages, even though he produces a clear counter example: the sentence 'Tell me about your trip' is clearly not a question, but is presumably stated to elicit a response. What is useful here is the struggle with the CA problem of pragmatic definition of structures, which Atai relates to 'difficulty levels'. Lado

(Chapter 1 above) predicted that out of CA one would emerge with a 'hierarchy of difficulty' based on NL and TL differences. After many attempts to give reality to this intriguing idea, this endeavour was prematurely abandoned. Learners tell us that some things are harder than others and as Atai hints, such things may relate to interlingual identifications where structural comparisons yield 'holes' as described above.

(4) A semanto-grammatical model

The CA dissertation by Hoi (1965), completed at Columbia, is an attempt to identify the differences between the expression of time and time relationships in the English and Vietnamese verb systems, by using the framework suggested by Allen. I suppose one cannot get a topic more quintessentially semantic than 'time' and Hoi struggles with the CA problem of initially starting a CA model from meaning criteria. Hoi builds a strong case that a major difficulty of Vietnamese students learning the English verb system is due to the different elements and 'devices' used in the two languages to show time and time relationships. The aim is to identify the devices in English and the corresponding devices in Vietnamese that signal time relationships. Her view of CA is View 1 above and there are no problems concerning what is 'the same' across linguistic systems, since these are 'given' by Allen's English analysis.

Some of her conclusions are as follows. In English the main verb in a 'complete sentence' is most always time oriented, but in Vietnamese every verb is 'non-committal' with respect to time. On the basis of form, according to Allen, English is a two-time verb system, whereas Vietnamese is a one-time verb system, with time identified by context and/or by time expressions. In Vietnamese, time expressions are the main devices for orienting predications with respect to time, whereas in English, time expressions are only one device used for time reference. Auxiliaries are used for expressing time relationships in both languages, but it is more complicated in English where with earlier-time time relationship to a past time, had is used; to a present time, have is used; and to a future time, will have is used. However, in Vietnamese, there is one auxiliary, da, that has the same function in all three kinds of time.

It is the basic assumption of Hoi's dissertation that differences between NL and TL verb systems seriously relate to persistent difficulties for Vietnamese learning English, and I interpret this work to make a plausible case for interlingual identifications involving semanto-grammatical correspondences. There is a complicating variable concerning aspect in the two languages – presumably Vietnamese has none (p.157). This latter should prove to be an interesting IL complication.

(5) A transformational/markedness model

The third Michigan dissertation considered here (Verma 1966) shows a more recent theoretical orientation. Verma presents a comparison of the English and Hindi systems of noun phrase in reference to their categorical structures, the nature and scope of their transformational operations, and their overall characteristic tendencies in manipulating the constituents of the phrase to obtain various kinds of strings. His general conclusions are that differences in the noun phrase structures of English and Hindi are 'more marked' in the behaviour of embedded structures and that the English noun phrase has a more 'complex' structure. This is one of the earliest CA treatments of markedness. There are many discussions of possible markedness constraints in SLA (e.g. *passim* in Flynn and O'Neal 1988; Gass and J. Schachter 1989) but none of them refers to this early work full of interlingual markedness detail.

In Chapter 1, Verma deals with the theoretical implications of CA, asking what is comparable across languages. His answer is that linguistic metatheories give comparable categories across languages, fitting into CA View 1. Additionally, he gets very close to the view of Sebuktekin discussed above, by his reference to the 'competent bilingual' who he claims is the source and justification for establishing equivalences between items across languages. In this view, one's linguistic metatheory provides comparable categories across languages by recognizing certain universals, but the data are set up by bilingual equivalence.

Chapter 2 sets up essential characteristics of the English noun phrase, discussing such items as proper names, appositive and relative clauses, determinate and indeterminate nouns, quantifiers, numerals, specified nouns, emphatics, predeterminers, negation in the noun phrase, the wh- constituent, and nominalizations – a fair amount of useful detail. His emphasis is on an important IL area, the determiner of the noun phrase and the distinctions of specificity shown in the determiner system. Pronouns for him are derivatives rather than basic formatives, involving different kinds of determiners and falling within the scope of the same kind of basic generalizations as nouns with different determiners. Chapter 3 discusses the noun phrase structure of Hindi, using the same mode and scope of description as for English: the indeterminate, the determinate, quantifiers, numerals, the constituent wh-, nominalization, etc.

Bilingual intuition does in fact enter the analysis and as an example of one of the CA or 'looking across' models, this is a plus. Verma claims that English shows three degrees of definiteness: indeterminate, non-specified determinate, and specified determinate. He believes (p.146) that the case of non-specified determinate may be classified as indeterminate, but his decision to associate it with specified determinate is motivated by the fact that Hindi, in its dichotomy of indeterminate/determinate, implies that non-specified determinate is determinate. This analysis is motivated bilingually by the fact that at times English 'a' goes untranslated in Hindi and at times appears as 'eh', the latter needed to make a particular sentence grammatical.

Verma thus uses Hindi categories to set up English ones and this is another example of one of the characteristics of his CA model. The researcher interested in article structure in all the English ILs that exist would do well to look at this material for detailed insights in the use of grammatico-semantic categories in one linguistic system to set up grammatical categories in another (see below). The article in English IL has been thought about in SLA research, e.g. in the morpheme studies as obligatory categories (e.g. Dulay and Burt 1973, 1974); by Seliger (1977) to distinguish 'high input generators' from 'low input generators'; by Huebner (1983) in his detailed study of the Hmong speaker's English in Hawaii in a 'dynamic paradigm'; Selinker and Douglas (1989) suggest a global English IL constraint for articles, etc., but none of these studies has used this model of interlingually identifying an article by abstract categories in another linguistic system.

Verma presents (Ch.4) a systematic comparison of the two systems, setting up their similarity as follows: in categorical structure; in the inventory of categories; in the possibilities of embedding; both distinguish between appositives and relatives with almost the same restrictions on their occurrence; and in both, adjectival modifiers are obtained by similar transformational operations. Differences occur within this framework of general similarity: in the categorical structure, Hindi lacks the dichotomy specified–non-specified; it has no system of articles; it has no category like the predeterminer of English; and the category quantifier is not identical in the two languages. Also, Hindi (unlike English) does not allow the constituent NEG in the noun phrase, but both allow the constituent 'wh-'. The result of the former is the absence in Hindi of negative determiners, negative pronouns and negative NPs, e.g. in an adverbial function. Concerning the behaviour of embedded structures and transformational operations that can be carried out on them, unlike English, Hindi makes all its adjectival modifiers precede the noun head, no matter what the internal structure of the modifier. Also unlike English, Hindi forces all its modifications in the adjectival function to assume adjectival form. Verma states that 'this explains the general absence of nominal modifier and nominal head sequences in Hindi'. One wonders if explanations such as these are reasonable for IL modification structures.

(6) A diaglossic grammar model

An important dissertation for the theory of CA is that by Dingwall (1964) done at Georgetown. The title of his thesis shows its scope: 'Diaglossic Grammar'. This is an attempt to determine which set of 'analytic procedures' provided by linguistics is most effective in determining the relative similarities and differences when two grammatical systems are compared. He presents a general model of a three-component diaglossic grammar which is sketched in detail, with examples provided from various languages. Dingwall's domain of study is morphotactics, an area of SLA with which I am convinced many learners have trouble.

Let me outline several key parts: typology of languages and Component I, which relates to indices of various kinds (p.83); outline of grammar and Component II (p.123); details of Winnebego (p.147) and English and Winnebego (p.153); approaches to morphotactics and Component III (p.162); English and Melanesian from a morphosyntactic approach; a transformational approach (p.191); some points about application of his model concerning German (p.247) in an attempt to 'align' his material with Lees's grammar of English nominalizations (Lees 1959, which has a most interesting CA appendix of Turkish nominalizations); proposal for a diaglossic grammar of German and English (p.275).

Dingwall faces the equivalence issue by using translation equivalents in setting up his categories. He is convinced that there must be a generative component in setting up interlingual identifications.

(7) An eclectic generative model

Otanes (1966), whose work was done at UCLA, presents a CA of verb complementation in English and Tagalog. He begins with Tagalog grammar, then presents patterns of verb complementation in both languages and concludes with a summary of the 'main points of difficulty' for learners. The analysis is based on Chomsky's generative transformational theory but, interestingly, is openly eclectic, which, given the IL evidence to date, is a plausible approach.

Otanes adapts some of Chomsky's 1965 model and retains some of his 1957 model. He retains the context-restricted rules in the base of phrase structure component of the grammar, since he says that such rules reveal co-occurrence restrictions more immediately (pp.6–7) than a system of context-free base rules plus transformations that 'filter' the deep structures. He adapts from the 1965 model the use of generalized phrase markers, instead of two string transformations, that allow the reintroduction of the initial symbol 'S' in generated strings. He also adapts to his description syntactic features, i.e. feature specifications and not categories. His data, too, are translation equivalents in both languages which employ verb complementation in their surface structure. He presents patterns of verb complementation in terms of Tagalog vs English structures (50ff) and English vs Tagalog structures (179ff). He presents the contrasting patterns in each direction respectively and compares them with translation equivalents respectively.

There is much detail here concerning the languages and points of difficulty predicted by the analysis in an area of IL grammar little understood. It appears that translation equivalents become a consensus methodology for a large number of CA studies. Explorations of theoretical eclecticism in CA grammars is most important for, in this case, co-occurrence restrictions are certainly an L2 learning problem and highlighting that aspect of grammar in CA is reasonable. Highlighting feature analysis is reasonable too since in some cases it looks as if it is features that are identified interlingually.

(8) A cognate syntactic model

Cohen's (1967) thesis, presented at Texas, presents a CA of the grammar and constituent structure of the order classes of prenominal and postnominal modifiers in Spanish and English. The order classes are described in terms of their constituents, the constructions into which they enter, and their relationships with each other. He emphasizes the many similar grammatical patterns that exist between Spanish and English that can be a source of language transfer from one language to the other. He relates his analysis to the 'frustration' of learning a language (p.3), believing that 'cognate syntactic patterns' indicate patterns of grammatical correspondence that can be transferred effectively. This is not too remote from Corder (1967; see Chapter 6 below), where it is claimed, for one of the first times in the literature, that mother-tongue influence can be a positive force in language learning.

This is another dissertation with a great deal of data and hypotheses which could be carefully studied in an IL framework. The notion 'cognate syntactic pattern' may prove to be a useful one in dealing with some problems of equivalence across linguistic systems. We should investigate whether the notions kernel and derived sentences, whose grammar and constituent structure are similar in two languages, make sense in the interlingual domain, even though they have been superseded in linguistic theory. They may make some sense in the grammatical area Cohen is talking about – word order – since the level of abstraction of IL cognate syntactic patterns may be very surfacy indeed.

(9) An intonational/functional model

Radaravanija's (1965) thesis, presented at Columbia, is an analysis of the elements in Thai that correspond to the basic intonation patterns of English, in order to identify potential difficulties for Thai students learning English. (Her data for English are derived from the Kenyon and Knott pronouncing dictionary of American English, and Pike 1944; Thai sources are herself and recordings of NY Thai students.) The phenomena of intonation in a tone language and its effect on ILs, including the potential of miscommunication, is a topic which is, unfortunately, not dealt with in the SLA literature to my knowledge, though millions of L2 learners clearly are affected. In fact, the intonational difficulties of a Thai student learning English and attempting to perform successfully in a pharmacology seminar are what first led me to propose fossilization and its contextual basis (this is reported in Selinker 1980).

In Chapter 2 she discusses tones in Thai, a complicated subject since they interplay with stress and intonation patterns: tones may be changed under different degrees of stress, and different types of terminal contours may cause modifications of tones. In Chapter 3 she discusses tones, stresses, rhythm, junctures and terminal contours in

Thai. Concerning the 'relativity' of tones in Thai, she states (p.42)
that 'no two records of the same tone are precisely alike in pitch,
though the pattern of the curves and their general relation to each
other are remarkably constant'. Her review of the literature concludes
that there are five distinct tonal phonemes in Thai (p.44), but there is
a question as to whether there is a sixth. To complicate matters,
weakest stress occurs on a 'syncopated syllable', which is characterized by very short syllable length, and several things 'disappear', e.g.
the distinction between short and long vowels, the first member of a
vowel cluster, etc. (pp.53–4).

She presents detail regarding the Thai 'suprasegmental' area: the
relevance of frequency of usage (high frequency words undergo
changes in tone more than do rarely used words) (p.58); stresses
(arguments are presented as to whether they are phonetic or
phonemic) (pp.59–61); how the rhythm unit may determine the
degree of stress on syllables (pp.70–2); other factors which affect the
degree of stress in syllables (they include form classes, position within
a word or a phonemic clause, a vowel, final consonant and tone of
that syllable) (pp.74–6); ways of identifying Thai stress (p.77); and
junctures, terminal contours and sentences without sentence particles
(pp.86–8).

She writes (p.90) that a terminal contour conditions allophones of
the tone immediately preceding it since it is difficult 'or perhaps
impossible' to 'convert a tone in a direction incompatible with a
following terminal contour, the terminal contour simply causes a
slight raising or lowering of the pitch on that syllable, but not to a
degree great enough to produce a different tone' (Radaravanija 1965,
p.90). Is this why Thai speakers are often so incomprehensible to
NSs of English? Could it be that Thai–English IL speakers are
allowing terminal contours to affect the quality of allophones that
precede them? One long weekend in Bangkok I tried to investigate
some of this with clearly fossilized Thai–English speakers. My
tentative conclusion was that these speakers were *not* transferring the
tones of Thai to their English but were *transferring the principle of
tonality* to create in their IL a tonal/intonational system that was just
not the same as that in their Thai. It now seems to me in rereading
this dissertation that the key to what these IL speakers were doing
relates to the apparent impossibility (and this constraint is probably
transferred) of converting a tone in an 'incompatible' direction – the
incompatibility here not being terminal contours of the Thai type but
the approximations of the intonational endings of English utterances.
I hope some researchers with a strong knowledge of both Thai and

phonetics will look carefully at all of this in detail. We need to know more about the transfer of NL abstract principles and constraints in addition to the transfer of units and concatenations.

At times, she comes close to being ahead of her time by almost describing IL data when she is doing her CA (e.g. in discussing stress in English and Thai (p.107) and terminal contours in English and Thai (p.124)), and when she is discussing some of the 'difficulties' Thais have in English (pp.143–59) in terms of functions of basic intonation patterns in English, and a comparison with elements in Thai sentences having similar functions. Given this functional perspective, she is able to break the strong Lado mould (see Chapter 1) of CA and there are no 'holes' of the kind discussed several times in this chapter. As she is doing her CA, she uses the strategy of comparing different means of signalling 'the same thing'. In retrospect, seeing her struggling so hard with CA problems and missing the relevant data is one of the detailed threads which led me to the postulation of IL, since it became clear to me in the 1960s that all these intelligent people were not looking at the right data. In fact, one of my earliest IL talks, at AILA in 1969, was entitled: 'The psychologically relevant data of second language learning', published as Sclinker 1971. This point is picked up in Chapter 8 on the discovery of IL.

Summary

In this chapter we have been considering problems of CA comparison. We addressed the question of the relationship of CA to a theoretical linguistics in a constant state of flux by discussing in some detail two basic views one could take, either by accepting the theory chosen as given and thereby solving the CA equivalence problem of units of interlingual identifications (View 1), or by using the CA to challenge the theory chosen, thereby leaving the equivalence problem open (View 2). We have looked at the CA problem of whether a deep-structure grammatical transfer is possible, and concluded that it is. This is a different sort of interlingual identification than that described in the last chapter. Given the IL idea of a partially separate linguistic system, we wonder if in deep-structure transfer, learners create *partially separate linguistic systems*. We have seen no literature on this possibility, though it appears reasonable.

In considering 'questions' vs 'primary questions', we entered into the tricky problem of size of linguistic structure to be compared. We also saw that this was solved in a clever way by Atai. We also saw that a major CA problem involves the name of what is set up as 'same' across linguistic systems. Is what is named the same in fact the same? We see this as a major learner problem in consciousness raising in grammar learning (cf. Rutherford 1987), since students might be misled by names across linguistic systems. Most of the authors discussed here do not in fact face this problem, which is a shame for it is a problem in describing IL, since, as Klein and Perdue (e.g Purdue 1984) have pointed out, it is often hard to know even what is a verb in early IL.

We discussed the problem of contrastive challenges, looking at units across linguistic systems identified as same in terms of their relationship to the correctness of a linguistic theory, for us the linguistic systems being not only NL/TL but also NL/IL and IL/TL. We wondered about how solid a particular constraint was in terms of such challenges and how that would affect IL description. We worried about the problem of what to include in a particular CA; partly this is a problem of size of the CA, but mostly it is a matter of theoretical judgement. We wondered, for example, whether to include the 'let' sentences in 8–11, i.e. whether all of the like-subject constraint is included in the interlingual identification of subject raising in object position. How, then, are we to take the case of 'related data' – namely, if starred sentences regularly occur in IL, as they do, then must all the data related by theory to these sentences be included in our CA? Especially, should the creation of a 'simpler' syntactic component in theoretical linguistics mean that we should be looking for a 'simpler' IL core grammar? One of the key problems this may boil down to remains unsolved. The CA literature provides some detailed discussion of the serious question (a dilemma really) of the relationship of translation criteria to transfer criteria to structural criteria. We have seen above that it is hard to know at times whether the L2 learner is transferring an abstract principle or is translating actual sentences. This relates to the CA problem of whether one starts one's analysis with structural criteria first or meaning criteria set up by translation.

Finally, there is the CA problem of how many fundamentally different CA models there are! There is first the structural model of Lado and Kleinjans which leads to the IL hypothesis that interlingual identifications are made by learners based on structural criteria. We know this is sometimes true, but study of the model shows 'holes', as discussed by Harris. Kleinjans accepts as same across linguistic systems the structural unit of immediate constituents and provides tables of the concatenation of such units. These units provide holes in the other system and it is clear that we have to look in interlingual identifications for more than the structural.

A different model is provided by Harris with an in-between grammar, called a Z-component, with translation correspondences becoming a good candidate, in addition to those mentioned at the end of Chapter 3, for interlingual units. Harris's Z-component is one of the strands leading to IL with the hypothesis that there is an ordering to interlingual identifications, where the learner, at least in the area of morphology, looks first for structural correspondence and then for translation correspondence. One now has the IL question of whether translation criteria are imposed on structural, or the reverse. Also, is there a point at which learners onset this learning strategy?

Sebuktekin also studies morphological processes and also employs translation as a tool intersecting with functional and structural criteria, but his model with diaforms is quite different. Like Sebuktekin, Verma's CA data are set up by bilingual equivalences as are Otanes's, but each of them suggests different models, as does P. Schachter who superimposes translation criteria upon generative criteria. Since there are no holes in any of these analyses, bilingual intuition thus enters centrally in the setting up of the model. Dingwall, who provides still a different model, also uses translation equivalents in setting up his CA, perhaps the consensus position. If so, we do need to investigate translation a little more in SLA.

Sebuktekin provides a unique solution to problems of comparability: diaforms (hinted at in previous linguistic literature) as interlingual units. In his model they are forms identified consistently as same across languages by translation, a methodology possible for IL. He noted the variable nature of his interlingual units long before SLA variation became vogue. It may be that in early IL that seems strongly controlled by interlingual identifications, the diaform is a particularly strong unit.

Atai provides a different model, using a pragmatic definition of CA structures studied, though he notes problems with this sort of definition. He also notes that the structures he studies – questions – may prove to be possible fossilization phenomena. He includes in the model a learner hierarchy of difficulty which may relate to interlingual identifications in terms of structures and the holes that are so identified.

Hoi struggles with the problem of starting the CA analysis with semantics first. He builds a case that a major difficulty with Vietnamese students learning English is due to devices used in the

two languages to show time. He provides information on semanto-
grammatical correspondences. From this study we can suggest that
the elements and devices used to signal a semantic category are units
of interlingual identifications. Verma's model, though, uses semantics
in a different way; he uses such categories in one language to set up
categories in another in a way that seems reminiscent of some sorts of
interlingual identifications. Radaravanija's research strategy is also
semantic, different ways of signalling the same thing – in this case
different ways in Thai of signalling the basic intonation patterns of
English. Lattey also chooses a semantics-based model in which there
are again no holes in this way of doing CA.

Verma's is the first CA model to suggest markedness as a factor in
interlingual identifications. This factor is still open to investigation in
SLA. He provides a generative component which suggests deep-
structure transfer, a suggestion that seems plausible in terms of the
IL evidence. Dingwall's question involves the set of linguistic
analytical procedures that are most effective in CA. He provides a
three-component diaglossic grammar, including generative processes,
a suggestion unfortunately not followed through in the SLA
literature. Otanes uses generative procedures in an eclectic model; in
each case his chosen analysis highlights IL fact, an entirely
reasonable position. Note that with the Radaravanija model one also
can talk about the transfer of underlying categories, this time a
phonological one, the principle of tonality.

Cohen studies word order and order classes, an important IL area
and one studied in depth in Chapter 7 below. The order classes he
studies are pre- and postnominalization in Spanish and English, a
salient area in the learning of these languages. He incorporates into
his model the notion of cognate syntactic patterns, a useful notion
reflecting similar grammatical patterns in the two languages which
may be the source of transfer. He uses discarded generative notions
which I suggested may have validity in the interlingual domain.

Radaravanija also provides one of the strands leading to IL. This
work includes in the model not only looking across linguistic systems,
but looking at what learners actually do in a more or less systematic
way. This leads to the question of what the relevant data of SLA
might be, a question taken up in Chapters 7 and 8. By looking in
detail at an important but tricky area of SLA in a CA framework, the
basic intonation patterns in English and what corresponds to them in
Thai, Radaravanija shows that different ways of signalling the same
thing have to be taken into account in any model that looks across
linguistic systems.

These models are important in terms of the paradox raised at the beginning of Chapter 3, of individuals in language contact situations consistently violating the constraints of units within previously learned linguistic systems, of identifying and grouping across linguistic systems units which break up the prior, usually native, system. We conclude that this breaking up of systems and reuniting in new systems (ILs) through interlingual identifications is an important mechanism in SLA. We need to know whether there is a manageable number of CA models out there to compete for models of interlingual identifications; our conclusion is that there are some eight to ten depending on grouping, and in this chapter we have presented exemplars from the large CA literature.

It is a pity that the CA literature, especially the CA dissertation literature, is a buried literature and thus so unknown. It is perhaps an intellectual tragedy of sorts, since so much detail is worked out in this literature (along with detailed presentations of other relevant literatures). From this literature, the interested language teacher or SLA researcher can create scores of testable hypotheses about what L2 learners are doing and be helped by CA detail to investigate IL.

We have now looked at units and equivalence across linguistic systems through study of bilingualism (Chapter 3) and to problems of comparison in CA (Chapter 4). In the next chapter we look in detail at some CA and EA data which could also possibly be IL data.

Points for discussion

(1) In the current second language acquisition literature one finds many attempts at comparison: IL with NL; IL with TL; earlier IL to later IL; N/N interaction with N/NN interaction; N/NN interaction with NN/NN interaction; input to NSs with input to NNSs; Spanish speakers learning English, with Japanese speakers learning English, etc. Choose three of these and describe possible relationships to the classical CA genre of research described in this chapter. Try to see the effect on our understanding of IL and IL learning by this comparison.

(2) Consider the CA problem of 'how many fundamentally different CA models there are', as presented in this chapter. Do you accept the solution proposed? Provide an example of how each model might relate to IL and IL learning. Are there in fact other 'fundamentally different' models you could propose? And how might these relate to IL and IL learning?

(3) Describe the two views presented in this chapter of the

relationship of linguistic theory to CA. Illustrate each with an
example from the chapter. With an original example, discuss the
limitations vs the good points of each as it is related to IL and
IL learning.

(4) Using the examples of 'He is certain to win' and 'He wants me
to speak French,' presented at the beginning of this chapter,
discuss the possibility of 'deep-structure grammatical transfer'
in SLA. Choose one of the other models that seem to argue for
some sort of 'underlying' language transfer and evaluate the
argument. Gather original IL examples to bolster either side of
the argument.

(5) Now consider the important theoretical questions of equivalence, comparability and units of CA. Evaluate whether the
discussion presented here begins to clarify Weinreich's notion
of interlingual identifications and its importance to second
language acquisition, namely, as possibly *the* basic learning
strategy in SLA. Be sure to note Harris's ordered hypothesis as
to interlingual identifications: translation correspondents after
morpheme correspondences in early IL grammar. You might
want to consider P. Schachter's detailed example of relative
clauses, above, where it seems to be the case that translation
criteria are imposed on structural ones. You might then want to
consider some of the other ordering possibilities mentioned in
this chapter – functional over structural, for example.

(6) Now focus on some of the studies that would have been
impossible in the 1950s and 1960s: contrastive rhetoric and
contrastive discourse analysis. Repeat the exercise in (5), once
again trying to see the effect on our understanding of IL and IL
learning.

(7) Here we considered the major CA problem of the name of what
is set up as 'same' across linguistic systems, i.e. is what is named
the same in fact the same? Do you consider this a major learner
problem in consciousness raising as stated in the chapter? Do
you agree that learners might in fact be misled by names across
linguistic systems, provided by either teachers or textbooks?
Note the point made in the chapter that names across linguistic
systems produce a problem in describing IL, since it is often
hard to know even what is a verb in early IL.

(8) Rethink the Lado/Fries approach to CA as presented in
Chapter 1 and compare it with the models presented in this
chapter. Now describe how CA attempts to handle the manner
in which language transfer is due to either NL structure or NL
rules.

(9) Now consider multiple language acquisition. How would the models presented here handle language transfer from a first IL to a second? How would Fries, Lado and Weinreich? In a consideration of multiple language acquisition and the models presented here, how would the bilingualism categories presented in the last chapter now affect your view of language transfer?

(10) In light of the models presented in this chapter, re-evaluate the paradox discussed at the beginning of Chapter 3 coming out of the work of Weinreich as discussed in Chapter 2. How might each of these models suggest a way out of the paradox of individuals in language contact situations consistently violating the constraints of units within previously learned linguistic systems?

(11) Now reconsider your previous answers to the question of multiple language acquisition. Specifically with the models presented in this chapter, does the interlingual identifications answer, as an important mechanism in SLA, satisfy the SLA cross-linguistic experience of identifying and grouping units which break up prior systems, reuniting in new systems called interlanguages?

5 Some CA and EA (and possibly IL) data

Predictive IL data

It is time to provide some detailed CA and EA data to gain a deeper understanding of the contrasts discussed so far in this volume. Our continuing aim is to inspect their 'value', in the Saussurian sense discussed above, as potential units of IL and IL learning. The point of classical CA is to predict 'errors' that would (or could) be made by an L2 learner of one NL specifically attempting to master another NL, called the TL. Even with the difficulties of the enterprise of error prediction as discussed above, the success of that research enterprise is that it (especially through empirical calls by Lado) inspired researchers actually to go out and look at learner speech with specific predictions in mind. Classical CA, EA and bilingualism studies gave those predictions a framework, provided empirical training to SLA scholars and helped in no small measure to bring us to IL and the flow of studies we currently see in SLA. In particular, CA and EA data lead to predictive IL data in terms of possible interlingual identifications.

In this chapter I will build on a study begun quite some time ago in the classical CA mould to predict some of the difficulties that speakers of Israeli Hebrew (IH) *might* have learning English, especially American English (AE), on the phonological level (Selinker 1960). This study, a step in the discovery of IL (Chapter 8), is presented here to provide linguistic detail in terms of *predictive IL data* for possible empirical study. Next we will look at several EA studies from the PAKS project mentioned in the last chapter, ending with a detailed look at the classical EA study done by Coulter and reinterpreted in the IL framework presented here. These studies also provide predictive IL data; such data are necessary since we know that learners do not transfer all of their NL systems to IL but select in some way the structures to be identified interlingually, and this must be connected empirically to other processes, e.g. universal ones.

Scholars in universal grammar argue whether the particular

parameters suggested by UG are still available in second language acquisition. We have argued throughout this book that going back to Palmer (1921), it has made sense to argue that some sort of universal principles are necessary to account for SLA. But which universal principles, under what conditions, and how do selective language transfer phenomena intersect? As I understand the debate, although it is more complicated than this, one set of scholars insists that the only possible conclusion from the data to date is that universal parameters operate only if 'instantiated' in NL structures (e.g. Bley-Vroman 1989; J. Schachter 1988, 1989, forthcoming). The other position, in which I see a directionality argument, argues for the prime role of UG and that language transfer operates in the case parameters mismatch between NL and TL. (Cf. *passim* in Flynn and O'Neal 1988, Gass and J. Schachter 1989 and Eubank (forthcoming) for discussions of this ongoing debate.) But maybe there is another position in IL, at least at times. Looking at Weinreich's claim (Chapter 2 above), that learners do not transfer all their NL (especially morphological) system to IL but *first* identify interlingual units across linguistic systems, leads us to a counter hypothesis:

(a) that learners draw on universal principles if transfer equivalents do not first activate, and

(b) that it varies, that both directions are true but that they operate under different (still to be discovered) contextual conditions.

To help decide issues such as these, because of the reality of interlingual identifications, we first need detailed understandings of what CA and EA contrasts look like, and thus what form predictive IL data might take. My feeling is that current theoretical debates handle a small percentage of potential types of IL data. For example, we note that in Coulter's detailed work discussed below, avoidance phenomena are identified and described in such a way that they may be independent of and precede language transfer developments in SLA. This would presumably place the accessing of universal principles at a later stage. Detail of the technical derivation of predictive IL data is necessary in order to understand learners when they are transferring NL material (whether units, concatenations of units, abstract principles or constraints) to IL and when transferring TL material to IL, and when they are not, as well as in multiple language acquisition when the predicted transfer presumably would be from a first IL to a second.

We start the chapter by integrating with Selinker (1960) the study by Blanc (1960) – a useful structuralist attempt to create a course for Americans learning Hebrew. We draw from the pedagogical information presented at the beginning of his volume 1. Blanc's approach is stated as: 'The teaching techniques . . . are the result of the application of modern linguistic theory to language learning' (Preface by Binda to Blanc, 1960). This fits in with the CA recommended way of doing things advocated by Fries and Lado and presented in Chapter 1 above. The motivation for the study presented here fits into the Fries/Lado paradigm, the basis for the CA study being the 'widely accepted [view] among linguists' that materials to be used in teaching ESL should be based on a comparison of the NL and TL. Lehn and Slager defended such a comparison, which included both phonology and grammar, by stating that it 'is essential because it locates the areas of difficulty for the learner (the Thai does not have the same problems learning English as the Turk), and because it makes possible proper grading' (Lehn and Slager 1959).

The Lehn and Slager study was portrayed to graduate students of that period as a paradigm example of how to do CA and it serves as a model for some of the CA statements that follow. We follow Lado's procedures as outlined in Chapter 1 above by first presenting segmental phonemic information not in clusters, including allophonic information where helpful. This is followed by a comparison of the consonant clusters, with some information on their distributions. The goal is to predict some of the problems an Israeli would have learning English since in this CA, Hebrew is the NL and English is the TL. Our aim is to provide predictive Hebrew–English IL data which could then be tested, but presenting empirically gained IL data here would obfuscate the techniques and predictions we are trying to highlight.

CA data as predictive IL data

Here is one way classical CA is done. Table 5.1 presents a comparison of the segmental phonemes of the two languages not in cluster. Segmental phonemes are contrasted because there is some evidence (presented above) that at times these are the units of interlingual identifications. The Hebrew table in 5.1 is adapted from Weiman (1950) and made to correspond to the English table adapted from Gleason (1955). Gleason, one of the seminal texts of structural linguistics, presents a descriptive approach that might still be correct for some IL phenomena.

From the table we can see that Hebrew has twenty-two consonant phonemes and English has twenty-four. In the following discussion,

TABLE 5.1   A comparison of the segmental consonantal phonemes not in cluster

		Bilabial	Labio-dental	Dental	Alveolar	Alveo-palatal	Velar	Glottal
Hebrew*								
Stops	vl	p			t		k	
	vd	b			d		g	
Affricates	vl				ȼ	č		
	vd					ǰ		
Fricatives	vl		f		s	š	x	h
	vd		v		z	ž	r	
Lateral	vd				l			
Nasal	vd	m			n			
Semivowel	vd					y		
English								
Stops	vl	p			t		k	
	vd	b			d		g	
Affricates	vl					č		
	vd					ǰ		
Fricatives	vl		f	θ	s	š		h
	vd		v	ð	z	ž		
Lateral	vd				l			
Nasal	vd	m			n		ŋ	
Semivowel	vd	w			r	y		

* One could claim that in slow style, very formal Israeli–Hebrew speech glottal stop is phonemic.

the consonants are grouped according to point of articulation. At each point of articulation the order is as follows: stop, affricate, fricative, lateral, nasal, semivowel. Not all of these types, of course, can occur at all points, e.g. Hebrew bilabials are only stop and nasal whereas English bilabials are also semivowel:

Bilabials:

Hebrew	p	b	m	-
English	p	b	m	w

What this chart indicates is the prediction that the speaker of Hebrew will have no trouble with English /p/, /b/, /m/ as each one of these segments has a 'phonemically equivalent' segment in Hebrew, where 'equivalent' is used in the sense that, although there may be some allophonic variation in the Hebrew /p/ and the English /p/, either /p/ may be substituted in the other's place without loss of meaning. The chart also indicates a hole (as discussed above) and the prediction is that the Hebrew speaker will have 'trouble' with /w/ as in English 'will', the /w/ not being in his phonemic inventory. The prediction is that at times s/he will 'substitute' for English /w/ the 'closest' NL phoneme, and that will presumably be labiodental voiced /v/. That structural prediction is enhanced by observations that in Hebrew borrowed place names, e.g. Washington, the Israeli speaker of Hebrew at times substitutes /v/ for /w/ as in /vasington/. However, note that from the chart itself this IL substitution would not necessarily have been predicted, since looking at allophonic information leads us to realize that English /w/ is both fricative and semivowel in nature (Gleason 1955) and is 'treated' as a semivowel in the glide or final portion of a syllable nucleus, as in English 'bout', /bawt/ or 'boat', /bowt/. One would thus not expect transfer in the latter case from the NL phoneme /v/. Therefore, English 'bout' would not appear as [bavt] in Hebrew–English IL, nor would 'boat' appear as [bovt]. Thus we are in the CA area of 'finer analysis' using allophonic information of the type Lado, Weinreich and Haugen spoke about (see Chapters 1 and 2 above). As has been pointed out several times already in this volume, the reality of CA predictions of selective substitution of the closest phoneme and the use of allophonic information on the part of the learner is quite important for the CA/IL link and something that must be accounted for in language transfer studies. Namely, we need a CA 'with safeguards' (cf. Schumann quote in Chapter 8) and this is appearing in the literature – see Zobl (1984), for example, who deals with this problem in terms of a 'richer' CA analysis with respect to empirical IL data.

Labiodentals

Concerning labiodentals in Table 5.1, the following can be extrapolated:

Hebrew	f	v
English	f	v

The chart would predict no problems and this may indeed be the case, but as we have just seen, in terms of IL as a system and the linguistic value of its units, the case of the IL /v/ as an interlingual unit is more complex than that of /f/. Thus, in this Hebrew–English IL, since the contrasts are going from Hebrew as the NL and English as the TL, the CLI value of /v/ will have to be different from that of /f/. The unit identified interlingually as /f/, it is predicted, will be substituted only for English /f/, whereas the unit identified interlingually as /v/ will at times be substituted for English /v/ and at times for English /w/, and only in some positions. I know of no IL studies in this area and for IL theory to handle information of this complexity in a principled way; it will have to become more sophisticated than it is at present.

Dentals

We can extrapolate from Table 5.1:

Hebrew	-	-
English	θ	ð

It can be seen that /θ/ and /ð/ do not occur in Hebrew and the prediction once again is that the Hebrew speaker will substitute the closest phonemes. But which are they? Table 5.1 provides two candidates: /t/, /d/ or /s/, /z/ respectively. What we have seen in Chapter 2 when discussing Weinreich's data is that *both* sets can occur as substitutes in different ILs. CA apparently cannot help us here, and this matter will be brought up again in Chapter 7 when discussing Nemser's results, for interestingly he finds different sets of forms perceptually vs. productively.

Alveolars

Concerning alveolars we can extrapolate the following:

Hebrew	t	d	c	s	z	l	n	-
English	t	d	-	s	z	l	n	-

It is predicted that the sounds /t/ and /d/ can be transferred to the Hebrew–English IL without any problems for TL communication except that the lack of aspiration would sound non-native. Because of the distribution of English /c/, for English speakers learning Hebrew, the phoneme /c/ in initial position may prove difficult, but the reverse should not be the case. The sequence [ts] appears in final position in English [kæts] 'cats' and the Hebrew phoneme /c/ should prove helpful when transferred. The substitution of Hebrew /s/ and /z/ for the English equivalents should not prove troublesome, though if these Hebrew phonemes are in fact substituted for English /θ/ and /ð/ respectively, they may complicate the IL phonological system, as hinted above. Substitution of the Hebrew /l/ for the English one should involve no loss in meaning but would result in clear non-nativeness. Hebrew, though the situation is a bit more complicated, has the so-called 'dark-l' in both initial and final consonant positions, so that the name 'Lill', if the Hebrew /l/ is transferred, would appear as [ɫiɫ] in the Hebrew–English IL. The identification of Hebrew /n/ with English /n/ should pose no difficulties, but /r/ is another problem entirely.

The English /r/ is listed in Table 5.1 as an alveolar semivowel, i.e. 'a slightly retroflex resonant continuant (a vocoid)' (Lehn and Slager 1959, p.29). Blanc states that the Hebrew 'sound /r/ has nothing in common with the American "r" and is most commonly pronounced like the voiced equivalent of /x/'. (Blanc 1960, p.19). Thus Hebrew /r/ is listed in Table 5.1 as a velar fricative that is voiced. Blanc, perhaps alluding to the influence of SAE on Israeli–Hebrew (see Chapter 3 above), then goes on to say that the Hebrew sound /r/ is 'like the Parisian French or Berlin German "r"' (*ibid.*). Should the Hebrew speaker substitute his /r/ for the English /r/, it will be one of the features that strongly mark him as non-native but, unlike other allophonic substitutions above, may cause intelligibility problems. This point is hard to handle in classical CA. In terms of bidirectionality, i.e. CLI going both ways (Gass and Selinker 1983a Ch.1), the substitution of English retroflex /r/ for the Hebrew voiced velar fricative would be the most obvious sign of an 'American accent' in the production of Hebrew. We will have more to say about this strange 'r-ness', where (in Weinreich's terms) things that are *not* the same become the same, below and in Chapter 7.

Alveopalatals

Alveopalatals are lined up this way:

Hebrew	č	dǰ	š	ž	y
English	č	dǰ	š	ž	y

As the chart shows, there is an exact equivalence in the two languages and the prediction based on this chart and on allophonic investigation is that there should be no problems in the transfer of the NL sounds. As was pointed out in Chapter 2, /č/, /dǰ/ and /ž/ do not occur in classical Hebrew and have come into the language as the result of modern borrowings. Blanc states that these sounds 'are relatively infrequent and occur only in recent loanwords, including some rather common ones' (1960, p.18), mentioning among others '/žaket/ "a jacket"'. This example brings up a confounding factor in interlingual identifications: one borrowed sound (perhaps from more than one donor or source language), in this case /ž/, may be substituted for another, /ǰ/, in the IL. It will depend on what the individual learner identifies interlingually in the particular case, either a phoneme or the whole lexical item *and* its phonemics. (Such a case was discussed in Chapter 2 concerning the difficulty of overcoming NL stress patterns in borrowed words and the accompanying reduced vowels.) In the borrowing process of recent loanwords, interestingly, for some speakers, these two phonemes may in fact have been interchanged, for example:

/žurnal/ *but not* /dǰurnal/	'journal'
/dǰentelman/ or /žentelman/	'gentleman'
/sabotadǰ/ or /sabotaž/	'sabotage'

It has to be predicted that some sort of variation will be transferred into the IL, but I see nothing in the NL that can be a guide. The structural facts of CA have let us down here. Finally, concerning /y/ there would appear to be no special problems.

Velars

Velar consonants are lined up this way:

Hebrew	k	g	x	r	-
English	k	g	-	-	ŋ

The phonemes /k/ and /g/ in English should not prove troublesome. The situation of Hebrew /x/ should resemble that of /c/ in the sense that for English speakers learning Hebrew, the phoneme /x/ may prove difficult, but the reverse is clearly not the case since English lacks the phoneme /x/ and a close phoneme for which it could be substituted. The case of /r/ has been taken up above and it is interesting. Why should a voiced velar (or with some speakers uvular) fricative (or even at times trilled) sound be substituted for a retroflex resonant? This is not a problem limited to English and Hebrew. It seems that many sounds of different phonetic qualities can be substituted for this retroflex. And in terms of bidirectionality, the retroflex English sound can be substituted for these other sounds as well. What is going on here? In light of the theory being developed in this volume, these substitutions happen when these different sounds are *identified* across linguistic systems *as same*, i.e. as 'r'. What I propose, then, is that there is in the bilingual and IL domains a psycholinguistically abstract principle of 'r-ness' (at least partially) independent of phonetic form, that gets transferred as an abstract unit. This is a new sort of unit category to be added to interlingual identifications. It seems to me that concerning units of equivalence across linguistic systems, the fact that so many sounds of different phonetic qualities – trills, flaps, retroflexes, velars, uvulars – are in fact substitutable for each other across systems is a strong empirical argument for the reality of abstract interlingual identifications. The fact that this substitution possibility was seen by CA is one of its strengths.

Returning to a consideration of the velar chart above, it can be seen that Hebrew has no equivalent for the English sound /ŋ/ (cf. discussion in the bilingualism chapter, Chapter 3 above, where at times two consonants are identified interlingually with one). It is here predicted from this CA that Hebrew speakers will tend to substitute for /ŋ/ a close NL sound, and we know from bilingual studies of modern Hebrew that Hebrew has no trouble borrowing English words with /ŋ/, substituting [n] for [ŋ], [bank] for 'bank', but substitutes at times in its place the phonemic sequence /ng/ as in /sleng/ 'slang'. This substitution may be the case for foreign names, e.g. /vasington/ 'Washington' (cf. Weinreich's analysis in Chapter 2 of this substitution by Yiddish speakers) and it is thus predicted that Hebrew speakers will substitute in a CLI sense, perhaps depending upon whether [ŋ] is followed by silence or [k], /n/ or /ng/ for English /ŋ/. The only sound remaining to be discussed for this chart is /h/, and no problems are anticipated.

Contrastive consonant data

We now move to Lado's phonemic CA question (Chapter 1 above) of distribution, and look at consonant clusters. Since the direction is from Hebrew to English and since thoroughness in description is not our aim, clusters that appear in Hebrew and not in English – e.g. /ps-/, /psalim/ 'statues'; /pt-/, ptuxim/ 'open' (masc. pl); /pk-/, /pkuda/ 'order'; /cl-/, /clav/ 'a cross', etc. (cf. Blanc 1960, pp.45–57) – will not be treated here. Our aim will be to provide *predictive IL data* for the following CA assumption. It is hypothesized that much of the learner's troubles on the phonological level will not stem from the production of individual phonemes that do not exist in the NL (here English /w/, /ə/, /ð/, and /ŋ/ for the NS of Hebrew) but will be 'largely those of learning *new uses* for old sounds' (Gleason 1955, p.225, emphasis in the original). In this view, then, the learner must acquire the characteristic way the individual phonemes cluster. We need to temper the hypothesis we receive from classical CA (as we did in Chapters 1 and 4), wishing to see whether in IL, the learning of new uses for old sounds can prove troublesome for some learners under some conditions. Importantly, we also wish to see whether this problem area could interfere with intelligibility in NN/N and NN/NN interaction; then we have, with IL consonant clusters, a serious SLA area of investigation with impetus, once again, supplied by CA. In this case, once again we do not find the expected SLA empirical studies.

Should we wish to do such studies, Fries (1945, pp.17–20) provides a solid base for the comparison of consonant clusters between English as the TL and any NL. His extensive listing with examples allows us to see whether 'similar shapes' exist in the NL. We will not be exhaustive since that would deter us from our goal of providing predictive data exemplars for CA assumptions and for SLA testing. In initial position, Fries lists thirty-nine combinations.

Table 5.2 compares the English and Hebrew clusters in initial position.

The first nine clusters list /r/ as the second member of the cluster and given the discussion of the abstract psycholinguistic category of 'r-ness' above, it is predicted that English /r/ in cluster will be an area of transfer for the Hebrew speaker. Also, given the CA principle attributed to Gleason in the last paragraph, it is predicted that even when an English-like approximation for /r/ is attained in isolated position, clusters will still prove troublesome. Furthermore, given the principles of bilingualism as applied to IL (see Chapter 2 above), it is

TABLE 5.2   A comparison of consonant clusters in initial position in English and Hebrew

(1) pr-	E	– /préy/, 'pray'; /prés/, 'press'
	H	– /prát/, 'detail'; /probléma/, 'problem'
(2) tr-	E	– /tréy/, 'tray'; /tríy/, 'tree'
	H	– /trémp/, 'hitch hike'; /transkrípcia/, 'transcription'
(3) fr-	E	– /fríy/, 'free'; /fráy/, 'fry'
	H	– /fránk/, 'a Sephardic Jew' (derogatory); /fraza/, 'phrase, empty words'
(4) gr-	E	– /gréy/, 'gray'; /grǽs/, 'grass'
	H	– /grúš/, 'an Israeli coin'; /groni/ 'throaty'
(5) dr-	E	– /dríp/, 'drip'; /dráy/, 'dry'
	H	– /draxím/, 'ways, roads'; /drišá/, 'demand'
(6) kr-	E	–/kráy/, 'cry'; /kríyd/, 'creed'
	H	– /kriá/, 'reading'; /krovím/, 'relatives'
(7) ɵr-	E	– /ɵríy/, 'three'; /ɵrów/, 'throw'
	H	–_____
(8) br-	E	– /bráwn/, 'brown'; /bréd/, 'bread'
	H	– /brógez/, 'anger'; /briút/, 'health'
(9) šr-	E	– /šrínk/, 'shrink'; /šréd/, 'shread'
	H	– /šraví/, 'hot and dry (weather)'; /šrirí/, 'muscular'
(10) st-	E	– /stéy/, 'stay'; /stíl/, 'still'
	H	– /stáv/, 'autumn'; /stén/, 'a sten gun'
(11) sp-	E	– /spénd/, 'spend'; /spíl/, 'spill'
	H	– /spórt/, 'sport'; /spesífi/, 'specific'
(12) sm-	E	– /smól/, 'small'; /smówk/, 'smoke'
	H	– /smixá/, 'blanket'; /smexá/, 'happy (fem. sg.)'
(13) sk-	E	– /skín/, 'skin'; /skáy/, 'sky'
	H	– /skirà/, 'review, survey'; /ski/, 'ski'
(14) sn-	E	– /snów/, 'snow'; /sníyz/, 'sneeze'
	H	– /sníf/, 'branch'; /snunít/, 'swallow'
(15) sf-	E	– /sfíyr/, 'sphere'; /sférikɨl/, 'spherical'
	H	– /sfarím/, 'books'; /sfirá/, 'era'
(16) sl-	E	– /sláy/, 'sly'; /slíyp/, 'sleep'
	H	– /slixá/, 'excuse me'; /slíl/, 'coil, spool'
(17) pl-	E	– /pléy/, 'play'; /pláw/, 'plow'
	H	– /plugót/, 'divisions'; /plitím/, 'refugees'
(18) kl-	E	– /klówz/, 'close'; /klúw/, 'clue'
	H	– /klavím/, 'dogs'; /klúb/, 'club'

(19) bl-	E	– /blúw/, 'blue'; /blǽk/, 'black'
	H	– /blí/, 'without'; /blók/, 'block'
(20) fl-	E	– /fláy/, 'fly'; /flów/, 'flow'
	H	– /flírt/, 'a flirt'; /flartét/, 'to flirt'
(21) gl-	E	– /glǽs/, 'glass'; /glów/, 'glow'
	H	– /glidá/, 'ice cream'; /gluyá/, 'post card'
(22) dw-	E	– /dwél/, 'dwell'; /dwórf/, 'dwarf'
	H	– _____
(23) kw-	E	– /kwík/, 'quick'; /kwél/, 'quell'
	H	– _____
(24) tw-	E	– /twélv/, 'twelve'; /twíg/, 'twig'
	H	– _____
(25) sw-	E	– /swím/, 'swim'; /swél/, 'swell'
	H	– _____
(26) hw-	E	– (doesn't exist in my speech)
	H	– _____
(27) ɵw-	E	– /ɵwórt/, 'thwart'; /ɵwæk/, 'thwack'
	H	– _____
(28) fy-	E	– /fyúw/, 'few'; /fyúwz/, 'fuse'
	H	– _____
(29) ky-	E	– /kyúwt/, 'cute'; /kyúwɾ/, 'cure'
	H	– /kyerušaláim/, 'like Jerusalem'
(30) my-	E	– /myúwzik/, 'music'; /myúwɨl/, 'mule'
	H	– /myuxád/, 'especially'; /myád/, 'at once'
(31) by-	E	– /byúwtɨy/, 'beauty'; /byúwrow/, 'bureau'
	H	– /byerušálim/, 'in Jerusalem'
(32) py-	E	– /pyúwpɨl/, 'pupil'; /pyúwr/, 'pure'
	H	– /pyuti/, 'poetic'
(33) hy-	E	– /hyúwǰ/, 'huge'; /hyúwmɨn/, 'human'
	H	– _____
(34) vy-	E	– /vyúw/, 'view'; /vyetnǽm/, 'Vietnam'
	H	– /vyerusalim/, 'and Jerusalem'
(35) str-	E	– /stríŋ/, 'string'; /stríyt/, 'street'
	H	– /stratosféra/, 'stratosphere'; /strixnin/, 'strychnine'
(36) skr-	E	– /skréw/, 'screw'; /skrípt/, 'script'
	H	– _____
(37) spr-	E	– /spríŋ/, 'spring'; /spréd/, 'spread'
	H	– _____
(38) spl-	E	– /splít/, 'split'; /splǽš/, 'splash'
	H	– _____
(39) skw-	E	– /skwéyr/, 'square'; /skwínt/, 'squint'
	H	– _____

predicted that borrowed words with 'difficult' sounds will prove even more difficult, e.g. /problema/ 'problem', /tremp/ 'hitch hike', etc. and the transferred sounds will probably fossilize. Number (7) in Table 5.2 is a special case in that we have two TL phonemes in cluster, one not existing in the NL, /ə/, and one troublesome, /r/. It is predicted that this cluster /ər-/, which occurs in common words in English, will prove especially troublesome. In more current jargon, what the Israeli tends to produce for English /ər-/ – most probably something like [sg-] – will become a strong candidate for fossilization. And all of this is testable.

We now come to a string of initial clusters which, if transferred from NL to IL, should prove to be no TL problem – (10)–(21) in Table 5.2, i.e. the sounds: /st-/, /sp-/, /sm-/, /sk-/, /sn-/, /sf-/, /sl-/, /pl-/, /kl-/, /bl-/, /fl-/ and /gl-/. This of course is the strength of language transfer, i.e. at times use of NL structural material in IL forms a solid basis on which to build knowledge and promote SLA (cf. Gass and Selinker 1983a, Ch.1). CA structural principles preview some such occasions.

The next set of initial clusters in English should all prove troublesome: /Cw-/, i.e. any of the permissible English cluster sequences with /w/ as the second member: (22)–(27) in Table 5.2, i.e. /dw-/, /kw-/, /tw-/, /sw-/, /hw-/ (if the learner tries to approximate this sequence), and especially /əw-/. It was predicted above that the Hebrew speaker of English will tend to substitute his/her phoneme /v/ for English /w/ in isolation, and given the predictions developed so far (see discussions of /r/ above), that even when an English-like approximation for /w/ is attained in isolated position, clusters with /w/ will still prove troublesome. Also, given principles of bilingualism as applied to IL and discussed above, borrowed words with difficult sounds will prove even more difficult. And perhaps equally difficult will be the case where two phonemes, neither of which is in the NL, cluster, i.e. when two non-existing NL phonemes pattern together in the TL.

Concerning phonemes (28)–(34) in Table 5.2, i.e. English consonant clusters whose second member is /y/, positive transfer should occur and there should be no problem. Foreign words borrowed into Hebrew, such as [fiord] 'fjord', provide a close enough approximation to avoid difficulty. Concerning the /sCr-/ sequences /str-/, /skr-/ and /spr-/, one prediction is clear: if the Hebrew speaker can produce these clusters in the IL, they will tend to be produced with an NL quality /r/ as discussed above. The only IH Hebrew words with /str-/ are borrowed words already assimilated to

TABLE 5.3   Some final consonant clusters in English and Hebrew

(1)	-nd	E	– /lénd/, 'lend'; /bénd/, 'bend'
		H	– /holánd/, 'Holland'
(2)	-nt	E	– /tént/, 'tent'; /hánt/, 'hunt'
		H	– /studént/, 'student'; /patént/, 'gadget'
(3)	-st	E	– /mást/, 'must'; /rést/, 'rest'
		H	– /artíst/, 'one who never does any work and gets away with it'
(4)	-ld	E	– /ówld/, 'old'; /kówld/, 'cold'
		H	– /mosád zóld/, 'Zold foundation'
(5)	-lm	E	– /fílm/, 'film'; /hélm/, 'helm'
		H	– /fílm/, 'film'
(6)	-ks	E	– /báks/, 'box'; /síks/, 'six'
		H	– /bréks/, 'brakes'
(7)	-mp	E	– /pámp/, 'pump'; /jámp/, 'jump'
		H	– /trémp/, 'hitch hike'
(8)	-ft	E	– /sóft/, 'soft'; /léft/, 'left'
		H	– /néft/, 'oil'
(9)	-rd	E	– /wə́rd/, 'word'; /bórd/, 'board'
		H	– /standárd/, 'standard'
(10)	-rn	E	– /tə́rn/, 'turn'; /bárn/, 'barn'
		H	– /modérn/, 'modern'
(11)	-rk	E	– /wə́rk/, 'work'; /tórk/, 'fork'
		H	– /nu yórk/, 'New York'
(12)	-rs	E	– /kə́rs/, 'curse'; /hórs/, 'horse'
		H	– /kúrs/, 'course'
(13)	-rt	E	– /hə́rt/, 'hurt'; /kárt/, 'cart'
		H	– /spórt/, 'sport'; koncért/ 'concert'

Note: for [ər], see the discussion under vowels.

NL phonological patterns, and given the IL borrowing principles described above, strength of fossilization should be high (cf. discussion of /pr-/ above). In a search of dictionaries, I have not been able to find borrowed words in IH beginning with /skr-/ or /spr-/. However, I would expect that a word such as 'script' is borrowable and that what holds for /str-/ would hold for the entire /sCr-/ pattern in IL. Concerning number (38), the English sequence /spl-/, all three phonemes are in the NL and transferable, with their transfer producing only the allophonic traces of 'dark-l' referred to above, NN but no problems expected. Finally, concerning the last cluster, /skw-/, I would expect the IH speaker to produce /skv-/ in IL.

Concerning final consonant clusters in English (Table 5.3), Fries (1945, pp.17–20) lists 151 and of these to date I have found only 15 in Hebrew, and importantly almost entirely in borrowed words. There is no point in listing all 151. In Table 5.3 I present corresponding Hebrew ones as a sampling of the kind of thing that can occur. Types 1–8 should not prove troublesome, and in 9–13 one can see /r/ in the pattern /-rC/. What is predictable, given the principles in the previous paragraphs, is that the NL sound will be transferred and the assimilated sequence of the borrowed words will be generalized to new TL words with that sequence. For example /- rn/ is produced as [-ɡn] in [modɛgni], the borrowed IH word for 'modern'; this will generalize to an IL pronunciation of [konsegn] 'concern' and like-sounding words – with an NL /r/ sound *and* an [ɛ], non-reduced vowel. Thus, given CA principles strengthened by bilingualism borrowing principles, it is predicted that speakers of IH will have problems with English final consonants, given, with the prevalence of NL phonology assimilating such borrowings, their probable transfer *back* into the IL. To my knowledge, there are no published listings of final consonant clusters in IH which include borrowed words in their assimilated forms, a useful listing to have.

There is a class of English words with bound inflectional morphemes added that we will look at now: the 14th 'consonant cluster' of Table 5.3 that matches an English one – the phoneme in IH /c/ as in /kec/ 'end'. The pronunciation [kets] should produce an acceptable cluster on English plural and third person singular morphemes such as /kæt, kæts/ 'cat, cats' or /hit, hits/ 'hit, hits'. The final Hebrew cluster to be discussed here that may prove useful when transferred from Hebrew to English is /-št/ as in /pušt/ 'hood, teenage gangster'. This cluster matches the case in English where in the preterite and the participle /-t/ is added to /-š/ as in [-št] 'rush, rushed' or 'push, pushed'. And in any case, there is an apparent rarity in native Hebrew words of final consonant clusters; thus the English ones with /r/, /ө/ and /ð/ should all prove problematical.

Contrastive vowel data

Concerning Hebrew and English vowels, Blanc, in a pedagogical mode, points out that Hebrew vowels have 'practically no real equivalents' in English. He suggests that the student 'who is able to draw on some knowledge of Spanish vowels, which are quite similar to Hebrew ones, should do so by all means' (Blanc, 1960, p.23). This is an interesting suggestion in terms of multiple language acquisition and the possible positive transfer from a first IL to a second. Note also that in terms of bidirectionality this is not too valuable a suggestion for going the other way. Though there is disagreement in the literature (Weiman 1950, p.22 adds /ü/ as phonemic), it appears that IH has a classic vowel configuration:

$$
\begin{array}{ccc}
\text{i} & & \text{u} \\[4pt]
\text{e} & & \text{o} \\[4pt]
& \text{a} &
\end{array}
$$

It is predicted that these will be transferred into English in ways not unlike that seen in other IL situations:

IH /i/, which is 'somewhere between that of English "slick" and that of English "sleek"' (Blanc 1960, pp.23–4), will presumably be substituted for both English vowels.

IH /e/, which is 'quite similar to the vowel of English "head"' (*ibid.*, p.25), will presumably be substituted for both English /e/ as in 'bet' and /ey/ as in 'bait'.

IH /a/, which 'has a sound that is somewhere between the vowel of English "come" and "calm"' (*ibid.*, p.24), should function with no problems if substituted for English /a/; but see below for English /ə/.

IH /o/ is 'perhaps the hardest to master' for the English speaker learning Hebrew. 'Its nearest English equivalent is perhaps the vowel of "shore", though the vowel of the British pronunciation of words such as "shock" is even closer.' (*ibid.*, p.24). Going the other way, it is predicted that this non-glided IH vowel will be substituted for the English (at least American) vowel glide /ow/ as in /bowt/ 'boat', and will sound very NN indeed.

IH /u/, which 'is analogous to /i/ in that it is somewhere between the vowels of English "full" and "fool"' (*ibid.*, p.24), will presumably be substituted for both those English vowels.

So far we have the following CA information: IH /i/ will be substituted for English /i/ and /iy/, etc. in the following way:

IH and IL	*English*
i	i as in bit
	iy as in beat
e	e as in bet
	ey as in bait

a	a as in the first vowel of father
o	ow as in boat
u	u as in full
	uw as in fool

The above eight English vowels and vowel glides involve only about half of the system in my NL English speech, however. Still unaccounted for are:

/æ/ as in bat	/ay/ as in bite	/ɨ/ as in wanted
/ə/ as in but	/ɔy/ as in Roy	
/ɔ/ as in raw	/aw/ as in bout	

plus the special vowel cluster [ər] in words such as word, bird, modern (2nd v), standard (2nd v). Beginning with the latter cluster, we have already seen that in two-syllable words spelled -ern (modern, concern), as well as in any word spelled -er, the Hebrew speaker will tend to transfer his pronunciation of [-eg] based on, we hypothesize, the pattern in his NL of borrowed words. It does become complicated, however. As pointed out in Table 5.3, a word such as 'standard', when borrowed, has the Hebrew /r/ and the English spelling vowel /a/, since Hebrew /a/ easily transfers to the Hebrew speaker's attempted pronunciation of English /a/ with no apparent difficulty, plus with the borrowing of that word as [standaɡdi] 'standard', we can expect to get in IL [standaɡd].

Concerning the single-syllable words with [ər], it is predicted that, given the spelling perhaps (cf. the discussion of French–English IL [ǰ-] for [ž-] in Chapter 1 above), the consonant which will be substituted in the IL will not be the off-glide but the Hebrew NL sound [ɡ]. But the vowel is unclear; it could be the 'closest' vowel which would be /e/ or some allophonic vowel of it. But I truly see no way to gain a precise prediction from classical CA. Now this is where IL can be of help since it opens new possibilities. Given the basic idea of IL, it is conceivable that a vowel which is in *neither* NL nor TL could be produced by the NS of Hebrew in an attempted production of TL English sound [əR] in monosyllabic words. This possibility should be investigated *empirically* in this case.

Concerning the vowel clusters /ay/, /ɔy/, and /aw/, no problems are expected since, as Blanc (1960, p.28) states: 'Any two vowels [in Hebrew] may occur in sequence in any order'. In Hebrew /ai/, /oi/ and /au/ occur and should be substitutable for corresponding English sounds with no difficulty.

The remaining vowels, /æ/, /ə/, /ɔ/ and /ɨ/, appear problematical in terms of CA, this indeterminacy being another of its weaknesses. For /æ/ as in bat the closest NL IH phoneme appears to /e/, i.e. phonetically [ɛ]. If NL /e/ is identified interlingually with /æ/, then quite a few English contrasts should be lost and intelligibility impaired. A similar problem exists for English /ə/ as in but. If it is /e/ that is substituted interlingually again, matters get much worse. But IL theory does encourage us to look for new possible sounds. For example, above we quoted Blanc when talking about the Hebrew vowel /u/, that it 'is analogous to /i/ in that it is *somewhere between* the vowels of English "full" and "fool"' (Blanc 1960, emphasis added).

A suggested 'in-between' principle

In rereading Blanc's CA descriptions of IH phonological structure in terms of the sounds of English, I am reminded that the 'somewhere between' principle could very well apply to IL. The principle is not as vague as it sounds since the phonetic spaces concerned are relatively small. The principle could work in IL this way: we begin with the CA principle that when there is a structural hole (as described in several places in this volume), the learner is programmed to seek interlingual identifications using other principles when the purely structural do not work. If too many TL sounds are identified interlingually as same with one NL sound, this could affect NN/N and NN/NN interaction with the IL vowel chosen transferred from the NL; but it will be *allophonic in the NL* (or, in terms of features, will be coloured by NL redundant features; see Ard 1984, 1989), i.e. phonetically somewhere in the space between the closest NL phoneme to the TL phoneme. If this does not work for communicative purposes and the learner has not yet fossilized an NL correspondence in the IL, then a *new sound*, one not in NL nor TL but somewhere in the referred to phonetic space, will be substituted for the TL sound in question. Here again, careful consideration of the details of classical CA leads us to an ordered series of hypotheses for IL which can then be empirically tested.

There are two English vowel sounds yet to be discussed: /ɨ/ as in wanted (2nd v), and /ɔ/ as in raw. The /ɔ/ case would predict that the NL /o/ sound will be substituted and this presumably will create problems of the type just discussed. Barred /ɨ/, since it occurs most often in bound morphemes, may relate to spelling conventions, as with the -er case above. Whether spelling conventions are indeed

118   *Rediscovering Interlanguage*

TABLE 5.4   Substitution of English vowels by Hebrew speakers as predicted by CA

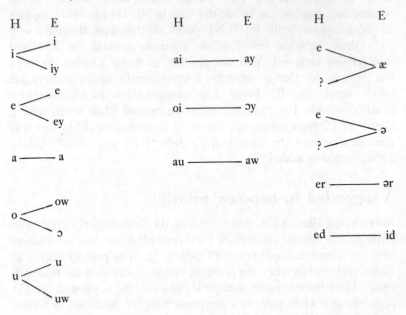

prominent, bound morphemes, as Weinreich points out (see Chapter 2 above), merits special attention. Thus, wanted will probably appear as [vantɛd]. The vowel substitutions as predicted by this CA are now summarized in Table 5.4. Thus CA predictions lead to IL predictive data and a better understanding of potential units of interlingual identifications.

EA as predictive IL data

We now turn to a consideration of some error analysis (EA) data which should also turn out to be IL data, since actually occurring errors should be in essence a *subset of IL data*. In this view, errors are that part of IL performance judged to be deviant from an idealized TL norm in some way. The EA literature, like the CA one, is vast, and a comprehensive survey as we move towards our understanding of IL and IL learning is unnecessary. Before moving to a detailed consideration of Coulter's EA thesis, I present first for the reader's consideration a sampling of EA material from the important Stuttgart German/English CA project mentioned in Chapter 4 above: PAKS (= Projekt für angewandte Kontrastive

Sprachwissenschaft, 'Project on Applied Contrastive Linguistics'). (I have been helped with translation of the German material by Jeanne Cox Lee, to whom I am most grateful both for translation and for insight. A general review of problems in this type of research is presented in Konig 1970.) As the title indicates, the EA material is done under the CA rubric. This should not be surprising and is one reason I have chosen to look in depth at PAKS since CA and EA have been intertwined as much as CA and IL, and EA and IL for that matter. All three attempt to relate to what learners actually do in creating IL and all three have drawn on each other for intellectual inspiration (cf. e.g. attempts by Eckman 1984 and Zobl 1984 to integrate CA and IL, and an update in Nickel 1988).

We will begin by looking at the goals of the PAKS project, as described in the PAKS Report Number 5, July 1970. As pointed out above in Chapter 3, they are interested in contributing to a general theory of language by investigating contrastively the characteristics of natural languages, especially English and German. They are also interested in carrying out a detailed CA of English and German in various structural areas with a third goal of preparating pedagogical materials from the analysis. Thus the project is not too different in its aims from some of the CA projects discussed to date in this volume. The advance they make is to look at actual learner data, but only the subset called 'errors'.

In the Foreword, they admit that they are missing some important factors for the evaluation of the source of errors and the rating of errors, factors such as motivation, teacher, teaching material and goals of the teachers and students. Nickel points out in his Introduction (1970; cf. also 1973) that there are two ways to look at errors, the first being the negative way, that students are lazy and unmotivated. A more modern belief would consider errors as part of the circular progression in learning, viewing them as a dynamic process involved in the learning process. Nickel claims that through this circular corrective function of error we can explain the relatively rapid progress in the learning of a TL. I believe that this has never been seriously tested in IL.

In this view, errors are necessary 'in-between stations', important for self-evaluation and, perhaps, therapy. This is not too different a position to Corder's (discussed in Chapter 6) of errors as a learning strategy. It may be, then, that the self-correction of error is indeed necessary as stated and the teacher can serve an important function here. At other times, the creative capacity may be interfered with if errors are noted. If this could be worked out, then the effect on the structure of IL of the learner's recognizing that his/her IL is deviant from expected TL norms can be studied. It is my view that such deviance is real for some learners, affecting interlingual identifications and thus ILs.

Nickel describes how errors in the corpus are determined by the manner of testing and the language level and here, presaging a current result, variation is found. In the dictations gained from the students there are hardly any syntax errors, but there are quite a few in the task where students are asked to rewrite a story they have listened to. There are also more errors here than in the translation task. (This result foreshadows the work of Tarone (1979, 1983, 1988) on variation in IL according to task and the inferred continuum of style shifting.) This result is important because, as pointed out in the last chapter, translation, even though it has not been sorted out unambiguously from transfer, is clearly basic to several of the possible CA models that learners might use as the basis for interlingual identifications.

The speculation is made that there are fewer errors in translation, perhaps because the learner's attention is more fixed on syntax in translation, also foreshadowing work by Tarone (1979, 1983), here on the attention variable (for the questioning of this variable cf. Sato 1985). Also of continued SLA concern is the possibility raised that the order of learning various structures is of significance and accounts for a series of errors in the areas of word order, tense and endings of verbs. Individual differences are also brought up in that there is a need, it is stated, to find out if the tendency of over-generalization of structures relates to different personality types; for example, it is hypothesized that over-zealous, conscientious students may create the common misuse of English participial construction with the function of connecting sentences. There is a hint of candidates for fossilization (though not said this way): what is learned first appears to be especially strongly fixed, thus uniting fossilization concerns with order of acquisition concerns. All this foreshadows a good deal of continuing debate in SLA, but once again we have here a basic source which is not looked at for insights in the SLA literature.

The concern of errors made in haste is brought up and the question is asked how one determines 'haste' – by a measurement of time perhaps? How should errors made in haste be evaluated, and what do they indicate? The distinction by Corder (1967; see Chapter 6 below) between 'errors' and 'mistakes in performance' is brought up, but the fundamental coding problems are not resolved. The introductory chapter also provides a useful list of issues: language norms (discussed above in Chapter 2) and the fact that there is no one perfect form of English (p.17); differences between oral and written language (p.18); the fact that NSs teaching the language appear to be more tolerant of learners' errors than NNSs who command the TL as an FL (p.19); the distinction between grammatical and lexical errors, though the distinction is often hard to maintain (p.20); problems in the task where students rewrite the story listened to, e.g. correctness of information, completeness of information and stylistic errors in language (p.22); the problem of gradation of errors into more and less serious ones and an examination of gradation schemes suggested by teachers (p.24); and a suggestion that teachers should learn from the errors made by students. All of these are useful researchable concerns for SLA.

Nickel (p.38) presents a statistical breakdown of errors in 100 student workbooks collected from various schools:

	Syntax/Morphology	Lexicon	Orthography
Task A	50%	30%	20%
Task B	1%	4%	95%
Task C	15%	75%	10%

where Task A involves students rewriting a story they have listened to, Task B is a dictation and Task C is a translation. These results surely add confirmation to Tarone's important claim (1983, 1988) that IL varies according to the elicitation task (see other references cited by Tarone for more evidence on this point).

The PAKS study by Kuhlwein (1970) is particularly revealing of this way of doing EA. He points out that errors arising from the relationship of spoken to written language show up most clearly in dictation, important if verified. His claim is that dictation is dependent on training in hearing and in spelling. Kuhlwein (p.40) provides some examples of errors resulting from false hearing and as a consequence false understanding:

*he has started wise	for	he thought it wise
*the art of grading is not a vulture	for	the art of reading is not a virtue
*he rubs no on (and *ropes no one)	for	he robs no one

To understand the EA motivation involved, he claims there are prerequisites for an auditory approach in FL instruction: (1) recognition of student errors in pronunciation, and (2) evaluation of the importance of some errors over others (e.g. a wrong allophone is not as bad as a wrong phoneme).

Concerning the possible combinations of errors in dictations (p.43):

	Hearing sounds	*Writing*
I	+	+
II	+	−
III	−	+
IV	−	−

(where + = correct; − = incorrect)

II and IV, it is claimed, are the most important for diagnostic purposes. To see if errors belong in category II, one needs to ascertain whether the student heard the stimulus correctly by having the student repeat the sentence. Then one can check for orthography interference between languages (as there seems to be in the /š/ case in Chapter 1) or within the TL. There may be some causes of wrong writing *despite* correct hearing. There may be (a) intrastructural errors where one has the same sound but different spellings in the TL, e.g. ee vs ea for /iy/ in English, and (b) interstructural errors where one gets the NL orthography for the TL sound. In both categories one needs to consider the semantic side as well as the phonetic/phonological in (a) to determine whether the wrongly spelled word is semantically in the NL. In (b) if the same sounding word is in the TL, one needs to find out whether there is a semantic similarity and/or a graphic one.

The possibilities for these criteria are as follows:

	Meaning	*Writing*
I	+	+
II	+	−
III	−	+
IV	−	−

(where + = same; − = different)

In case I, there are no problems; in case II, writing the TL word with the NL spelling is involved; in case III, one cannot tell anything from the dictation; and in case IV, errors from semantic divergence are less probable than in II, but if they occur one can expect NL spelling for the TL word. In terms of potential causes of wrong hearing, this can be determined only from a wrong written representation. Again one can distinguish between intra- and inter-domains. In terms of the intra-domain, wrong hearing is usually attributed to wrong hearing only, but in most cases errors can be handled linguistically through the means of frequency and distribution analysis. In terms of the inter-domain, it is useful to ask if there is in the NL an obligatory, optional, or no-rule situation opposing the one in the TL (reference is made here to the classical CA study by Stockwell and Bowen (1965)). Since the wrong hearing of a similar phoneme or word of the TL involves semantic criteria, one must ask similar questions to those concerning the causes of wrong writing despite correct hearing. It is often hard to tell the difference between intra- and inter-cases as structural errors and as a basis for predicting interlingual identifica- tions. The claim is made that one should use NSs here and the suggested methodology is reminiscent of that described in the previous chapter as one basis for several of the CA models presented there.

There are three aspects of error treatment (p.47): (a) description of errors, where it is suggested that one use Gimson's (1964) phonetic treatment for the system of cardinal vowels and a consonant matrix, (here the units are given by the description used); (b) explanation of errors, where 'psychological factors' are excluded and one tries to determine linguistically connected causes of error on a descriptive/ structural basis. Much detail is given by Kuhlwein on how this works in practice. Importantly, if errors are not recognized as intra- structural (and here I see a striving towards an IL-type idea), then comparison is made with the NL (German in this case) or with a third language known to the learner (French or Latin). Kuhlwein knows, of course, that it is not possible to fit everything into categories (a) and (b).

Some interesting examples are provided that begin to lead to the well-accepted view (cf. Selinker and Gass 1984, Introduction) that it is a mistake in looking at SLA data to assume that there exists a unique source for IL forms. Things are indeed more complicated than that. Kuhlwein shows that in some cases, intra- and inter- structural components work together in a seemingly equal fashion. For example, the error *'live' for 'life' could be an analogy error within the language (cf. 'alive') as well as an inter-structural one where there is not sufficient training for /v/ vs /f/. (This is close to what is called 'transfer-of-training' in Selinker 1972.) Kuhlwein claims that only subtle frequency and distribution investigations might explain this sort of error. For practical purposes, however, it is a lot to know what these different factors might be, that they might play a role, even if one cannot judge the exact amount of influence of each. Which leads to aspect (c).

The third aspect of error treatment is: (c) evaluation of errors. According to the importance of the particular error concerned, and also through the suggestions of exercises of correction based on (a) and (b), a multiple approach is preferred, where one decides from the kind of error whether to use a structural or generative explanation. As we have seen above with CA studies in the language contact domain, one is often pushed by the data, it seems, towards some sort of eclecticism (hopefully principled). Put in another way, it is not entirely clear in this new area of IL and IL learning, and in CA and EA where it touches on IL, exactly what is a 'good' theoretical explanation for the often very messy data one finds in SLA, and, perhaps more fundamental, what is a 'good argument' for coming to theoretical conclusions from IL data. There will be more of this concern when we look at the philosophical underpinning of some current comparative studies in IL and IL learning below in Chapter 8.

On p.50 Kuhlwein provides his taxonomy for major categories of errors: (1) wrong written variant, e.g. * 'rools' for 'rules' – this seems interesting since it is a theoretically possible spelling for the /uw/ sound in the English phonological system; (2) non-English phoneme/ grapheme correspondence rule, e.g. * 'attaced' for 'attached'. Kuhlwein provides criteria for telling the difference between (1) and (2): if the word is read as spelled, it still produces the correct sounds, as in the example in (1). Such would not be the case for the example in (2). The author states that (2) is a worse mistake than (1). The third category of errors is: (3) a phonetically possible but non-TL rule spelling, unlike category (1); the student is not applying English phonological rules but appears to be merely guessing. Examples are: * 'oun' for 'own'; * 'casle' for 'castle'; * 'peopl' for 'people'. Category (4) is homophone errors, e.g. * 'she road' for 'she rode'. Here there are semantic or syntactic difficulties involved. Like category (1), if students do not know that their wrong spelling exists semantically in English, there is an extension of English patterns or what is often called 'over-generalization'. Kuhlwein admits that from the data it is hard to distinguish category (1) from category (4). Additionally, one of the most common types of errors results from the divergence rule of the written representations of /iy/ (p.51): /iy/ → ee, ea, e, ie, ei, ey, ae, oe and i. Examples abound in the data collected in this EA study for this well-known discrepancy, e.g. *speek, *dreeming, *cheaks, *preavious, etc. A second common error type resulting from this sort of spelling/phonology divergence (p.53) is that of /ər/ as in ir, yr, er, err, ear, ur and urr. Spelling errors recorded are of the

following types: *determined and *jurney. It appears that cross-
linguistic phonology/orthography correspondences are at times
sources of interlingual identifications.

We now turn to Drubig (1970), a PAKS EA study in the area of
morphology. His data (p.86) involve 850 errors culled from a
technique mentioned above, that of having students rewrite a story
they have listened to in the TL. He begins discussing morphological
errors with nouns where there is not much variation in the errors.
There is a small number of plural errors; most in this category occur
with the genitive. The highest probability error occurs in the case
where for ____'s, one gets ____s. The following (p.87) was made by
about 75 per cent of the students in one sitting of the task and was
repeated by 48 per cent of the group later:

* This he fastend round the *dogs* neck.

The author attributes this type of error primarily to the situation
where the learner docs not command 'graphic differentiation' in
English, but also when the diacritical apostrophe is left out due to
lack of concentration.

A second type of error occurs when for ____'s, one gets zero, as in:

*The King__ theatre.

The thought here is that the student has overlooked types of
discrimination where the definite article is related to the second
noun, and the first noun in this type of situation can be executed only
through one person, thus demanding the ____'s (p.88). Here we have
a hypothesis about IL where the overlooking of a type of TL
discrimination is a source of written IL form.

Leaving out the apostrophe is the most frequent error in the
genitive plural; 40 per cent of students in a particular class made the
following error (p.89):

*. . . for he didn't want in the least to be punished by losing his
friends [pl.] respect.

The reasons given are those above concerning the lack of command
of graphic differentiation in English. A total of 23 per cent of the
students in the same class produced the over-generalized error:

*. . . by losing his friend's respect

which, the author claims, exemplifies a process he has observed
frequently: the simple genitive singular is learned early, being
extensively repeated in class exercises so that it is eventually used to
excess in TL situations where it would not occur. It is interesting that
in the rewriting of the story task, few students make use of the
periphrastic paraphrase with 'of'. This could of course be an artifact
of the task and should be checked out through conversational data,

but there is a type of over-generalization error with the 'of'
construction based, it is thought, on the application of the pattern
'this is a book of John's' to 'ours', as in (p.90):
    *... may think this tradition of *our's* is nonesence ...
    The next group of errors discussed concerns morphological errors
with adjectives and adverbs. An -ly can be left out with adverbs, e.g.
(p.91):
    *... when usual__ dinner was ready ...
    *... but he helpless said ...
Also, the student may add the ending -ly to an adjective, e.g. (p.92):
    *... the impatiently lookers-on ...
    *... the furiously spectators ...
These are interesting errors because the exact interlingual identifications are not clear. Note that though unfortunately no statistics are
given, it is claimed that these errors seldom occur and then mainly at
the early stages of English instruction, with the second type, i.e.
adding the -ly improperly, occurring more frequently than the first.
    Getting close to the IL idea, the author discusses inter-structural
errors (pp.92–3) that are not morphological errors with the adverb,
e.g.:
    *... a stranger had rcnt(ed) the theatre one day = for one day
    *... when he had walked sometimes = for some time
These remind me of Corder's 'covert errors' (discussed in Chapter 6)
with perfect correspondence of NL/IL syntax but IL-particular
semantics. NL CLI (though not named as such) is credited with
causing sentences such as these, and NL data are provided.
Interestingly, backing up a result shown above to demonstrate the
positive effect that the NL can sometimes have, examples are
provided of the production of an almost correct pattern in English
based on NL German patterns, e.g. 'in a week' and 'in a distance':
    *... and when in a week the town was covered again with
        placards ...
    *... he saw in a distance a tall lion
Other frequent errors of morphology with adjectives and adverbs
involve the confusion of forms, as in (p.93):
    *... when he saw a crouch lion before him = crouching
    * The Saved Idea   = saving
The author believes that no systematic conclusions are possible here.
    The next group concerns errors in the verb system and we have
looked at the IL verb system above. In general the study confirms
what had been expected (p.94): especially in the early stages of
learning, the structure of the English verbal system produces the

most errors for German students of English, about 400 errors in the investigated material from the verbal area. There are not only purely morphological problems but also problems closely connected with questions of tense and aspect. There is in the data a good deal of repetition of errors of a morphological nature. Concerning ablaut forms in English, there are many more weak verbs than in German. Therefore, it is claimed (pp.94–5) that there are numerous errors in these forms made by the German writers of English. There are several types: first, the present stem occurs in the preterite very frequently (unfortunately no examples are given); second, the participated stem can occur in the preterite, though there is only one example in these data:

*Seeing his master struggling in the water he swum up to him
. . .

Third, a non-existent English form can occur in the preterite, and here too there is only one example that the author believes is orthographic (p.95):

*The poor animal immediately senk of course.

A fourth type produces the preterite instead of the present stem, as in (p.95):

*He couldn't ran away, because the lion was faster . . .
*The traveller couldn't *shot* him because some monkes had
    stolen his rifle.

One could assume here, the author claims, that it is a question of false application on the part of the learner of the preterite, *not* the mistaking a preterite stem for a present stem. Here we come to the heart of what continues to plague IL and SLA research – that data produced by learners are often ambiguous, in fact more often than not.

The author, Drubig, is groping with uncertainty here and clearly recognizes this dilemma. He claims that uncertainty in fact supports the hypothesis that the present stem, *learned in terms of vocabulary first*, is used for the preterite, however without a weak preterite meaning. Thus, his study comes out on the side of a view of IL that involves substitution of items across systems which, I would maintain, must involve prior interlingual identification of items. Once again a rethinking of the literature provides an ordered hypothesis, here lexical acquisition taking primary focus.

Other examples are provided and Drubig states (p.97) that in cases of uncertainty with irregular verbs, the probable explanation is that the learner in most cases is using the more familiar present tense stem. One cannot really say that the absence of an ending, for example, shows that the student knew he was dealing with a strong rather than a weak verb since there are weak verbs in English which take no endings. This reminds us of the Kellerman (1977, 1983, 1987) *principle of transferability* of psychotypology where what is accepted and rejected in the TL relates to what is accepted and rejected in the NL by the learner, regardless of 'objective' linguistic facts. Such an approach could be built upon Drubig's work when, to determine if the learner makes a break in tense sequence, for example, one criterion suggested is that the learner needs to have used a correct present tense in context with a correct preterite form. Numerous examples of this happening are presented (pp.97–8). I feel that the author is here ahead of his time and this is one of the reasons I have chosen to present this study as exemplary of the EA/IL link.

He recognizes ambiguity of data, for example by pointing out that one cannot tell whether the preterite ending was forgotten or the verb was interpreted as a strong verb in some cases, and that one must also consider whether the result is a graphic/phonetic error. To confuse things (p.98), a preterite stem occasionally is used in the present or in the infinitive:

*The traveller knews . . .

*. . . I should went behind some bushes . . .

Are examples such as these counter examples to the ordered hypothesis that problems with strong verbs usually involve forgetting the preterite stem and using the present stem instead, i.e. the first learned (or the first taught) stem? Drubig points out that there are clearly not enough data to decide. Coming close to IL again, he suggests that there is an indication here that there exists an intra-structurally oriented tendency to simplify. Note that with weak verb stems there is a tendency to make intra-structural over-generalizations of the V+ed type used with strong verbs, e.g. 'falled', 'flied'. This has been reported widely for other types of language acquisition and is often cited as evidence for the notion of system in learner language. Over-generalization as a learning problem has vexed researchers in both second language acquisition and primary language acquisition. The reader interested in an account within the framework of linguistic theory should consult Zobl (1987) where he handles the over-generalization problem in terms of the learner 'fixing the proper bounds of grammar'.

Showing that 'hearing' plays a role again in IL formation is the interesting confusion of feel and fall, as in (p.100):

*The lion felt down and was dead.

*Now the exhausted and breathless man felled very ashamed of himself.

*Now the exhausted and breathless man falled very ashamed of
   himself.
Also, it is claimed that in many cases where writing of the English is
'irregular', the erroneous orthographic interpretation reflects the
morphological interpretation of the students (p.100), as in:
   *maied = made; *saied = said; and *laied or *layed = laid
Concerning errors in tense, one must consider semantic factors (cf.
Gass and Ard 1984 where this has been shown to be true with strong
empirical IL data). In the task where students rewrite the story they
have heard, they often jump from past into present for one or two
verb forms, then go back to the original past tense of the story. In
some instances it appears that the influence is of the German use of
the present, while in others the same errors, it is claimed, are made
in NL writing. An example of the latter is given (p.105), including the
parallel German sentence:
   *. . . the lion . . . thought it were the man whom he wanted to eat
An example of the former (also, p.105) would be:
   *The man knew the lion springs to him at night
Another example (also, p.105), under the influence of German, is:
   *. . . he asked who would have done this = who did this
this time from the German colloquial:
   Er fragte, wer denn das getan haben wurde.
Pluperfect mix-ups are also blamed on the NL:
   *The day of the performance was come.
   *He said that the stranger was gone with a little suitcase.
This material is related plausibly to NL semantic notions such as
(p.108): 'looking back from the standpoint of the speaker' vs 'looking
back from the past' and provides a further sort of interlingual
identifications to those recognized so far in this volume.
   In discussing the learner's use of -ing in German–English IL,
Drubig foreshadows Kellerman's (1983, pp.126–8) *principle of
iconicity* as applied to ILs. The learner here appears to make a
durational tense in English – example from Drubig (p.110):
   *. . . and be looking forward to of being prising = praised by the
   men
Concerning the German use of the future in English, there are few
errors here and those appear to be mostly from NL transfer in the
use of the present with future meaning, as in (p.112):
   *I am back in some minutes.
   Moving to consideration of word order, the author says that these
investigations confirm the view among teachers that word order is a
major problem for German students learning English, and vice versa.
Word order has been studied in IL (See Chapter 7 below; J.

Schachter and Rutherford 1979; Rutherford 1984b; Zobl 1983, 1986; Wode 1978, 1983; White 1985; Rutherford 1989). Its importance as a central area for SLA research has long been appreciated. Lado and Weinreich, it will be recalled (Chapters 1 and 2 above) talked about word order transfer.

The data in Drubig (1970, pp.113–21) concern the placement of finite verb in second place and problems with the subject position and with dependent clauses with verb last, and errors in placing adverbs and objects relative to the verb. Although, in classical EA form, only one or two examples per point are presented – so that it is hard to come to grips with exactly how much of these EA data are actually IL data – one gets the feeling of the potential richness of the careful study of the structures hinted at here. For our perusal there is a useful section (pp.121–30) on compound sentences which surely need to be carefully studied in IL.

The final paper we will look at in the PAKS materials is Gnutzmann's (1970). In terms of the tasks used (see above), there were more lexical errors in the translation task (75 per cent), as opposed to grammatical errors, than in the task where one rewrites a story one has heard orally (30 per cent) and in the dictation task (4 per cent). He states (p.143) that there are more errors in the translation task of a lexical nature than grammatical errors due to the practice among teachers of giving drilled grammatical forms (i.e. attention to form) with new vocabulary in translation exercises, what is called *transfer of training* in Chapter 8 below. He claims that students feel the freedom to circumvent the structures (i.e. *avoidance*, foreshadowing Schachter 1974) which they do not know in the rewriting of the story task, but not in the translation task.

Gnutzmann (p.144) claims that, as expected, a large number of the errors in his corpus are based on German–English influence, but that there is not much influence of a second FL (French, Latin). This is an interesting result because an unresolved question in SLA theory is the place in language transfer of the most recently acquired language(s). For those who claim a strong influence on IL from UG, an important unresolved question is: What does the L2 learner *re*activate when using UG to approach the IL creation task? There appear to be two possibilities (White 1985 and pc): (a) something from the data that the learner received as a child, or (b) something from the data that the learner has now as an adult speaker of the NL. If the influence of CLI is as strong from a non-NL language (i.e. (b) on an L2 as from (a)), this suggests (but does not demonstrate) that there is (strong?) influence of recent language data of whatever source and the *non*-reactivation of L1 child data. Gnutzmann complicates this issue by claiming that there may be more influence from a second FL on *older* students, a variable, in terms of MLA, apparently not discussed in the UG/SLA literature. It is hard to know what the input data are in this case, whether or not in Lily Fillmore's personal communication terms it is 'junky'. The situation we are discussing here is of adult IL creation; the situation would be even more complex for *child* IL creation where what Fillmore calls 'junky data' (1983) appear to serve as important input.

Gnutzmann (p.145) discusses 'polysemi-relationships' that are based on German to English influence, e.g.:

*Very often he used to sit on that bank (bench).

*Did you hear (listen) to the radio last nicht?

*. . . take a place (seat).

He has a series of examples (pp.146–9) which he claims use word formation rules of German which are possible only 'in some modified form' in English, again presenting an idea close to IL. Though he does not highlight the fact, he also presents (p.150) some examples of TL grammatically correct sentences which, in terms of the learners' intended meanings, are still erroneous:

*Finally, he arrived at his destiny (destination)

– what Corder (1967 and next chapter) calls 'covert errors'.

Problem in error analysis

In order to continue to 'get our hands dirty' with actual data, I suggest we look in detail at an EA study – Coulter (1968), influenced by Corder (1967; see next chapter). After Coulter's data were collected but before the study was written up, Corder (1967) became available and influenced the final product, giving us one of the first EA/IL connections. In the event the reader may wish to examine the original – I highly recommend this since I believe that Coulter's study should be a 'highly valued text' in the training of SLA researchers; page numbers are extensively provided in the discussion below.

In Coulter two native Russians are the subjects of the study – F, aged sixty-five at the time of the study, and L, seventy-three. Their knowledge of English was acquired outside the classroom after they had come to the United States in 1949 and 1950. At the time of the study (1966) they were both able to converse fluently in English without resorting to NL, except for an occasional lexical item. The method of data collection, ahead of its time, was taped free discourse (p.17) and the corpus consisted of 28,000 words. Coulter used a

methodology to classify errors that was indeed ahead of its time. He
gathered retrospective secondary data (Selinker and Douglas 1989)
from the informants by gaining Russian glosses to their Russian–
English IL data, classifying errors on the basis of these NL glosses
and on a careful evaluation (I can personally attest to this) of the
situational context. The fossilized subjects in Coulter's study were
involved in what is today called 'untutored' learning, or sometimes,
misguidingly I think, 'natural' acquisition. Unfortunately, Coulter's
work, an insightful study, is not referred to in the current SLA
literature.

In order to help the reader get 'hands on' experience with these
EA data, I present the Coulter material in a different form from that
used to date in this volume, in terms of a 'Problem in EA' (written in
1969 when I had the honour of a visiting professorship at the
Department of Applied Linguistics, University of Edinburgh with Pit
Corder). I ask readers to suspend linear reading patterns and actually
do the problem to reach their own conclusions before moving on to
the analysis that follows. Following the problem, I will present a
discussion which is primarily intended to guide the reader towards
rethinking Coulter's views.

Instructions to the reader:

(1)   Relate errors in (A) below to generalizations in (B) and (C)
      where possible.
(2)   Consider how strong a claim one can make regarding CLI
      based on this limited corpus. Consider the role of CA, but bear
      in mind that learners of an L2 often over-generalize the rules of
      the TL.
(3)   Work out some general statements regarding the system of
      knowledge underlying this IL. Consider how much you might
      wish to call this IL 'transitional', 'stabilized' or 'permanently
      fossilized'.

(A)   Sample errors
These errors are from Coulter 1968, as described above. (F) and (L)
identify the individual speaker, so that the 'more advanced reader'
may wish to make statements about individual variation where
appropriate. Words in italics represent the errors to be accounted for,
with ˆ indicating that something is missing in TL terms.

1   Where *the* should have appeared:

It was dark on ^ tornado. (F, p.22)
2 Where *a/an* should have appeared:
It was ^ nice, nice trailer, ^ big one. (F, p.22)
3 *This* where *the* should have appeared:
I forgot *this* name, double name like Palo Alto. (L, p.22)
4 *The* where *a/an* should have appeared:
And I work from farmer on *the* farm there. (F, p.23)
5 Do you have *some* rest of bread? (L, p.25)
6 He was *our this* best man [at his wedding]. (L, p.26)
7 The formant *of* should have been placed between two determiners:
So I got for my command *six* ^ *this* . . . and so we have *five* ^ *this* rifles.(L, p.27)
8 Occurrence of double determiners such as:
one this, some this, every one boy, this the as in: *this the* legumes (F, L, pp.27–8)
9 I have many hundred *carpenter* my own. (F, p.29)
10 Yes, it was some *day* some *days* colder. (F, p.30)
11 He is in Tolstoj committee, too. (F, p.32)
12 Then she *transcribe* different music what is on television. (L, p.33)
13 He *catched* bad sickness and died. (L, p.38)
14 Omission of *be*: That ^ right. (F, p.42);
They ^ too late. (F, p.42)
15 I *been* seventy-three, yeah, seventy-three now. (L, p.44)
16 My parents *was* Russian (F, p.46)
17 Any time he is *living* in Nice. (L, p.52)
18 I *was* in Frankfort when I *fill* application. (F, p.36)
19 He *speak* little Russian because he *was* Russian family. (F, p.36)
20 We know what we *will* be when we *will* come to it. (L, p.54)
21 They wrote before they *will* meet them in New York. (L, p.55)
22 Then come German. (p.8)
23 I know some camps without UNRRA was organized. For example, in this Kuenzelsau start *one camp*. This all Poland [that is, Poles]. (F, p.59)

(B) Linguistic generalizations
1 There is an absence in Russian of articles. (p.21)
2 Russian 'etot' has a wide range of meanings. The first translation given in dictionaries is 'this', but it is often translated 'the' and 'that'. (pp.23–4)

3   A sequence of two determiners – not separated by a preposition – is permitted in Russian if one of them is a possessive personal pronoun or possessive adjective. (p.27)
4   The Russian equivalent of 'of' occurs in translation of 'some of these'. (p.27)
5   American English regularly reduces 'of' to [ə]. (p.27)
6   Russian has five separate plural forms in nouns. (pp.30, 87)
7   In Russian, the present tense form (est') of the verb byt' is regularly omitted whereas past and future tense forms are required. (p.41)
8   Verbs are marked for aspect (perfective–imperfective, and for verbs of motion also determinate–indeterminate), for tense (two simple tenses plus a periphrastic future in the imperfective), for person and number in the present and periphrastic future, and for gender and number of the subject in the past tense. There are many participial forms. (p.19)
9   In Russian, the verb in a subordinate clause introduced by a temporal conjunction is in the future. (p.54)
10 In Russian, the tense of a verb in a subordinate clause is the same as it would be if that clause were an independent sentence. Note (p.55):

On pojdet   'He will go'
On skazal, cto pojdet   'He said he would go'

11 A common surface pattern in Russian: Conjunction + V + Indefinite N. (p.8)
12 In (literary) Russian, the verb–subject order appears when the subject is to be elaborated in a following clause or sentence. (p.59)

(C) Frequency information
(Applies to the IL performance of both informants unless they are identified):
1   Definite article where context requires its use: L 80 per cent; F 23 per cent. (p.21)
2   Indefinite article where context requires its use: L 55 per cent; F 5 per cent. (p.21)
3   *That* either as a determiner or a demonstrative pronoun occurs very seldom. (p.23)
4   Noun plural morpheme where context requires its use: L 90 per cent; F 34 per cent. (p.29)

5   One half of F's plural forms were represented by the words
    years, days and *weeks*. (p.29)
6   Possessive morpheme in nouns: almost totally absent. (p.31)
7   Omission of various forms of *be* where their use is required: L 5
    per cent; F 12 per cent. (p.41)
8   Past tense morpheme employed when required (p.35):

	All verbs	Be	Verbs other than be
L	59%	65%	57%
F	34%	83%	15%

9   L generally uses only three models: *will, can,* and *could*; F four:
    will, can, could and *should*.

Discussion of problem in error analysis

The data presented and described by Coulter show the dependency
of the study of EA and IL on CA. Coulter starts from painstakingly
transcribed EA data, then with the aid of situational context and
informant-provided glosses interprets the 'intended meaning' of each
utterance and relates each IL structure, where possible, to NL
structural, semantic and discourse information. As we have shown
throughout this volume, sometimes CLI is shown and sometimes it is
not. Language transfer as originally seen by Weinreich is once again
shown to be a selection process. Coulter's analysis may appear to
some to stick too close to surface data, but this effect has to be
understood in terms of his hypothesis: much of language transfer
takes place on a surface structure level. This point of view can be
seen when error phenomena are explained in terms of the general
hypothesis on p.8:

> It must be understood that *then come German* was not an
> inadvertent choice of word order. In substance it followed a
> familiar pattern in Russian: Conjunction + Verb + Indefinite
> Noun.
> (italics in original)

This surface structure formula reminds us of Weinreich's similar
formula to explain the German–English sentence: 'He comes
tomorrow home,' discussed in Chapters 2 and 3 above. This view
explains those cases where linguistic congruence and IL form
coincide and we will come back to this point in Chapter 7 below with
an empirical IL approach to language transfer.
   In the following, we will use Coulter's chapter headings as guides
to the discussion of the problem presented above.

Determiners (Coulter's Chapter 2)

Apparently, because of the absence in Russian of articles (B1), the informants often have no determiner at all where an article is required in English (sentences A1, 2). The speech of F especially shows a paucity of articles (C1, 2). Though there is variation other determiners are used in place of the expected TL article (A3, 4); the informants seem to be especially confused by the difficulty in explaining the distinction in English between *the* and *a/an* (A4). Generalization (B2) may explain deviation (A3) since the 'main meaning' of a word, whether the translation choice is lexically or co-occurrence motivated, often appears to show up in IL performance as against 'secondary' meanings. This result foreshadows Kellerman's (1977, 1983, 1987) empirical SLA work on the hierarchical CLI of polysemous lexical items. Though it is here noted and named by Coulter (p.24), plausible explanation of the informants' almost complete avoidance of *that* (C3) is not available. Coulter's noting of 'avoidance' phenomena foreshadows empirical SLA work by J. Schachter (1974) on this topic. See further discussion below.

The confusion *some/any*, though quite common among learners of English, does not explain A5. Sentences A6, 7 and the phrases in A8 are related to generalizations B3, 4 but except for A6 are not wholly explained by them. The occurrences of *this* for *these* in A7, 8 apparently involve phonological transfer (p.23). But why the informants say *some this* for *some of these* in light of B4 is unclear. Perhaps the [ə] in the reduction of *of* in rapid American English speech (B5) was not noticed by them (p.27). Presumably, this latter explanation is just as plausible when considering *one this* for *one of these*, *six this* for *six of these* and *five this* for *five of these*. What we do see, in any case, is systematicity of the type expected in IL. (Cf. Tarone *et al.* 1976 for discussion of systematicity/variability in IL. Preston 1989 places this in a wider SLA/sociolinguistics framework.) The IL forms *every one boy* and *this the* remain unexplained (p.28).

Noun and pronoun inflection (Coulter's Chapter 3)

The discrepancy between L and F with regard to the noun plural morpheme (C4) cannot be accounted for on the basis of CA information. (Note that this kind of discrepancy also occurs in C1.) Coulter believes that the plural morpheme is not necessary for the kind of communicating the informants indulge in (p.30); if so, then F's errors especially (e.g. A9) are to be explained as being part of his personal strategy of communication. CA traditionally would suggest that since Russian speakers learning English proceed from five forms of plural (B6) to the one of English, an example of moving to simplicity from complexity is manifested, and the English noun plural should represent no problem (p.87). This type of conclusion brought forth by classical CA is at times convincingly falsified by Coulter's data; details of Coulter's analysis should be paid attention to in SLA.

The error in A10 is related to C5 and most likely should be considered as a slip of the tongue and classified as a 'mistake' (Corder 1967, see Chapter 6 below). It should be noted, if it hasn't been already, that the exact classification of an error is at times difficult. F rarely uses articles (C1, 2) or the possessive morpheme in nouns (C6). Thus in A11, in EA terms, is the possessive or article absent? The 'hypothesized' American English norm for A11 is thus either 'He is on the Tolstoj committee, too' or 'He is on Tolstoj's committee, too' (p.32).

Verb forms (Coulter's Chapter 4)
Many errors in this category are straightforward, e.g. lack of third singular present (A12) and regularizing past tense forms of irregular verbs (A13). Explanations have to do with over-generalizing rules of English. The situation regarding the verb *be* and past tense forms of all verbs is extremely complex. Much of their difficulty seems to be due to Russian: equation sentences, the complexity of the verb system, and the lack of full-scale analyses. Sentences A14–19, as well as B7, 8 and C7, 8 may hint at the difficulties involved in description and explanation. One point that demands explanation is the unexpectedly low frequency of omission of *be* (C7) in light of B7. Perhaps est', usually absent in Russian, was directly equated with the sometimes absent *is* of their IL performance and thus they did not omit *am* and *are* nearly as often (p.43). Or perhaps this result is due to a variable mentioned above, salience of structure, namely the obvious centrality of BE to the surface structure of standard English.

Sentence A20 is explained in the relation to E9 as an example of the transfer to their IL of a Russian predictive illocutionary potential and though the CA does not state this, it may represent deep-structure transfer; as seen in Chapter 3 instances of underlying transfer regarding modality appear to occur. (See also A21 related to B10.) Unfortunately, occurrences in Coulter's corpus of surface exponents of modality are infrequent which in a way is not surprising since the conflation of forms occurs (C9); furthermore, the avoidance of these surface exponents appears to be common as well. In my

experience, learners of English are often consciously aware of the
seemingly hopeless complexities of the modal area of English
grammar, of the entanglement of subtleties and ambiguities.
Avoidance here would presumably be due to a deliberate strategy of
communication, but there is a methodological difficulty in identifying
and interpreting surface exponents of modality. The problem is
analogous to the analysis of Corder's (next chapter) superficially non-
deviant sentences: 'I want to know the English' and 'You must not
take off your hat,' depending on learner intention. Corder's problem
of 'plausible reconstruction' is indeed a subtle one, to be taken up
again in the next chapter.

Structure of clauses and sentences (Coulter's Chapter 5)
In many sentences in Coulter's corpus (e.g. A22) the positions of
subject, verb, object and adverb are different in the IL from what
they would be in standard English. Generally speaking, these appear
to be examples of surface structure transfer (A22 related to B11).
Another phenomenon is particularly illuminating and ahead of its
time, because Coulter claims it to be discourse related: using two
specific twentieth-century pieces of literature, Coulter concludes B12
as an explanation of A23, claiming that *this all Poland* elaborates and
explains ONE CAMP. I recommend Chapter 5 of this work, as
presenting further discourse material ahead of its time.

Given the advanced age of these long time speakers of NN English, it
is hard to believe that their IL would change and it did not, except
for the adding of some vocabulary. They were fossilized speakers of
Russian-English and not temporarily stabilized with a 'transitional
competence' (Corder 1972 and the next chapter). Most of the errors
described in this study appear in the speech of both informants, the
main difference being in frequency (p.84). Both informants tend to
avoid grammatical formatives such as articles, plural forms and past
tense forms (pp.7, 84). Though they clearly understand NS TL
English speech in which these forms occur, productively speaking
these forms may not be present in the linguistic knowledge which
controls their IL speech. Because of the tendency to avoid these
forms (even if they 'know' them but do not use them) in IL
productive performance, lexical items are often strung together
without overtly showing structural relationships between them, a
common occurrence in L1 acquisition data and pidgin/creole data. It
is hard to say if the same thing can be said about the informants' lack
of ability to produce 'modal-full' sentences, since it seems reasonable

that the proposition of a sentence may be interpreted independently of speaker beliefs or feelings about it.

Summary

As we have seen from this discussion, both CA and EA have the possible goal of accounting for L2 learner behaviour. If we ignore weaknesses already identified in each approach, both provide *predictive IL data* and hypotheses in terms of interlingual identifications that can be tested in careful SLA studies. By getting our hands dirty in the details of CA and EA, we have seen cases where linguistic categories match IL data and cases where they do not, and perhaps we have come to appreciate in more depth some older sources for the IL hypotheses they generate. The study of CA and EA, like that of bilingualism, serves at least five helpful purposes:

(1) teasing out of these literatures IL hypotheses that can be empirically tested;
(2) providing these hypotheses possible frameworks of theoretical thought;
(3) providing analytical tools for both old and new data sets;
(4) enhancing the breadth and depth of IL explanations;
(5) training scholars of SLA in descriptive IL analytical techniques.

We conclude this chapter by noting the importance of realizing that all SLA work stands on the foundation of the papers in EA and IL by Corder, papers which themselves stand on a clear understanding of previous CA, EA and bilingualism literatures. In 1967 I was called in to consult on the first draft of Coulter's EA thesis, discussed at length in this chapter. Coulter had spent two years collecting extensive amounts of data, but lacked a framework for pulling the material together. Fortunately for him, several months earlier, Corder's paper 'The Significance of Learners' Errors' (Corder 1967) had appeared. Its 'significance' for Coulter was the possibility, at long last, of the beginnings of a coherent perspective. Many works since have benefited thus, being informed by the strong speculative/philosophical approach of Corder, to which we now turn in the next chapter.

Points for discussion

(1) Describe your own experience with errors in learning a second language, especially when they have made a difference and when they have not. First, look at the situation from your point

of view as a language learner. What learning strategies do you use to deal with errors? Now look at it from the teacher's point of view. What teaching strategies concerning errors do you think prove useful, if any? In either case, can you think of ways of taking advantage of these strategies? Where might the re-searcher's point of view coincide and where would it not?

(2) Rethink (1) with the distinction oral/written language in mind.

(3) Next, consider the Binda, and Lehn and Slager quotes at the beginning of this chapter concerning CA as a necessary step in the language teaching process. Given the notion of a CA 'with safeguards' – i.e. a CA backed up by empirical IL studies – re-evaluate the CA recommended way of preparing for language teaching advocated by Fries and Lado and presented in Chapter 1. Now repeat the exercise by considering an EA with safeguards. (This notion of CA/EA with safeguards is further considered in Chapter 8.)

(4) In light of the CA and EA data presented in this chapter, first discuss the notion of contrasts in CA, EA and IL. Relate your answer to the Saussurian concept of 'value' as discussed in the first few chapters above. Next, differentiate between the frameworks provided by CA vs EA vs IL in dealing with predictions provided by each of the others.

(5) Re-evaluate Weinreich's view of language transfer as a selection process in light of Coulter's analysis of language transfer as occurring on a surface level. Integrate into your discussion the evidence presented in the last chapter of a possible underlying or deep structure view of this process.

(6) Given the following (simplified) contrastive data, predict those problems that an Arabic student learning English will 'tend to' have (remember the discussion of such terms in Chapter 1) in two linguistic domains. State your reasons in each case.

(a) *Phonological*

English		Arabic	
/iy/	'beet'	/ii/	long vowel phoneme with two allophones, one close to the English articulation and one further back.
/i/	'bit'		
		/i/	short vowel phoneme with two allophones, one close to the English articulation in English
/ey/	'bait'		

| /e/ | 'bet' | /iy/ and one close to the English articulation in 'bet'. |

(Note that the /-y/ in the English vowel data signifies a glide to a higher vocal position.)

(b) *Grammatical*

English	Arabic
who	
whom	ʔalleti (masculine)
which	ʔallati (feminine)
that	
whose	.

(7) Describe the learning problems that you predict a Portuguese speaker learning English will tend to have in the following two linguistic domains.

(a) *Grammatical*

There are three forms used in the affirmative patterns of the conditional in English. The semantic interpretations that are implicit in these three forms are: (1) the time element; (2) the idea of possibility in *Form A* below; (3) the idea of improbability in *Form B*; and (4) the idea of impossibility in *Form C*. The most important point is that although in the surface forms in English, these four semantic ideas are *implicit*, in Portuguese the same ideas exist but are *explicit* in the surface forms, i.e. the verb tenses used in *A*, *B* and *C* below in Portuguese immediately convey the desired meaning. In other words, the Portuguese verb tenses are directly equated to the four semantic interpretations stated above.

CA–Form A:

E: If + subj + verb (present) + obj + subj + verb (future) + adv phrase

P: Si + subj + verb (present conditional) + obj + subj (optional) + verb (future) (future) + adv phrase

Example:

| If | I | have | the car, | I | will go | to the movies. |
| Si | eu | tiver | o carro, | (eu) | irei | ao cinema. |

CA–Form B:

E: If + subj +	verb (past)	+ obj	+ subj +	verb + (future past)	adv phrase
P: Si + subj +	verb (past conditional)	+ obj	+ subj + (op- tional)	verb + (future past)	adv phrase

Example:

If	I	had	the car,	I	would go	to the movies.
Si	eu	tivesse	o carro,	(eu)	iria	ao cinema.

CA–Form C:

E: If + subj +	verb (past perfect)	+ obj	+ subj +	verb + (past future perfect)	adv phrase
P: Si + subj +	verb (past conditional perfect)	+ obj	+ subj + (op- tional)	verb + (past future perfect)	adv phrase

Example:

If	I	had had	the car,	I	would have gone	to the movies.
Si	eu	tivesse tido	o carro,	(eu)	teria ido	ao cinema.

(b) *Phonological*

Intonation: The contours presented here are those used in mid-western American English and in Portuguese spoken in Rio de Janeiro.

Contrastive Analysis (based on 4–3–2–1 pitch levels, 4 highest):

English examples:

(a) If I have / time \ I'll / finish \ my work.
   2   3   2   3   2   1

(b) If I don't / see you to \ morrow I'll / call \ you.
   2   3   2   3   1

(c) Would you / have washed \ the car if it hadn't been / raining?
   2   3   2   1   2   3 1

Portuguese translation of above examples:

(a)
$$\quad\quad\quad 3 \quad\quad\quad\quad 3 \quad\quad\quad\quad 3$$
Si eu tiver / tempo \ eu termi / narei \ meu trabalho.
$$\quad 2 \quad\quad\quad\quad\quad 2 \quad\quad\quad\quad 2 \quad\quad 1$$

(b)
$$\quad\quad 3 \quad\quad\quad\quad\quad 3 \quad\quad\quad\quad 3$$
Si ⌐ eu nao \ vir voce amanha \ eu te telefonarei
$$\quad 2 \quad\quad\quad\quad 2 \quad\quad\quad\quad 2$$

(c)
$$\quad 3 \quad\quad\quad\quad 3 \quad\quad\quad\quad 3 \quad\quad\quad\quad 3 \quad\quad 4$$
Voce teria lavado o carro si nao tivesse estad chivendo.
$$\quad\quad\quad 2 \quad 1 \quad\quad 2 \quad\quad\quad 2 \quad 1$$

6 Theoretical advances: Corder and Van Buren

S. Pit Corder

In 1984 at Edinburgh University, some thirty scholars gathered from Europe and North America to honour the retirement of Professor S. Pit Corder. The topic of the seminar was 'The Current State of IL Studies' and the results are published in a most useful volume (Davies *et al.* 1984). The atmosphere of the seminar was informal and much useful discussion ensued. IL studies appeared to be alive and well, and even thriving. It was a happy and festive occasion, or as Pit put it in his Epilogue: 'Somebody pointed out that this was in effect the "Fest" part of a "Festschrift", and that most so-called Festschrifts lack Fests. This for me has been a Fest' (*ibid.*, p.344). The seminar was an old-fashioned Festschrift; papers were prepared in honour of the retiring senior scholar, read orally and discussed. The published volume is a detailed statement of what is known about IL up to that date including an interesting record of discussion of each paper.

It is generally and genuinely acknowledged that the current vibrant state of SLA studies could not have come about without the pioneering theoretical and speculative work of S. Pit Corder. In fact, it was pointed out over and over again at the seminar that 'speculation', i.e. *disciplined speculation*, is a most positive endeavour, necessary to the advancement of scientific thought. I heartily agree, and it is clear that over the years Corder's insights on theory and on research methodology in EA and IL studies, standing on previous work in CA and EA, have regularly provided breakthroughs allowing empirical and then further theoretical advances to occur.

One of the original breakthroughs, in my view, was the insight that reframed our conception of 'errors' from something negative showing lazy unmotivated students to something normal and important for learning to occur, a 'window' on the learner's internal grammar, a learning strategy perhaps neces-sary to promote SLA. Corder's idea, brought up several times in previous chapters, leads directly to the view of a highly structured learner language (cf. Chapter 8 below).

Much is owed to S. Pit Corder intellectually as well as for his ability to set up a context for creative work for younger scholars, a contribution which has been acknowledged in several places, e.g. in the dedications to Widdowson (1978) and to this volume. In conversation with Corder and others during the Edinburgh seminar, it was agreed that credit for the important insight concerning errors just mentioned should go also to Paul Van Buren and that this has not been generally recognized, although in Corder (1967), Van Buren's contribution is acknowledged in the last line of the paper. Thus, in discussing theoretical advances from CA to IL through EA, I wish to bring together the work of Corder and Van Buren. The Van Buren paper on which we shall here concentrate (Van Buren 1972) is entitled, plainly enough, 'Contrastive Analysis'. This paper should become 'highly valued' in applied linguistics for it weighs carefully the argumentation used in classical CA, theoretical linguistics and IL.

Van Buren's grafting component

Van Buren investigates the classical CA hypothesis attributed to Lado in Chapter 1 above, and provides us (p.294) with a 'grafting' component (reminiscent of Harris's 'Z-component' in transfer grammar discussed in Chapter 4 above) which he claims is necessary to an explicit CA. This is an 'in-between' component, unique to each language. It specifies conditions under which 'secondary categories' are 'grafted on to' the 'primary categories' which contain the semantic information common to the two languages being compared. He sets as a goal for CA that it 'should convey as many insights as possible into the differences and similarities between the languages being compared' (p.279), and investigates the sort of linguistic theory that can best accomplish this.

He begins by looking at assumptions underlying comparison in Lado (1957), pointing out that these assumptions conceal 'fundamental problems' of CA (p.280). In terms of his detailed example of tense in English and French, the concept 'tense' may not be the same in both languages (cf. the title to Lattey 1982, which is discussed in Chapters 3 and 4 above). His point is that the concept 'tense' is not a fact about English or French ('the only facts at our disposal are the two utterances in English and French') but 'belongs to the realm of theoretical terms which should be sharply distinguished from the realm of fact' (p.281). This is a good reminder which we shall pick up again in Chapter 8.

He then reminds us of the basic CA problem discussed in Chapter 4 above: to set up 'satisfactory contrastive procedures' one must first of all postulate 'common categories' between the two linguistic systems concerned. Van Buren summarizes the contrastivist's basic dilemma, which we have discussed before in this volume, that many linguists who 'champion' 'the cause of contrastive analysis fail to acknowledge the logical necessity of common categories (or, a fortiori, universals)' (Van Buren 1972, p.294), attributing the failure to 'the characteristically structuralist assumption', namely that each language is a self-sufficient system in that each element in that system has a value, in the sense described in Chapter 2 above, a value 'uniquely determined' by the structural relations of that system. Van Buren goes on to point out that: '[A] descriptive technique which is confined to an analysis of the internal relationships of a single language is, strictly speaking, incompatible with the notion of comparison between two or more languages.' Much of the paper is devoted to resolving this problem, one which, in order to understand IL, must be continually faced. He begins with equivalences in meaning, more specifically translation equivalents across languages, as pointed out in Chapter 4, an apparent consensus CA procedure. Concerning his tense/time example, he sets up a series of parameters, pointing out that these parameters are semantic in nature, that they are common to both languages (perhaps universal), that they are implicit in the utterance, that this can be ' "spelled out" by the device of paraphrase' (p.239), and that the common semantic principles are 'coded differently' for English and French, which results in different syntactic categories on the surface. He sets up a 'notional grid' (which we reproduce here as Table 6.1). With this grid, Van Buren adds to the technology of CA. He shows how CA data and 'permutations' are 'heuristically useful' in forcing the analyst to produce *principled sets of data* (analogous to predictive IL data; cf. Chapter 5) and to check out theoretical categories concerned against these data. The detail is interesting and is recommended for study, but in this chapter I wish to concentrate on the CA/IL principles involved.

He next brings us to a discussion of 'auxiliary' in English and French (p.294), showing that 'the auxiliary expansion rule is different for English and French'. He asks the important CA question: Is auxiliary a common category or not? If not, 'then the common label is highly misleading'. He concludes that if it is, then there must be *cross-linguistic justification* for its existence, logically a prior step to claiming CLI when comparing NL with IL. What one needs in a

| | POINT START | | | CONTINU-ING | | POINT STOP | | | POINT ORIENTATION | | | |
| | *Past specified* | | | | | *Past specified* | | | *In Past* | | | |
	1 Point inferred	2 Point named	3 Past unspecified (but relevant)	4 Past	5 Present	6 Point inferred	7 Point named	8 Past unspecified (not necessarily relevant)	9 Time specified	10 Event specified	11 Event unspecified	12 In present
1	X											X
2						X						X
3		X										
4					X							
5				X								X
6			X	X								X
7		X										X
8	X											X
9				X		X				X		
10		X				X				X		
11		X		X		X					X	
12		X		X		X				X		
13		X		X			X			X		
14	X			X			X			X		
15		X										X
16	X											X
17		X							X	X		
18	X								X	X		
19									X	X		
20	X							X	X			

Source: Adapted from Van Buren (1972, p.291)
Note: 1–20 on the left refer to 20 sentences in English and their translation equivalents in French.

TABLE 6.1 Specimen grid for CA

principled CA then is an 'identity condition on deep components'. A 'notional approach', such as shown in Table 6.1, 'reflects' this condition which, Van Buren argues and I agree, provides a set of useful heuristic constraints on CA statements and predicted IL data.

Van Buren provides a detailed example of how this works, contrasting selected aspects of yes/no questions in English and Chinese. His analysis *necessitates* the grafting component; his conclusion, like others in SLA, is that 'no version of any grammatical model in existence . . . is adequate to describe the data'. This mirrors the conclusion that keeps coming up in language contact and IL studies: that as soon as one leaves the strictly monolingual domain of inquiry of grammatical judgements, then the units postulated by currently available linguistic theories need to be rethought and new types of interlingual units are called for. It would be interesting to see a carefully developed theoretical linguistics including a Van Buren grafting- or a Harris Z-component along with units of interlingual identifications *and* the resulting new IL hypotheses generated for empirical testing, a linguistics that paid more than lip service to the fact that the world is far from a set of monolingual languages. (As mentioned in the last chapter, this failure of theoretical linguistics is discussed at various places in the literature, e.g. Selinker 1972. Long and Sato 1984 provides a summary of attempts to establish this point, and Wode 1984 makes this point with regard to language transfer; see Selinker 1984, Issue 6 for an attempt to summarize this discussion.)

Van Buren 1988 is an interesting addition to cross-linguistic thought. He considers Zobl's (in press) suggestion that, with modification, the 'subset principle' concerning 'marking' of UG parameters is useful in understanding acquisition of the verb phrase in English by Japanese speakers. Contrastive information is discussed using such Lado-type phrases (discussed in Chapter 1) as what the learner 'has to learn', and Van Buren rejects Zobl's suggestion on technical grounds, showing that the learner has a binary choice – fossilize or adopt a movement grammar 'totally constrained' by UG. I read Van Buren's argument as one more bit of evidence that we need a wider linguistics that more intimately includes language contact data than what we now have.

Corder's basic papers

Van Buren's cross-linguistic theoretical thinking, going back many years and way ahead of its time, was central as input to Corder's

work; the latter is conveniently collected in the twelve papers in Corder (1981):
- 'The Significance of Learners' Errors'
- 'Idiosyncratic Dialects and Error Analysis'
- 'Describing the Language Learner's Language'
- 'The Role of Interpretation in the Study of Learners' Errors'
- 'Error Analysis and Remedial Teaching'
- 'The Elicitation of Interlanguage'
- 'The Study of Interlanguage'
- 'Simple Codes and the Source of the Second Language Learner's Initial Heuristic Hypothesis'
- 'Language Continua and the Interlanguage Hypothesis'
- 'Language Distance and the Magnitude of the Language Learning Task'
- 'Strategies of Communication'
- 'Formal Simplicity and Functional Simplification'

In the discussion to follow, I also consider a later paper (Corder 1983), produced for a conference on language transfer (Gass and Selinker 1983a):
- 'A Role for the Mother Tongue'

Also helpful is the review of Corder 1981 by Sharwood Smith (1984).

It is important to note that Corder 1967 is *the* paper that began current interest in SLA and IL studies. Whenever I feel that we are not making fast enough progress, or that our data are too messy, or that our theoretical concepts are not precise enough, etc., I reread this paper and think of sibling fields. The study of grammar, for example, is 2500 years old at least, as is the thinking and talking about language pedagogy. On the other hand, the study of IL, it is generally agreed, is no more than twenty-five years old, dating from Corder 1967. I have searched the literature for several centuries back and there exists no previous systematic study of learner language, under any name. We have to be patient while we are struggling with a way to do things given data that are enormously complex.

But we have come a long way; in the late 1960s we would have cheered if we had even seen an empirical EA study such as Coulter's thesis (1968; discussed in Chapter 5 above). Like most colleagues today, I can hardly keep up with the literature. I feel that this is a success, and not a trivial one. We have without doubt shown that there is structure in learner language. Also, there are now many things we do not have to 'call for' any more:
- careful descriptive and analytical studies are being done;

- longitudinal studies are being done;
- methodology, in most cases, is being clearly stated;
- pidgin and creole studies are not being ignored;   and so on.

We have thus solidified a subject matter with Corder's inspiration and help.

Significance of learner errors

In Corder's seminal paper (Corder 1967 = Ch.1, Corder 1981), errors are viewed as highly systematic, serving as 'windows' to the learner's progress in the second language, or in Corder's highly influential terms, as windows to the learner's 'built-in syllabus'. In a recorded dialogue of mother/child interaction, errors are shown to provide insights into the child learner's development of language. Corder (1967, pp.167, 170) attributes this dialogue and CA/IL insights related to it to Paul Van Buren, as discussed above.

Mother: Did Billy have his egg cut up for him at breakfast?
Child: Yes, I showed him.
Mother: You what?
Child: I showed him.
Mother: You showed him?
Child: I seed him.
Mother: Ah, you saw him.
Child: Yes, I saw him.

Corder uses this example to claim that the child – and, by extension, the adult learner – tests hypotheses. In this case, the child, according to this analysis, tests three hypotheses: '... one relating to the concord of subject and verb in a past tense, another about the meaning of "show" and "see" and a third about the form of the irregular past tense of "see"' (Corder 1967, p.167 = 1981, p.11) These hypotheses are presented by the analyst in the CA/EA sense as a result of comparing the learner data with the expected target data. Corder adds to our thinking by discussing *the function of errors for the learners themselves*. This latter is one of the major themes of this volume. In Corder's early view, and I still believe this position to be correct (at least, for some learners under some conditions), for learners themselves errors are 'indispensable', since the making of errors can be regarded 'as a device the learner uses in order to learn'. Corder goes on to say that the making of errors is: 'a strategy employed by children acquiring their mother tongue and by those learning a second language ... is a way the learner has of testing his hypotheses about the nature of the language he is learning' (Corder,

1967, p.167 = 1981, p.11). We have two highly significant contributions: that the errors of a learner, whether adult or child, are (a) not random, but are in fact systematic, and are (b) not 'negative' or 'interfering' in any way with learning a TL but are, on the contrary, a necessary positive factor, indicative of testing hypotheses. Such contributions in Corder 1967, done in the EA vein, began to provide a framework for the study of adult learner language. Along with the influence of studies in L1 acquisition and concepts provided by CA (especially language transfer) and by the IL hypothesis (e.g. fossilization, backsliding, language transfer, communication and learning strategies), this paper provided the impetus for hundreds of SLA empirical studies. Several other important and influential themes also appear in this paper. One is the call for studies which provide longitudinal description of the adult learner's language, as analysts describe the longitudinal development of a child's language throughout its maturation. Corder convincingly argues that *only longitudinal studies* can answer certain theoretical questions (1981, p.11) and this theme, which I am sure is still correct, is picked up throughout the 1981 collection. For example, on p. 20 (originally Corder 1972) he points out that longitudinal studies of the language development of an adult L2 learner rely on the techniques of error analysis, as longitudinal study of infants learning the NL 'depends on the analysis of his idiosyncratic sentences'. Then, in a statement that has proved most influential, Corder writes: 'Furthermore, I believe that until we do attempt to undertake the longitudinal study of *free-learning* second language learners, we shall not make much headway with finding out how people learn second languages' (Corder 1981, p.20, italics added). This revolutionary suggestion is the first of its kind in the literature and such studies are continually being carried out (e.g. the 'guest-worker' IL studies summarized in Perdue, in preparation).

Then, in a bold move, linking up longitudinal studies with studies of input (the latter a growth industry in SLA), Corder provides reasons why 'we need to make a regular series of checks on [the learner's] grammar to see the effect that exposure to certain data has had on the state of his grammar.' (1981, p.27, originally Corder 1971b). Importantly, and I am sure that this is true and not trivial, 'we can make certain inferences about the learning process' by describing 'successive states' of learner language, comparing these states, noting changes and correlating these with input. Such empirical studies immerse in the techniques of CA as we search for interlingual identifications connected with input. This continuing research programme is Corder's.

In a methodology paper (1981, Ch.4 = Corder 1972), he discusses 'the role of interpretation' in the study of IL and once again calls for longitudinal studies of the adult L2 learner 'similar to those of the infant learning his mother tongue'. He calls errors that the learner makes the 'most important source of information about his linguistic development' (pp.35–6), providing an account of the 'built-in syllabus'. In this paper he discusses the central position of EA in 'applied linguistic studies' and discusses how we can develop better techniques for the identification and description of errors. We will return to these points later.

Corder calls the learning system a 'dynamic' one, claiming, in a current vein, that it is 'a process of interaction' between the learner and the input data. He links up the longitudinal with language transfer (*not* restricted to NL transfer) (1981, p.58 = Corder 1971c) by stating that we need to make 'a regular series of checks' on the learner's grammar to discover the effect that exposure of particular data has on 'the state of his grammar'. Concerning the 'optimal' logical sequencing of input data, these longitudinal checks could be related only to a particular learner or, perhaps, group of learners. Corder believes it necessary to make this qualification because: 'clearly what the learner already knows of a language (his mother tongue and any other languages he has) is part of the learning device itself' (Corder 1981, p.58) Notice how different his view is of *what the learner already knows*, and its place in the SLA process, from that of Lado as discussed in Chapter 1.

One should study this learning device in a longitudinal way (pp.58–9), *not only* for 'captive learners' who have been exposed to particular syllabuses in classrooms, but also for 'non-captive learners' who presumably have been exposed to no planned syllabuses at all. In the latter case, Corder wrote in 1971 that 'we have little idea at present of what the nature of the potential input to the device is'. Here there is progress in SLA: several researchers, and research teams, have devoted themselves to studies of *non*-tutored learners. (For a summary of the European Science Foundation 'guest-worker' language project, see Perdue 1991, and for a summary of the work on artificial pidgins, also called here 'pedagogical pidgins', see Cushing *et al.* (forthcoming). Van den Berg (1988) focuses interestingly on the process of 'depidginization'.)

The final mention of longitudinal studies that we shall look at in Corder (1981, p.72) is where he is looking at SLA and 'the nature of' IL 'as a type of language' and its relation to other types of languages. The study of IL, in a view of which I highly approve

(Corder 1981, Introduction), becomes part of the study of language or linguistics 'in its broader sense'. The call for longitudinal studies of language learners, particularly in informal settings, is motivated by the *goal* of IL studies, to discover 'the way language learners process the data of language to which they are exposed, whatever the superficially different properties of the data may be, as well as to discover what the "natural" sequence of development is' (Corder 1981, p.72 = 1976), making a practical argument for the 'central relevance' of IL to teaching, that if we find general principles of second language development, then we can apply these principles to the 'selection, organization and sequencing' of material for learning in teaching situations (Corder 1981, p.72). We here return to consideration of Fries/Lado in Chapter 1: language teaching materials and teaching methodology as an important impetus for looking at what learners actually do. In the Corder Festschrift, it is stated that we are concerned with what IL studies tell about the language learning processes, enabling teachers to 'contrive the most effective conditions possible in classrooms for this process to take place' (Widdowson in Davies *et al.*, 1984, p.324). This is still a powerful motivation for studying IL, for I would maintain that teachers, in order to make intelligent pedagogical decisions, need to have a principled way of contemplating the speech and writing of learners that pour out of the learners in front of them. (One situation in which Corder's applied IL programme has been carried out is at the University of Copenhagen and can be seen in a volume with a nice title: *Learner Language and Language Learning* (Faerch *et al.*, 1984).)

Another influential theme brought up in Corder 1967 is the important distinction: input vs intake. It is easy to show the continued relevance of this distinction. For example, the Xth University of Michigan Conference on Applied Linguistics, held in October 1983, had as its topic: 'Input in second language acquisition: Learners' use and integration of language in context'. One of the key questions addressed at this conference was: 'Appropriate methodologies for investigating the relationship between input/intake/output' (Gass and Madden 1985 = Proceedings). Corder offers the caution that introducing a qualification 'about the control of input' would be wise. He points out that input relates to the 'external syllabus' presented to the learner. In a most influential statement, he notes that presenting a particular linguistic form to a learner in the classroom 'does not necessarily qualify it' as input, because input 'is "what goes in" not what is *available* for going in, and we may reasonably suppose that it

is the learner who controls this input, or more properly his intake'
(Corder 1981, pp.8–9, emphasis in the original). All this control may
well be determined, speculates Corder, by 'the characteristics of his
language acquisition mechanism and not by those of the [external]
syllabus'. Corder's notion of 'intake' leads to the important concept
of 'built-in syllabus', i.e. the idea that 'the learner is using a definite
system at every point in his development' (p.10), a phrasing that is
close to the notion of IL (cf. Selinker and Lamendella 1978).

Corder brings up the input/intake distinction again in Chapter 6 of
Corder (1981 = 1971c), a widely quoted paper for its methodological
suggestions, and we come back to these below. It was basic to some
of the early work in the Toronto French-immersion research (e.g.
Tarone *et al.*, 1976). Corder points out that there is not a 1:1
relationship between input and output, which means we have to make
a 'systematic distinction' (1981, p.58) between input and intake,
shown by the fact that, on first exposure, learners do not immediately
learn 'what the syllabus prescribes should be learnt at that point'.
Two possible reasons appear as valid today as when first proposed:
(a) the data or their presentation are 'defective' in some way, or
(b) even in those cases where the data are adequate, the state of the
    learning device is such that 'it cannot take them in'.
This leads to the idea that learners are 'programmed' to take in and
process data in certain (still unknown) ways, and, importantly, that
the teacher is 'not in control' of the learner's programme (cf. also
Pienemann 1989). Corder points out, though, that the learner can
influence this learner built-in programme and what may be bad for
the learner is that this influence can manifest itself in interfering
ways. A reason for teachers to know about IL is that they may present
data 'prematurely' so that they will not form part of the intake.
Another possible way in which the teacher can interfere with natural
processes is *not* to present data when intake demands that they are
'logically required'. (I am open to correction here, but I do not
believe that this latter point has been researched in the literature.)

In a most influential pronouncement, Corder calls for research
which investigates the nature of input data and the current state of
the learner's grammar in the dynamic learning system. Here I believe
we can see that disciplined speculation leads to a research
programme, the details of which will be spelled out below in this
chapter. For now, we will note only that this seminal discussion is
crucial to developments in IL theory.

An important theme in Corder 1967 is that of transitional
competence (1981, p.10), the learner's 'underlying knowledge of the

language to date'. The notion 'competence', of course, comes from Chomsky (1965) and the idea that this competence in the L2 is 'transitional' is meant to capture the dynamic nature of the learner's developing system. I have some problems with this term and will discuss them while comparing it with Nemser's notion of 'approximative systems' in the next chapter. For now I mention that it does not appear to cover the type of IL speaker with an entirely fossilized competence, studied by Coulter (1968) and discussed above in Chapter 5.

Corder on p.16 of the 1981 collection of papers discusses the idea that a learner's language is 'normally unstable' and why this should be the case. When a learner is not understood, he or she: 'has a motive to bring his behaviour into line with conventions of some social group, if he is able'. This is an important idea and one that is widely accepted. This means that IL learning will cease when learners believe they are able to get intended messages across with the IL system they have. The interesting idea that the learner 'may not be able' to match the norms of a target social group brings up important questions of 'inevitability' and 'innateness' of fossilization; cf. Chapter 9 below. (Also, this is discussed in Selinker 1984, Issue 3, and Selinker 1985–6.)

Corder (1981, p.56) links up the idea of transitional competence with the database (i.e. grammatical judgements) of NS studies on monolingual linguistic competence. In an influential statement Corder writes that if IL researchers are describing the learner's (transitional) grammatical competence, then 'we must also accept that he will have "intuitions" about the grammaticality of his language which are potentially investigable' (Corder 1981, p.56). Interestingly, Corder adds: 'The fact that he himself may regard them as intuitions about the target language is neither here nor there'. I am of two minds about this issue. In Selinker 1972, fn 9 I argued that: 'the analyst in the interlingual domain cannot rely on intuitive grammatical judgements since he will gain information about another system, the one the learner is struggling with, i.e. the TL'. (For a similar methodological problem in another domain, see Labov 1969, p.715). Many colleagues were unhappy with this position; for example, J. Schachter *et al.* (1976) argued strongly against it and, following Corder's suggestions, produced interesting and significant results using intuitional data. Other colleagues have followed Corder's advice and used learner intuition as a methodological tool, including myself (cf. Selinker and Douglas 1985, 1989). So in some sense I was very clearly wrong! On the other hand, I find that the Labov caution is still worth considering. His point is as follows: that when two forms of a language are in a subordinate and superordinate relationship, the intuitions one gets from those in the subordinate relationship will (or at least may) reflect the superordinate system. I believe that this does happen at times in IL studies and that the caution holds, Corder's assertion in the quote above notwithstanding. There is an important theoretical issue which comes out of consideration of the Corder speculation: it is a possibility that in some learners at least, co-existent IL systems are not to be discounted. In Chapter 2 above it was pointed out that long ago, Fries and Pike (1949) raised this issue in a neighbouring domain. They showed convincingly that co-existent phonemic systems are likely in some IL cases. Their study should be reinvestigated using newer methodological tools.

There is another angle here, too: even if it is a valid tool at times, one has to ask how far IL intuition can get us. We should judge each claim of intuitional data on its merits, especially since Tarone has strongly argued (1983, 1988) that intuitions about linguistic form as shown by grammatical judgements underlie *a different sort of competence* from the competence which controls language use in conversation and writing. Those who use intuition as a tool (myself included) have a burden to temper claims made about what ILs are like and what they are not like, especially since, as discussed above (see Tarone, *ibid.*, for references), different tasks with the same learner regularly produce different IL facts.

In Corder's masterful 1967 paper we find still another theme seminal to IL studies: the distinction covert vs overt error (in Corder 1981, p.12), though the terms 'covertly erroneous' and 'overtly erroneous' do not seem to be used until the 1972 paper, which is Chapter 4 in Corder 1981. Corder has given us a famous sentence here – 'I want to know the English' – and he discusses it more fully on p. 38 in Corder 1972. The learner who produced this sentence is French. The plausible interpretation of 'I want to get to know the English people' was ruled out on contextual grounds; the IL-particular semantics was retrievable in this case. Language transfer as an explanation is raised and it is claimed that the incorrect use of the definite article 'was derived from its normal use in French before the names of languages'. So the 'plausible reconstruction' is: 'I want to know the English [i.e. the language]'.

Another example Corder brings up to show the same phenomenon (p.21) is: 'After an hour it was stopped.' Corder explains that the context shows that 'it' in the above sentence refers to 'the wind', thus the *expected TL interpretation* 'was unlikely', the correct interpretation being, in TL terms: 'After an hour it stopped.' Here Corder puts it slightly differently, raising the issue of translation from IL to TL; the translation into the TL was: 'After an hour it stopped.' In Chapter 5 above, recall that there is a similar example from PAKS: 'Finally, he arrived at his destiny' when the intended meaning was, in TL terms: 'Finally, he arrived at his destination.' Corder calls such sentences 'apparently "well-formed"' (p.21), and 'superficially well-formed' (p.39). He states (p.39) that: '. . . a sentence may still be erroneous and show no outward and formal sign of this. It may be perfectly well-formed and yet be erroneous in context'. He adds profoundly that: 'Purely superficial formal correctness is no guarantee of absence of error'. And, slightly differently (p.41): 'superficial well-formedness alone is not a guarantee of freedom of error'. One needs sentences which are not only well formed but also 'appropriate' to TL contexts to be error free.

Suggested research procedures

As a consequence of the above, Corder produces for us a 'general law' for doing EA and IL research: *'every sentence is to be regarded as idiosyncratic until shown to be otherwise'* (Corder 1981, p.21, emphasis in original). 'Idiosyncratic' here means *not* of the target system – in our phraseology, 'IL-particular'. Culminating this discussion of 'covertly erroneous' and 'covertly idiosyncratic' is the following crucial methodological point (p.44): we must surely carefully study what the learner intended to say, for that is what provides us with a means of 'determining whether an error is in fact present or not'. Even in more current IL work, where the notion of error plays (perhaps unfortunately) a minor role, Corder's methodological suggestion of studying intended meaning is still quite strong. There have been numerous techniques suggested; the one we like has been called 'grounded ethnography' (cf. Selinker and Douglas 1985). Hawkins (1983) shows that without some such technique, analyst guessing about learner intentions can go seriously astray. In fact, studying learner intention systematically is the next step suggested to carry through the important work on units of second language acquisition in the French-immersion programmes (eg. Harley and Swain 1984).

The final theme in Corder's initial paper (1967) is the important notion that regarding the NL only as negative and interfering (see discussion in Chapter 1 above) is a serious mistake. The 'learner's possession' of the NL in fact should be regarded as *facilitative*. He returns to this theme in one of his final papers (1983, p.95), concluding that the NL acts 'as a heuristic tool' as the learner attempts to discover the formal properties of the TL, 'facilitating especially the learning of those features which resemble features' of the NL.

If this is the case, and I see no empirical reason why it should not be, then we are forced to return to CA. The learner must have *a means to identify* which features of the TL 'resemble' features of NL, since the learner must be constantly comparing NL, TL input and his developing IL and making interlingual identifications if Corder's conclusion is to hold. Thus the learner must establish units of comparison between these three systems (cf. Selinker 1972). I would suggest that it is one of the main jobs of SLA to discover what these comparative and contrastive units are. Does the learner use one or more of the many such units which appear in the CA, bilingualism, and EA literature, or is there variation here as well and do different learners create in fact new sorts of interlingual units? What we have now in the literature are 'if-statements', i.e. 'if learners create an equivalence' or 'given that learners create x or y equivalence', then such and such follows. These are useful generalities to have. What I am calling for is a deeper investigation of the conditions under which learners create equivalences and exactly what those equivalences are. This will take a kind of patience with qualitative individual case-study data and may at present be intractable to cross-sectional group studies.

For example, Kellerman looks at IL lexis in terms of NL transfer in a probabilistic framework. He produces statements of relative probability on the grounds that we cannot predict the specific occurrences of transfer in specific situations due to reasons which Weinreich discussed long ago (see Chapter 2 above): the intervention of non-linguistic variables. This may be true, but may miss the issue under discussion here. Discussing the 'transferability hypothesis' (Kellerman 1983), as applied only to a subset of IL lexis, Kellerman carefully states: *'Given that the learner establishes a correspondence* between L1 surface form F and L2 surface form F', where F is polysemous, the less marked the meaning in the L1, the more likely it is to be attributed to F' in the IL' (Kellerman 1987, p.66, emphasis added). Building on Kellerman's work, I would like to see investigated the italicized part of the subordinate clause in the above quote. Which learners establish such a correspondence, under what conditions, etc.? One of the main themes of this volume is to uncover the assumptions of a contrastive nature buried in the literature.

On pp.15–16 of Corder (1981 = 1971a) we have the beginnings of another major contribution, namely the discussion of the problems of *interpretation of IL sentences*, for 'without interpretation, of course, analysis cannot begin'. One of the general laws of interpretation of such sentences was mentioned above (pp.6–19), that every sentence of the IL is to be regarded as 'idiosyncratic until shown to be otherwise'. This relates to the issue of 'superficial well-formedness' and for me, when I first heard Corder lecture on this point (about 1969), it proved most insightful and eventually helpful in developing the IL hypothesis (see Chapter 8 below).

Corder points out the difficulties of interpretation of idiosyncratic sentences, but then (1981, p.33) notes one of the advantages we have in IL. We have 'recourse' to the learner's NL when we wish to establish the speaker's meanings. He first establishes (pp.36–7) that the traditional description of errors is 'superficial' and inadequate. This material is well known and there is no need to repeat it here. He next brings in an important methodological CA point: the way we identify 'or detect' errors is by *comparing* what the learner 'actually said with what he ought to have said to express what he intended to express'. That is, the 'starting point' for EA is a pair of sentences which by definition are '*synonymous* in a particular context, i.e. translation equivalents' (1981, p.37, emphasis in the original). In order to pair up the actual learner sentence with the 'reconstructed sentence', interpretation of the learner sentence is crucial.

How do we interpret the meaning or intentions of learner sentences? We can, of course, ask the learner to translate his IL utterance into the NL, and then the analyst can translate it into the TL (this was essentially the procedure of Coulter 1968; see previous chapter). Note that this procedure depends on analysts being aware, in the first place, that they have perceived an error, for many of these are 'covert' (see discussion above). As pointed out in the LSP area (Selinker 1979), we are here often in the situation of 'we don't know what we don't know'.

He then asks in typical Corder fashion: How do we gain 'plausible interpretations' of erroneous sentences in situations where the learner is not available for consultations? (The reader should note that this is the normal situation in the interpretation of learner writing in tests and is too often the situation regarding the database of SLA studies.) Once again Corder makes the important point that superficial well-formedness is no guarantee of the learner's IL data being free of error. He also points out that even where there is no overt error, 'social appropriateness' is often difficult to judge. He makes the point that it is often 'only later' that one realizes what the learner intended to convey. Here (p.42) he gives an example of an English learner of German and another one of a German learner of English who was overheard saying: 'You mustn't wear a hat at the party', a well-formed, non-erroneous sentence on the surface, when she intended to convey the meaning: 'You don't need to wear a hat at the party.' Corder summarizes: 'It may sometimes be difficult to detect errors of this sort, since only an extended context can provide the information for the correct interpretation' (Corder 1981, p.42).

He then provides examples of other possible situations, e.g. an acceptable utterance in TL terms but one that is ambiguous; utterances which are well formed in TL terms but uninterpretable in the context. A good question is then asked: Can analysts make a 'correct' plausible interpretation of the majority of overtly erroneous learner sentences? Corder believes we can (p.43), but cites another caution: that one may still make an incorrect interpretation on an erroneous sentence because we may be satisfied with the first plausible interpretation, not seeking alternatives.

All of this is related to his extensive contributions to considerations of methodology in IL studies. In Corder (1971c = 1981, Ch.6) he makes the point (p.59) that we must 'supplement' the textual data produced by learners with intuitional data 'and devise systematic methods of investigating these'. Textual data are biased primarily because learners 'place limitations' upon the data we work with '. . . by selecting from his actual repertoire, where possible, only those aspects of his knowledge which, rightly or wrongly, he has most confidence in' (Corder 1981, p.60), a lesson that I, at least, always seem to forget, that our sample is what the learner chooses to show us, not what we choose to discover from the learner *if we are bound* by the methodological requirement of textual data only. This point has been most influential in the way we work. Summarizing, Corder points out that we need techniques which allow us to 'correct' the sampling bias, techniques that 'will enable us to elicit information about the learner's interlanguage which he is not required to reveal by the ordinary tasks we set him or which he does not care to reveal to us voluntarily' (*ibid.*). Corder suggests that we must use 'elicitation procedures', defined as procedures which cause 'a learner to make a judgement about the grammatical acceptability of a form or provokes him into generating a linguistic response' (Corder 1981, p.61). Criteria for elicitation procedures are made more precise; they must force the learner to make a choice so that they reveal very specific facts about his IL, i.e. they must be designed 'to find out something specific about the learner's language, not just to get him to talk freely' (*ibid.*) The procedures demonstrated for the empirical study of language transfer in the next chapter meet this criterion.

At this point in the argument (p.62), Corder returns explicitly to the CA/EA link by stating that the hunches that the investigator may wish to test with specifically designed elicitation procedures will derive from the two 'systematic' techniques already mentioned: formal EA and CA; these two are 'complementary'. The following 'logical sequence of procedures' in the investigation of IL has proven influential in literally scores of studies: (a) textual data are collected which provide useful hypotheses about the IL; (b) hypotheses which were formed on the basis of (a) are refined by CA and EA, providing an important auxiliary source of data about the IL; these hypotheses are validated or refuted by means of an elicitation procedure. It is important to note that not all researchers, though influenced by this formulation, accept that elicitation procedures (especially those that go after grammatical judgements) are the final arbiter for acceptance or rejection of hypotheses about the nature of IL. The counter argument was given in Chapter 5, where the fact that different elicitation tasks regularly elicit different IL data from the same learner was discussed (cf. Tarone references there along with her idea that competence underlying grammatical judgements is of a different sort from that underlying language use).

Corder's formulation of elicitation procedures (1981, 62ff) has proven helpful indeed, giving researchers ideas on how to proceed, as well as confidence to explore new techniques. He discusses, for example, the use of an informant as being part of the traditional methodology of linguistic fieldwork and of studies in child language acquisition. However, he notes that these three areas of study are 'differentially constrained' (p.63) and that we who are looking at learners' language are in a 'relatively favourable position' for the use of elicitation procedures. Studying adult L2 learners vs the study of infants, first, the adult L2 learner can make judgements about the acceptability of forms, about possible synonymous sentences, etc., which the infant cannot; second, the adult L2 learner can provide a translation equivalent (in the NL) of his or her learner sentences, which the infant cannot; and third, most adult L2 learners can acquire a metalanguage, something that is necessary to understand instructions in elicitation tasks and reports introspections about grammatical judgements. In fact, learners who have had formal L2 classroom instruction have already been exposed to the teacher's and the textbooks' metalanguage comments. And infants cannot gain such a metalanguage.

Myint Su's study

In the original version of Corder (1972, pp.43–6) he discusses three research papers done at Edinburgh in the early 1970s using elicitation procedures. I will briefly discuss the work of Myint Su (1971), an interesting study on the lexical competence of university-level students learning English in Burma. Following Corder (1971c, p.44), we concentrate on suggested use of elicitation procedures and do not discuss results. Myint Su's study, unfortunately, was never published and my feeling is that it is a shame that one of the few detailed studies on the acquisition of IL lexis, one that follows exactly Corder's suggested sequence, is not better known.

Concerning investigator characteristics, Myint Su is the perfect 'bilingual' of Burmese and Burmese English, her English rarely exhibiting non-nativeness. She is also an experienced teacher of English at the level she was studying. Corder (1981, p.59) makes a rather large point of these characteristics for IL studies. He states, describing the limits of an approach which uses only textual data, that such a teacher has (a) 'considerable insights' into the linguistic development of the subjects studied, and (b) is usually bilingual in the subjects' NL and the TL. And then, in an important piece of speculation so typical of Corder, he concludes that the researcher 'at some point in his career' actually has been a NS of his pupil's IL.

If this teacher is the person actually carrying out the study, s/he is in a 'similar position' to the 'linguist when he is describing his own mother tongue who consciously or unconsciously makes use of his native intuitions about it' (Corder, *ibid.*). If this is correct, or at least a reasonable working hypothesis, then the status of IL as a language, i.e. 'the second language learner's language' (Corder 1981, Introduction), is more secure. This is diametrically opposed to the position which Corder continually disparages, one which denies structure to the learner's developing second language knowledge, this latter position being more and more difficult to hold. Structure is shown in this case by the fact, which I here assume is fact, that most teachers can predict 'fairly well' what their students will 'regard as acceptable or unacceptable forms, what they will regard as good paraphrases and what sentences they will understand as being related in one way or another' (Corder, *ibid.*). Also Corder concludes that most EA studies 'implicitly incorporate' a large amount of intuitional data, there being 'considerable confidence' in the interpretations assigned to learner utterances in most EA studies. All of this, if correct, strongly supports the position of Corder as outlined in this paragraph.

Corder's methodological point is: Myint Su is 'intuitively aware of idiosyncrasy in the use of English lexical items by her students' ('idiosyncratic' here, remember, is IL-particular use). In her procedure she first carries out an EA of a set of compositions, from which she sets up several lexical sets in which non-TL use is most evident to her as someone knowledgeable about the particular interlingual situation, 'having been there', as it were. Her initial database consists of lexical sets derived from students' IL Burmese–English sentences *paired with* postulated 'equivalent sets' for the NL Burmese (recall the discussion in Chapters 2, 3 and 4 above concerning 'hypothesized' or predicted IL data). These latter are arrived at by a series of 'plausible' interpretations or translations into the NL of the IL sentences, as discussed earlier in this chapter with regard to Corder's views on interpretation of IL sentences.

She then sets up hypotheses about the relationships between the two lexical sets and does a semantic/syntactic/functional analysis of items in both sets. This is pure CA; as we have discussed in earlier chapters, she needs a 'common descriptive framework'. Once again, as we have seen for others working in CA, EA and IL, she finds that none of the available theoretical models can handle the interlingual data. As with others, she has to make a principled choice related to the reality of her IL data: (a) modify existing models; (b) fuse existing models, which may imply modification; or (c) create a new model (cf. Van Buren's grafting component). Like several CA studies in Chapter 4, she chooses a fusion approach.

Another methodological claim concerning Myint Su's work is that: 'The common applicability of these models was assured by the fact that the investigator was a competent bilingual' (Corder 1971c). This claim is too strong, but her CA, based on her previous EA, yields information about similarities and differences between NL and IL, expressed in a common descriptive framework and, thus, predictive IL data as testable hypotheses. These hypotheses are then tested by elicitation procedures aimed at seeing how the learners studied use items from each IL set in a written mode and how they translate the Burmese lexical items arrived at by Myint Su's NL translations. In other words, the investigator's 'useful hypotheses' about specific aspects of learner language are tested by Corder's procedures.

Careful study of Myint Su's work is recommended as it yields useful information about IL lexical acquisition, the types of choices practical IL researchers have to make about the relationship of IL data to available theoretical linguistic models and Corder's elicitation procedures aimed at 'gaining access' to the learners' intuition about IL.

View of interlanguage and interlanguage development

Corder, in a series of papers (the last five in Corder 1981 and Corder 1983), proposes a view of IL and IL development that moves away from the idea of IL as a 'hybrid' between NL and TL (Corder 1981, Introduction). Corder's proposal has interesting and interwoven themes to consider. The following picture of Corder's proposals is drawn from these references, from Sharwood Smith's review of Corder (1981), and from many discussions with Corder, though he is surely not responsible for this interpretation.

In this view of IL, the learner begins L2 acquisition (i.e. the learner's 'initial IL hypothesis') *not* from a 'fully developed' form of the NL – ie. it is not full adult NL knowledge upon which further IL development is based; this fact is clear from most bilingualism, CA and EA scholars from Weinreich on, as discussed in previous chapters. The research problem is to 'discover' (cf. Chapter 8) what this initial IL hypothesis is, and where language transfer fits in.

For Corder, the initial IL hypothesis is a 'stripped down' version of the NL, a 'simple', possibly universal code. Central to this view of things is the clever idea that 'simple' does not mean 'simplified', i.e. simple codes do not necessarily mean that the learner has simplified anything. The argument is that learners cannot simplify the TL, if only for the reason that one *cannot simplify* what one does not know. Corder states that the explanation for this simple code is that: 'we all know a simple basic code because we ourselves have created one in the course of acquiring a first language' (Corder 1983, p.91). He also states that the starting point of the SLA 'developmental continuum' is a 'basic, simple, possibly universal grammar', either which is learned in some unexplained way or, more probably, 'created and remembered' from the learner's own early linguistic development. Thus, SLA insights on latent universal structures from Palmer's insights onwards (1921; cf. Chapter 2 above) are drawn upon. In this scheme, the learner 'reverts' to this basic simple code and begins to 'elaborate' it. This elaboration takes place in the 'direction' of the TL, though permanent non-learning, or fossilization, is recognized as having an important role.

Interestingly, Corder recognizes that the learner's simple code very often acts together with fossilized ILs in other languages. This is shown by the well-attested fact that 'interference' takes place in some cases not from NL but from other second languages, and Corder believes that EA is convincing regarding this transfer from IL1, IL2

... to ILn. Elaboration takes place when the learner is faced with the data of the TL and with growing communicative needs. The NL is a facilitator, a heuristic tool, having the role of helping the learner to discover in the TL, NL-like features. Language distance plays a role (cf. the many Kellerman references cited by Corder and in this volume), with the NL maximally facilitating the acquisition of those features in languages which are structurally close.

In looking at L2 acquisition one has to distinguish carefully between phonology on the one hand, and other levels of language on the other. Phonology, unlike IL grammar, is not susceptible to reverting to a basic code and successive complexification: 'No one would seriously suggest that a second language learner replicates the phonological development of the infant acquiring its mother tongue' (Corder 1981, p.96). Phonology alone in IL involves the successive restructuring of the NL.

Thus, concerning the seeming contradiction between L2 simplification and L2 complexification, for Corder the former does not exist for reasons listed a few paragraphs back and the latter is central to IL development. In several places Corder makes the analogy of L2 acquisition being like the development of a flower: many aspects develop simultaneously. This is contradictory to the common conception of L2 development as linear.

Corder's view of language transfer is as follows: for transfer to exist, it has to take place between two mental structures, NL and developing IL (or between ILn and previously known ILs). He distinguishes between 'transfer' and 'borrowing', the latter being a performance strategy whereas the former relates directly to acquisition (cf. Adjemian 1983). Structural transfer, all that can only properly be called transfer in this view, involves 'incorporation' of an item or features into the IL system. Items and features are often borrowed into the IL from the NL, borrowing being conceived of in the same fashion as in the discussions on bilingualism in Chapters 2 and 3. Borrowing 'refers to the use of items from a second language, typically the mother tongue, particularly syntactic and lexical, to make good the deficiencies of the interlanguage' (Corder 1983, p.92). Use of the NL in this way is a communication strategy, facilitating communication by borrowing items and features from the NL. For transfer to occur, i.e. the incorporation of these NL items and features into the IL, 'successful communication' has also to occur. This may have unforeseen consequences for the learner, and often does; as Corder so cogently puts it, it is clear that successful communication 'does not entirely depend' upon formal correctness, so that 'items and features which have been borrowed but which are *not* similar to the target language may get wrongly incorporated into the interlanguage system, giving rise to error which may sometimes be fairly persistent' (Corder 1983, p.95, emphasis added). Thus potential fossilization is invoked. One weakness in all of this is that Corder does not address the complex issue of how the learner knows if the attempted communication has in fact been successful. (For discussion of some of the complexity involved in the learner actually knowing if a communicative intention is actually successful in an on-going conversation, cf. Selinker and Lamendella 1978.)

Of course, Corder is aware that for this perspective one must *not* revert to the classical CA position on transfer and errors (see discussion in Chapters 1 and 4 above). Thus, he integrates *learner perceptions* of structure with transfer/borrowing concerns by stating that the learner's 'willingness to borrow' may be determined by the learner's 'perception of the linguistic distance between their mother tongue and the target language' (Corder 1983, p.95). Empirically and theoretically, this view has most clearly been shown to have validity for some aspects of lexical transfer by Kellerman (cf. 1983 and 1987; also Gass and Ard 1984 for application of this principle to the acquisition of verb tense information). Kellerman's concept of psychotypology begins to get at the explanatory issues here by detailing how this perception of distance is in fact constrained.

Sharwood Smith, in his review of Corder 1981, deals critically with several of Corder's positions, most importantly his position on transfer as related to borrowing as a performance strategy. Corder in his 1978 paper 'Language Distance and Magnitude of the Language Learning Task' (= Ch. 10 of Corder 1981) had apparently not yet sorted out what appears as his 1983 position described above, i.e. the clear theoretical distinction between borrowing as a performance phenomenon and structural transfer as incorporation of some results of borrowing into the IL system, though Corder does admit (1983, p.96) that sorting out the two empirically will not be easy. At this point in his review Sharwood Smith usefully distinguishes Corder's position on language transfer from Wode's well-known (1981) position: 'where a similarity between a developmental form and the learner's L1 will bring about a delay: the learner may get stuck at that stage for a while' (Sharwood Smith 1984, p.70), thus also invoking potential fossilization.

But Wode's position is indeed quite different from what appears in Corder's work. In comparing the two versions, Sharwood Smith comments on the apparent lack of constraints in Corder's perspective as to what actually will get borrowed/transferred: 'The only condition seems to be that the learner must arrive at the point where the rule in question becomes a candidate for acquisition in the order as dictated by the built-in syllabus' (*ibid.*, pp.70–1). Put this way, though, Corder's position may be on the right track but its lack of precision leaves us with a good amount of empirical work. Sharwood Smith concludes that, according to Corder: 'L1/L2 correspondences . . . are presented as being relevant to the development of (IL) competence' (*ibid.*, p.71), with the proviso that the built-in syllabus be taken into account, but Corder leaves it to us to figure out how. Finally, important to the argument being developed in this volume is Sharwood Smith's conclusion, which I take to be correct and basic to SLA: 'there is nonetheless some sense in which learners *compare* competence systems' (*ibid.*, p.71, emphasis added). That is, given the basic interlingual identifications argument of this volume, Corder, after much observation of and speculation upon empirical IL data, comes to the conclusion that NL/TL comparisons by learners (or, rather, comparisons of perceived NL/TL structurings) exist and play a facilitative role in complexification that starts to operate on one's basic core simple grammar. IL development continues as a response to sociofunctional communicative needs and ceases when such needs are met. This in a nutshell is the Corder position, as I interpret it for this volume.

Summary

The account presented here of Corder's views provides a rich perspective, or perhaps metatheory, much of which was not there before and from which clear, precise and testable hypotheses have been and continue to be gleaned. We are beholden to his disciplined speculative accounts of IL. Corder has been called by French colleagues 'le père fondateur' (LANGAGES, 1980, 57), the 'founding father', of SLA. One sees why by listing important, influential concepts and maxims discussed here. Even if one believes in only a part . . .

(1) *Errors as a window to the learner's IL competence*
(2) *Errors as a learning strategy*
(3) *Covert vs overt errors*
(4) *Language teaching concerns as a motivation for studying IL*
(5) *Teacher input as possibly interfering with acquisition*
(6) *Input vs intake*

(7) *Learner system as dynamic system*
(8) *Longitudinal studies*
(9) *Successive stages of learner language*
(10) *Learner using a definite system at each point*
(11) *Transitional competence*
(12) *Learner's underlying knowledge of language to date*
(13) *Learner language as normally unstable*
(14) *Idiosyncratic competence*
(15) *Investigation of learner intuitions*
(16) *Interpretation of IL sentences*
(17) *Translation equivalents of sentences synonymous in a context*
(18) *Methodology of using learner mother tongue*
(19) *Study of learner intention*
(20) *Using bilingual former speakers of earlier IL*
(21) *Elicitation procedures*
(22) *Logical sequence in investigating IL*
(23) *CA and EA as complementary research procedures*
(24) *NL not as inhibitory but facilitative*
(25) *NL as a heuristic tool to match NL-like phenomena in TL*
(26) *Transfer as incorporation of items and features into IL system*
(27) *Transfer takes place between two mental structures: NL and developing IL*
(28) *For transfer to occur, successful communication has to occur*
(29) *This may give rise to persistent error*
(30) *Internal (or built-in) vs external syllabus*
(31) *Learner is programmed to process input data in a certain way*
(32) *Relationship of input to current state of learner's grammar*
(33) *Study of non-tutored acquisition*
(34) *Study of IL as part of study of language*
(35) *Basic core IL (possibly universal) component*
(36) *Importance of conventions of a social group in shaping IL*
(37) *IL development as complexification, not simplification*
(38) *IL development continues related to communicative needs*
(39) *IL development ceases when communicative needs are met*

How could we manage without this and Van Buren's input into it?

From CA (Chapters 1, 4 and 5), from bilingualism (Chapters 2, 3 and 5), from EA (Chapter 5), even from theoretical linguistics (Chapter 4) and now in this chapter, from IL studies we see that we need to rethink available linguistic categories to account for IL data, even for the predictive IL data of classical CA. We need to include in our general linguistic thinking the fact that in language contact situations, language users and learners 'compare competence systems'. At least, one needs to add a Van Buren grafting- or a Harris Z-component in order to begin to account for the principled role of NL. With what we have seen to date regarding units of interlingual identification and analytical cross-linguistic problems, how can we experimentally study the phenomenon of language transfer?

To this we now turn.

Points for discussion

(1) Describe Van Buren's 'grafting component' and compare it with Harris's 'Z-component' as discussed in Chapter 4. Relate each of these notions to the concept of interlanguage as we have developed it in this volume to date. Specifically, relate your answer to Van Buren's attempt to resolve the Saussurian paradox described at the beginning of Chapter 3 and elsewhere in this volume.

(2) Discuss Corder's view of errors as a 'window' to the learner's underlying system. Specifically, do you agree that errors are most important sources of information about the learner's linguistic development, providing an account of the 'built-in syllabus'? Relate your response to discussion point 1 in Chapter 5.

(3) Corder expounds the view that making errors as a strategy is 'indispensable' to the learning of a language. In light of what we have learned about interlanguage in this volume, how would you evaluate this position? Consider in your discussion your own experiences with errors.

(4) Refresh your memory of Lado's discussion of what the learner already knows vs what s/he has to learn. Now see how different Corder's view is of this distinction and its place in the second language acquisition process. Make that distinction relevant to your understanding of your own (attempted) second language acquisition.

(5) Evaluate Myint Su's study as discussed in this chapter. How does she follow Corder's suggested research procedures? Specifically, argue the proposition that she is the 'perfect bilingual' between the native language and the interlanguage, given the criteria that Corder sets up. Is this indeed the best way to do IL studies? Now compare this study with Coulter's as presented in Chapter 5, keeping in mind that with Coulter's study we were concentrating on EA/IL data.

(6) Look at the list of thirty-nine influential concepts attributed to Corder above. The argument in the chapter is that this is an

immensely significant set. Discuss its importance. Choose one concept, for example Corder's concept of 'covert errors', and relate it to one of the others, for example Corder's concept of 'the learner using a definite system at each point', and state how the significance of one entails the significance of the other.

(7) So far in this volume we have had several extensive discussions on the 'significance of learner errors' and in this chapter we have a long section with this title containing the views of S. Pit Corder. Integrate the latter discussion with the previous ones. See if your answers to previous questions would now change and, if so, how.

(8) In Corder's view of IL, the learner begins L2 acquisition (i.e. the learner's 'initial IL hypothesis') *not* from a 'fully developed' form of the NL. What evidence is there that this is fact, and what does it mean for Corder that it is not full adult NL knowledge upon which further IL development is based? Now integrate into your response Weinreich's idea that learners do not transfer the full morphological system of the NL to the IL. Given this, how is it then that researchers should proceed to 'discover' the learner's initial IL hypothesis and where language transfer fits in?

7 The quintessential CA/IL notion: Language transfer

Some history

The question of the principled role of the NL in the SLA process is one that was central to CA (Chapters 1, 4, 5 and 6), bilingualism (2, 3 and 6) and EA (5 and 6 above) and has become once again central to SLA, to theoretical and empirical work in understanding the creation by learners of IL. It is the major claim of Gass and Selinker (1983a and b) that knowledge of the NL plays an extensive role in SLA; evidence presented in studies reported there strongly supports this view, which can now be stated as SLA fact.

A widely held view of classical CA (cf. Chapter 1 above) was that language transfer worked this way: the vast majority of learners' errors could be predicted by a comparison of the NL and TL, the differences being attributed to language transfer, which was thought to be 'inhibitory' to learning. In the 1960s, several things happened to this view. One was that Corder challenged the inhibitory claim, presenting solid arguments, in a disciplined speculatory framework, that NL often plays a 'facilitative' role in the SLA process (cf. Chapter 6). Another thing that happened to this CA view was experimental testing at the urging of Lado (see Chapter 1 above), one of the routes to interlanguage.

There were three early attempts to test experimentally predictions made by CA theory: two attempts on the phonetic and phonological level (Nemser 1961a and Briere 1964) and one on the syntactic level (Selinker 1966). The main thrust of this chapter, as we work our way towards an understanding of the continuing discovery of IL in the next chapter, is to present a reinterpretation of these three early attempts in light of current knowledge. As far as I know, all three attempts were made independently, none of the three being aware of any other work or of the planning of that work. Also, all three conclude by proposing something like IL, or at least being consistent with the view that in the SLA process there are more systems than the two postulated by classical CA: NL and TL. In this chapter we are continuing to link things through time – here CA and EA to IL through language transfer *experimentally*. The chapter will end with an appraisal of language transfer, tying in these early experimental approaches. In brief it is claimed, among other things, that the evidence supports the view that the NL serves primarily a facilitative role in creating IL where NL and TL are perceived by the learner to match in some property through interlingual identifications, discussed in detail above.

Traditionally the NL in the form of language transfer has received the majority of attention as *the* major influencing factor on the shape of IL. One could even say it was assumed knowledge, going back centuries, that one's NL affected how one spoke a particular TL. Recall the logic represented by the Lehn and Slager (1959) quotation at the beginning of Chapter 5: 'The Thai does not have the same problems learning English as the Turk'.

Lado, as we saw above in Chapter 1, viewed second language learning as overcoming differences between NL and TL, as primarily a process whereby 'habits' from the NL are systematically replaced by habits from the TL. Even without the concept of habit, Lado's position can be viewed as one extreme language transfer position, the view that second language learners rely almost exclusively on their NL in the process of learning a particular TL. With attacks on this position gaining currency in the early 1970s (cf. most particularly Dulay and Burt 1973), the other extreme of the transfer hypothesis came to the fore, the view that language transfer is unimportant in creating IL. Both these extremes have been successfully assailed by a number of scholars. For example, Gass (1979, 1984) has argued that language transfer is *not* an 'all or nothing' phenomenon; use of NL information in the formation of ILs is a 'selection process', and certain principles make some NL structures more likely to be transferred than others. Thus Gass's experimentally derived view matches Weinreich's view of language transfer as a selection process a quarter of a century earlier (cf. Chapter 1 above). Through these papers and through organization of the IXth Conference on Applied Linguistics on the topic, 'Language Transfer in Language Learning' (Ann Arbor, March 1981), she helped revitalize and restructure this central research area. In the words of Schumann: 'Last year [research in language transfer] was given a big impetus at the Michigan conference on language transfer, and now it's a fascinating and very vital area of research, and it's being looked at quite differently' (Schumann, *English Language Teaching Journal*, Interview, 37.2, 1982). In the next chapter we return in detail to the interview in which Schumann's comments appear. This comment is interesting in that it shows revitalization and renewed interest in the concept of language transfer.

I stand to be corrected here, but there appears to be a rather large gap of a decade in which experimental studies on language transfer were not conducted. Then, Kellerman (1977) presented an experimental language transfer study of lexical acquisition, and Gass (1979) presented an experimental language transfer study of syntactic acquisition. Like the earlier 1960s studies mentioned above, these two were performed without knowledge of each other. These two, and the many more that have followed, stand on the shoulders of the three early experimental studies to be discussed in this chapter. The earlier studies provide an empirical anchoring and an intellectual foundation on which the large amount of recent studies on language transfer stand. Thus, in order to understand how we have come to the consensus position of (a) denying both extremes of the language transfer claim, and (b) of experimentally studying the what, where, how and why of language transfer, i.e. *constraints on transfer*, it is necessary to explore early experimental attempts to test CA predictions.

Nemser's experimental phonological studies

On the journey of CA to IL, one scholar stands at a crucial methodological point: William Nemser. He recognized, as also did others described here, that informal observation of L2 learning using CA principles is defective, but he was the first to choose instead precise perception and prediction tests of various phonological contrasts across language contact situations. Studying Nemser sheds detailed light upon an important background goal, an unknown in the early 1960s: whether conducting experimentation in this kind of language research is even possible. Now, when experimentation on IL data is commonplace, it is difficult to recall that this was ever an issue. In the earlier period, the tradition of normative descriptive studies was so powerful that any alternative was looked upon as radical.

Nemser's experimental studies, using phonological and phonetic data, conducted in the early 1960s, were presented first as a Columbia University dissertation in 1961 under the title 'The Interpretation of English Stops and Interdental Fricatives by Native Speakers of Hungarian' (Nemser 1961a). A slightly revised version of the experimental portions of the thesis was published as 'Hungarian

Phonetic Experiments' in xerox form (Nemser 1961b). It was then published in a more widely available form a full decade later under the title *An Experimental Study of Phonological Interference in the English of Hungarians* (Nemser 1971a). In the latter the literature survey is updated and, important to this chapter, Nemser provides an extensive critical discussion of Briere's experiments (*ibid.*, pp.26–35). His theoretical perspective is summarized in Nemser 1971b, where he defines approximative systems as: 'the deviant linguistic system actually employed by the learner attempting to utilize the target language' (Nemser 1971b, p.115). This is a concept which is close to IL but differs in several important respects, a central one being Nemser's emphasis on the learner's language being 'deviant'. (See Tarone *et al.* 1976, p.96, and the next chapter, for other points of contrast.) The strong point of concurrence that I wish to emphasize here is Nemser's assumption that: 'Learner speech at a given time is the patterned product of a linguistic system ... distinct from [NL] and [TL] and internally structured' (Nemser 1971b, p.116). This assumption derives directly from his experimental work. Moreover, like several studies mentioned already, Nemser's approach has inherent in it one of the central concepts of the IL hypothesis, fossilization: '... effective language teaching implies preventing, or postponing as long as possible, the formation of *permanent intermediate systems and subsystems*' (Nemser 1971b, p.117, italics added). Identical with the IL hypothesis, Nemser argues for the 'structural independence' of approximate systems, i.e. structurally independent from NL and TL, by citing from his data 'the frequent and systematic occurrence in non-native speech of elements not directly attributable to either [NL] or [TL]' (Nemser 1971b, p.118). His particular phonological example is the common occurrence of 'intermediate phones' in his data, as Hungarian subjects attempting to approximate English [θ] often produce [fθ] or [sθ] instead.

We will look at Nemser's original study in terms of the corrected 1971a version. He presents detailed experimental results on NN production and perception of interdental fricatives (pp.57–81) and stops (pp.91–120). Five tests are presented to the informants, eleven NSs of Hungarian recently arrived in the USA with no prior knowledge of English; these learners were 'estimated' at from 'low' to 'low intermediate' to 'intermediate' proficiency in English (p.56). Test (1), a discrimination test, and test (2), an identification of English orthography test, were both designed to test Hungarian–English perception; test (3), an identification test of Hungarian orthography, was designed to test Hungarian perception of English sounds; test (4), a production test, was designed to test Hungarian–English perception and production (Nemser 1971a, pp.52–6 and *passim*). Nemser's goal is 'the construction of a battery of complementary tests' (p.129), a goal that fits in with the accepted position of the inadequacy of one testing situation, given learner variation in IL performance (cf. Tarone 1983 and *passim* in Eisenstein 1989 and Gass *et al.* 1989a and b).

In test (1) informants listened to sets of English nonsense syllables, each one differing minimally in terms of the fricative or stop distinction being studied. A multiple-choice format was used to ask the subjects to mark the 'aberrant form'. In test (2) informants were asked to transcribe recorded English sounds, again in nonsense words, using a provided transcription system. In test (3) informants were asked to perform a similar task as in (2) but, cleverly, this time they were asked to interpret English sounds in terms of their familiar Hungarian orthography. In test (4) they were asked to 'retranslate' from Hungarian, English words containing the key sounds. (This, it must be noted, is a special use of the term 'production' in SLA research.) In test (5) they were asked to repeat recorded English nonsense syllables containing the key sounds. A sixth test was used to test specifically for English stops – a 'residual stop' identification test – where informants were asked to judge English stops from a tape where the preceding sibilant had been removed by Haskins lab technicians. However, a different elicitation technique was used to elicit production of English stops than was used for fricatives. Informants were asked to produce English stops by adding to what they heard on the tape an initial stop which appeared on a script they received. This methodology is in line with the stated goal of 'ascertaining how Hungarian speakers with a limited knowledge of English perceive and produce the English stops and interdental fricatives' (Nemser 1971a, p.51). Nemser's methodology reaches this goal through experimental techniques going beyond but building on the technology of CA discussed above.

Results are interestingly mixed, in light of a CA which predicted that speakers of Hungarian, in a hedging form typical in classical CA statements, 'would probably tend' 'to identify English stops with the analogous Hungarian stops, although tenuis-media confusions were likely, and to identify the English interdentals with the Hungarian labial fricatives, apical stops or hissing sibilants' (p.51). (Problems associated with this theoretical position are described in detail in Chapter 1 above.)

Results with interdentals, where Hungarian has none, show

asymmetry between perception and production. For example, for English /ɵ/ the 'preferred perceptual reflex' is labial fricative /f/ but the 'preferred productive reflex' is 'apical stop', the latter represented by a capital /T/. In trying to capture units of phonological learning he finds, like the bilingual data in Chapter 3 above, that 'blends' are common in learner productive data. The symbol /T/ subsumes a large set of phonetic outputs: [t], [d/t], [tɵ], [d/ð], [ɵ̂], [tɵ], [sɵ], [t'] and even [ts] (pp.60–1, 72 and 81–2). For the voiced English phoneme /ð/, a *parallel asymmetry* is found: the preferred perceptual reflex is labial fricative /v/; the preferred production reflex is stop /D/, an analogous wide range of blends subsumed. As we shall see, sɼ_h widespread variation is typical of Briere's data. What could be the unit of interlingual identifications for such cases?

Though interlingual identifications on an individual level with these cases remain an important problem for SLA theory in the neglected area of IL phonology, an important result holds true: for both English /ɵ/ and /ð/, concerning units of phonological learning, *perception* results show a preference for a fricative, /f/ and /v/ respectively, whereas *production* results show that /f/ and /v/ are 'totally excluded' (pp.82–3). Thus, Nemser's general conclusion is that, *asymmetrically*, Hungarian speakers usually perceive English interdentals as labial fricatives but almost always produce them as apical stops. The actual perception and production speech behaviour in these tests, then, hints strongly that perceptual and productive mechanisms are *not* isomorphic, a fact not taken proper account of in classical CA (although Lado, as discussed in Chapter 1 above, did see such differences as possible) nor in SLA.

The predictive power of CA is stronger when we look at stops in the Nemser data, with English and Hungarian pairs matching more. Both languages have stops, the same category, which is not the case with English interdentals just discussed. Reinterpreting Nemser, with stops the learner already appears to have categories upon which to base interlingual identifications (called 'intersystemic identifications' in Nemser 1971b, p.47), thus facilitating L2 learning. However, where stop errors are made, categories appear *reversed* within the already established categories, i.e.: 'a surprisingly large proportion of these errors represent misinterpretations of tense and (redundantly) voiceless phonemes as lax or voiced' (Nemser 1971a, p.130). In terms of finer detail, there is a distinction in production deviances with regard to place of sound, with apical and velar stops most subject to errors of the above type; labial stops, however, where errors were made, were more subject to aspiration errors, 'usually of the *under-*

aspiration variety' (Nemser 1971a, p.127, emphasis in the original; see also p.130).

Nemser, in a useful discussion section (pp.129–52), looks at classical CA in terms of a question underlying much of SLA work: What are 'the relationships established by bilingual speakers between the units of the two systems', NL and TL? His experimental results show unequivocally that in terms of the learning of phonological units, classical CA predictions can sometimes lead to correct results and sometimes to incorrect results, when IL behaviour is actually tested. This empirical finding remains valid and is important in light of the classical CA assumption that 'sounds of a foreign language are perceived and produced in terms of either the primary or secondary system' (Nemser 1971a, p.132). Why this is only sometimes true remains one of our greatest mysteries.

Reinterpreting Nemser, then, we can say that learners in creating IL sometimes make NL/TL categories equivalent and sometimes do not. Blends are to be expected and *not only* from NL and TL material. Nemser provides evidence for at least partial autonomy of IL systems, since 'the test data contain numerous examples of elements which do not have their origin in either phonemic system' (Nemser 1971a, pp 134–5). Thus, interlingual identifications from NL and TL are essential to only some parts of IL, with perception and production at times acting differently. Some parts of the remainder of IL are the result of different interlingual identifications between items in the developing IL with items in the TL, often unexpected blends occurring here using previously learned IL material and perhaps autonomous material.

Perception and production at times also act differently here. Nemser summarizes, stating that Hungarian NSs in English 'often use distinct and different perceptual and productive phonological patterns' (Nemser 1971a, p.141). He here poses *the* question of language transfer, which we discussed initially with Weinreich's work (see Chapter 2): 'The interesting question, of course, is how this curious disjunction between the [NL and TL] patterns can be tolerated' (Nemser 1971a, pp.141). Note that whether ILs are facilitative or inhibitory to communicative success in the L2 seems to be a separate, though related, question.

Briere's experimental phonological studies

Briere's experimental phonetic and phonological studies, done independently of Nemser's work, were also conducted in the early

1960s, being presented first as a University of Washington dissertation in 1964 under the title of 'On Defining a Hierarchy of Difficulty of Learning Phonological Categories' (Briere 1964). A shortened version was published later as an article in *Language* (Briere 1966) under the title 'An Investigation of Phonological Interference', becoming one of the few SLA articles ever published in *Language*. The material was later made available in a Mouton monograph under the title *A Psycholinguistic Study of Phonological Interference* (Briere 1968).

In testing the predictions of classical CA, Briere deals, as does Nemser, with actual behaviour of L2 learners doing phonological tasks on selected experimental data. In looking at Briere's work as relating to the important question of relevant phonological units in SLA, it seems to me that Briere has demonstrated that for his data there are several relevant units, lending credence to the position we took at the end of Chapter 3.

For Briere, the relevant units do not always correspond to known linguistic units but rather depend on the sound involved: sometimes the taxonomic phoneme appears to be the relevant unit, but the unit in other cases seems not to be describable in purely linguistic terms. As we shall see, this also argues for the partial autonomy of IL systems, and we can ask here, as Nemser has done above:

(1) What exactly are the relationships established by L2 learners between the units of NL and TL and the developing IL and TL?

And, given the empirically discovered evidence:

(2) How can the disjunction observed between the developing IL, on the one hand, and the NL and TL, on the other, be tolerated by the learner?

Briere developed an experimental technique which, to a large extent, imitates actual methods of instruction: listening to TL sounds, attempted imitation, use of phonemic transcription, physiological explanations, etc. He was working with exactly the three systems incorporated in the IL hypothesis. NL utterances for Briere are hypothesized utterances in American English (Briere, with one or two exceptions, differs here from Nemser and Selinker in not trying to establish experimentally an NL base line). TL utterances are actual utterances in the 'composite language' as described below. IL utterances are actual utterances produced by NSs of American English attempting to produce the particular TL norm.

Regarding the sounds /ž/ and /ŋ/ in Briere's TL corpus, the unit identified interlingually across NL, TL and IL is the taxonomic phoneme defined distributionally within the syllable as opposed to within the word (p.73). For some other sounds, the relevant phonological unit of interlingual identification is not the taxonomic phoneme but may be based on phonetic parameters, some of which, he says, are probably not known (pp.73–4). It seems to me that Briere's references here are to autonomous material of the type described as blends by Nemser.

Briere's experimental procedure is interesting and we will look at it in some detail. He sets up as the TL a 'composite language' based on sounds from three phonologically different languages: French, Arabic and Vietnamese. From Arabic /h/, /ḥ/, /x/ and /ɣ/; from French /u/, /ž/, /ɛ̃/ and /e/; and from Vietnamese /t'/, /t/, /ɨ/, /ɛ/ and [ɛ], (p.35), relating each of these to 'learning problems' for his subjects, twenty monolingual speakers of American English. The learning problems were determined by a classical CA, of the type described in earlier chapters of this volume, between the composite TL and the NL. Six logically different sets of learning problems set up by CA are:

(1) /ž/ and /ŋ/ were looked at in terms of distribution, since in recalling Lado's discussion (see Chapter 1 above): 'There is a 1–1 correspondence between [NL] and [TL] sounds from the standpoint of articulatory features, phonemic status and privilege of occurrence within the respective systems' (Briere 1968, p.38). But the real difference between these NL and TL sounds is not the word differences claimed by Lado, but syllable differences. That is, Briere wishes to test the claim that /ŋ/ would be harder to learn than /ž/ *if* the syllable is the correct unit of L2 phonological acquisition. In experimental tests with American English speakers, where Briere did try to establish a NS baseline, /ŋ/ never appears in syllable initial position whereas /ž/ is most often placed there; in CA terms using the syllable as the learning unit, there are no differences between NL and TL as regards /ž/, whereas with /ŋ/, NL /ŋ/ never occurs in syllable initial but TL /ŋ/ always does.

(2) TL [ɛ̌] vs NL /ey/. Both of these sounds are phonetically similar and occur in syllable initial distribution. As shown by the symbols, [ ] vs / /, they differ in phonemic vs allophonic status.

(3) TL /h/ and /ɛ̃/ have 'partially similar' NL allophones 'now being learned as phonemes in new positions (Briere 1968, p.41).

(4) TL /ü/ and /ɨ/ involve 'regrouping' of existing NL phonetic features into new combinations.

(5) TL /e/, /x/, /ɣ/ and /ḥ/. These do not occur in the NL either as phonemes or as allophones. In phonetic terms, the TL vowel

/e/ must be 'monophthenized'. He intends to test the 'usual argument' that the learner will substitute his 'nearest phoneme', in this case /ey/. In the case of /x/, /a/ and /ḥ/, uvular or pharyngeal articulation must be learned.

(6) TL /t'/ and /t/. The NL has the sounds [t'] and [t] but has them as allophones. Classical CA would predict here that NL /t/ with its two relevant allophones would 'split' into the two TL phonemic categories, sometimes producing one, sometimes the other in the same TL phonological environment (Briere 1968, pp.44–5).

I find this careful categorization of predicted learning problems, prior to experimentation, to be one of the clearest and best argued in the literature, and urge readers who are interested to go back to the original and work through the details as a most useful exercise. This would be especially true if the interest is training, i.e. in preparing future colleagues to do empirical work in the realm of contrastive thinking.

Briere prepared the TL composite material (1968, pp.48–55) in the following way. The four informants chosen for each language are NSs of the language concerned. They were pre-tested as to their ability to judge consistently various degrees of native vs non-native speech (a most important methodological innovation) and as to their reliability with each other and with the experimenter. A master tape was made of the contrasts to be studied in terms of four Arabic, six Vietnamese and four French utterances. Learning tapes and testing tapes were then made from these . Further tapes were then made which had a learning stimulus followed by a testing stimulus in turn followed by the learner's response for each trial. Learners mimicked TL sounds and matched up memorized symbols with TL sounds. Explicit TL and CA instruction was given on each of the sounds, primarily in terms of particular errors committed. The NS informants were trained 'to listen only to the specific sound being tested', judging the tapes without first consulting each other. Disagreements were meticulously gone over, and disagreement brought down to less than 1 per cent of 6720 responses.

One of Briere's major objectives was to attempt to establish a 'hierarchy of difficulty', a goal based on Lado's notions of difficulty of learning discussed in Chapters 1 and 4 above. Establishing such a hierarchy plagued the efforts of classical CA and was considered a notably difficult task. Briere tries to establish such a hierarchy by statistical means, a procedure which Nemser (1971a, pp.30–2) challenges. He particularly challenges, and I think in retrospect correctly, Briere's assumption that 'different from' in statistical terms equals 'harder than' in learning terms (cf. comparative discussion in Chapter 8 on SLA and experimental psychology). That said, I believe that Briere's results are suggestive and illuminating. His results include the following (Briere 1968, 60ff):

(1) The learning of a completely new articulatory feature not in the NL is very difficult – here learning the pharyngealization in TL /ḥ/.

(2) Equally difficult, though, was 'regrouping' a set of features which already exist in the NL, in this case high-back-unrounded in TL /ɨ/, i.e. back to front and unrounded to rounded.

(3) For some unknown reason, front-rounded vowels are significantly easier to learn than back-unrounded vowels.

(4) TL aspirated /t'/, as a phoneme, is quite difficult for American speakers. Success with this TL sound would require the 'inhibition of the feature fortis and the substitution of the feature lenis' (Briere 1968, p.62). Productively speaking, this sound was more difficult than TL /t/ which was an unexpected result, since [t-] is an allophone not found in initial position in the NL.

(5) Another unexpected result is that NL /t/ was the most frequent substitution for TL /t'/.

(6) Though there were unequal learning problems in the production of TL /t'/ and /t/, in perception they formed a pair with the learners in retrospective sessions saying they had had a difficult time telling them apart. This result begins to back up Nemser's conclusion of production vs perceptual differences in some cases.

(7) Sounds in the NL, whether NL status is phonemic or allophonic (e.g. /h/, /t/, /ŋ/, /ey/, [ẽ], /ɛ/) are significantly easier to learn than sounds which are not in the NL system at all, e.g. /ḥ/ and /ɣ/. Briere puts it slightly differently in his general conclusions: '[TL] sounds which are close equivalents of [NL] system sounds, whether phonemic or allophonic, are easier to learn than [TL] sounds without such equivalents' (Briere 1968, p.73). It seems to me that this latter result empirically supports Corder's contention as stated earlier in this chapter that the NL primarily performs a facilitative role in L2 acquisition. We have seen a similar result with Nemser's work, where if the NL has a category existent in TL, in his case stops vs interdental fricatives, then the results are 'far from uniform'

(Nemser 1971a, p.130) in following CA predictions.

(8) For some reason, /ɣ/ is significantly more difficult than /x/. Neither is in the NL and both have the same articulatory features, with the exception that /ɣ/ is voiced.

(9) For TL /ɣ/, the most frequent substitution was NL /g/, but, parallel to the Nemser data, other sounds were also produced: [ʔ], [0] (= nothing produced for /ɣ/), [r] and [R]. The latter result, a sound not even in the NL system, also parallels the Nemser finding of 'autonomous sounds' in learner production, i.e. sounds not in NL or TL (Briere 1968, pp.65, 68).

(10) Given 'proper' explicit instruction, learners were able to produce in isolation members of the 'perceptual confusion pairs' /h/ and /ḥ/, and /tʼ/ and /t/ 'long before they were able to perceive accurately which particular sound was being given as a stimulus when the item occurred in random order on a test tape' (Briere 1968, p.70). This production/perception *asymmetry* is noteworthy because it is perhaps the first time we have firm evidence that production *can* precede perception.

(11) /ž/, which 'indicated complete positive transfer' from NL to TL, was significantly easier to learn than /ŋ/, a result which in Briere's eyes sets up the syllable rather than the word as the unit of L2 phonology learning (cf. Briere 1968, pp.72–3).

From all of the above results it is clear that language transfer effects do occur, but not in the classical CA absolute 'all or nothing' fashion. What is also clear is the correctness of Nemser's and Briere's general conclusion, paralleling Weinreich's and Haugen's (Chapter 2 above), that predictions and empirical study of the learning of L2 phonology must be based on 'exhaustive information at the phonetic level'. But such classical linguistic concepts as 'distinctive features' or 'allophonic membership of phoneme classes' provide far from the whole story (Briere 1968, p.74) concerning the learner's creation of IL. There's more to it than that. In addition to gathering (a) information on NL phonology from a language transfer point of view, and (b) information on TL phonology, we can conclude from Briere as well that fine details of IL phonology, *as they cross linguistic systems*, must be studied in their own right in order to understand in Weinreich's terms (Chapter 2) how in interlingual identifications what 'cannot be the same ... becomes the same'. These must be studied in terms of abstract categories such as Nemser's /T/, given the large numbers of forms that can be identified interlingually as same. This abstractness matches that of several of the CA models identified in Chapter 4. What would be updated in current SLA work (Perdue 1984) is that, from an SLA input point of view, the phonological information should be gathered from *actual TL speakers* whom learners meet.

Selinker's experimental word-order studies

We move now to consideration of Selinker's experimental language transfer *syntactic* studies, done independently of and without knowledge of Nemser's and Briere's work. These were conducted in the mid 1960s, being presented first as a Georgetown University dissertation in 1966 under the title 'A Psycholinguistic Study of Language Transfer' (Selinker 1966). A shortened and revised version of the experimental portions of the dissertation was then published as an article in *General Linguistics* (Selinker 1969) under the title 'Language Transfer'. The historical portions of the dissertation entitled 'Four Strands of Inquiry' in Selinker 1966 were incorporated into the first ten pages of the Introduction to Gass and Selinker 1983. Additionally, the experimental parts of the study are discussed by Andersen (1983) and linked in a comparative fashion to more recent experimental work discussed later in the chapter.

Given syntactic variables, Selinker's methodology is quite unlike the methodologies of Nemser and Briere and that is why congruent results reported at the end of the chapter are all the more believable. Like the other two, he uses the predictions of classical CA by studying the actual speech behaviour of L2 learners doing controlled tasks. In looking at Selinker's work as relating to the question of relevant syntactic units of L2 learning, his studies take a contrastive perspective of units applying at one and the same time to three linguistic systems – NL, TL and IL – whereas recall that classical CA confined itself to two – NL and TL. In the experiments to be reported on here, subjects respond orally in their NL to questions presented orally in the NL and attempt to respond in English to parallel questions presented in English. The questions come from an interview designed to elicit manifestations of specific types of surface structures in certain syntactic domains. The only experimental instruction given was for each speaker to speak in a 'complete sentence'.

Replicated results show that the syntactic interlingual unit which is transferred from NL to IL is an *abstract* surface structure unit at times roughly equivalent to the traditional direct object or to an adverb of place or time, but at other times with pronominal constraints and/or discourse/pragmatic constraints (cf. discussion below on arrangement/combination). This unit has a behavioural unity in the experimental situation and informal observation reflects the view that this unit exists in natural interaction. The surface domain considered is constituent concatenation after the verb. Results show statistically significant parallel trends for NL and IL word-order arrangements.

It is important to point out that some of the results in the Selinker study have been replicated in other interlingual situations. For example, Zobl (1984) reports that one of these results, the transfer of time–place (Ti–Pl) structures has been discovered to be widespread in interlingual situations. This is a particularly surprising result for Zobl, since in terms of more current thinking in UG, the preferred universal order should be Pl–Ti, the reverse of what is discovered empirically in IL. Also, in light of the view that interaction in SLA is what can shape IL syntax (cf. e.g. Hatch 1984), the studies reported on here, a syntactic unit *tied to semantic/discourse content* is presented. Replicated results show that responses concerning a topic such as 'subjects studied at school', as opposed to other topics, affect the surface concatenation of some of these string arrangements in NL and IL word order, statistically demonstrating language transfer. When experimentally derived responses concern this topic, there occurs an almost absolute statistical trend towards the NL order place–object noun (Pl–Obn) which is paralleled in the IL. But when the responses concern other topics in the experimental interview, there occurs an almost absolute trend toward the NL order of Obn–Pl, once again paralleled in the IL word order. This is one of the first times that such semantic and discourse effects on word order were reported in the literature and it is significant to a general view of language that it came about in a CA/IL study.

The methodology used in these studies is now discussed. Like Nemser and Briere, the starting point is classical CA and the initial framework (Lado was a member of the dissertation committee) is very much that of Lado (1957), as discussed in Chapter 1 above. Picking up our discussion from examining CA detail in Chapter 5, the relevant CA *statement* takes the form:

> Whenever an NL place (Pl) string (e.g. Hebrew bair 'downtown') occurs in the same sentence with an object (Ob) string (e.g. Israeli Hebrew (IH) et hagluya 'the postcard') and, furthermore, both occur after the verb, the order is Pl–Ob as in the NL sentence below.

A comparable descriptive statement of TL Pl and Ob string order would be:

Whenever a TL Pl string (e.g. English 'downtown') occurs in the same sentence with an Ob string (e.g. 'the postcard') and, furthermore, both occur after the verb, the order is Ob–Pl.

NL (Hebrew): kaniti   bair   /   et hagluya
            I bought   downtown   the postcard
TL (English): I bought the postcard   /   downtown
(The slash symbol / is used to separate surface syntactic strings.)

The relevant CA/*language transfer statement* is as follows:
A speaker of IH tends to transfer the distribution of NL Ob and Pl strings to production of TL Ob and Pl strings. The NL IH word order, Pl–Ob, is different from the TL order, Ob–Pl, and is thus an error when produced:
Predicted IL data: I bought downtown / the postcard.

As for many others working within the framework of classical CA, though the predicted IL data matched the structural facts they were not entirely hypothesized; I knew where to look. As pointed out in the bilingualism chapter (3 above), before conducting the experimental research I had had occasion to listen to large amounts of Israeli talk, both in their IH and in their English. This particular predicted IL data sentence was spoken by an Israeli woman with a vast knowledge of English who had lived in the USA for about two years. This type of construction is *not* an isolated event in her English. The problem with this sort of 'hypothesized sentence' is not its hypothesized status, for like other CA statements it has shown us where to look empirically. The problem is that, as discussed in Chapter 1 above, such statements can be taken as IL fact without seeing the need for empirical studies, and as this study shows, *not* all such predictive statements proved entirely accurate. As we will see in Chapter 8, CA analysis has greatly helped us to look at actual L2 behaviour, leading directly to the *continual discovery* of IL.

In the Selinker studies, the first six experiments (132 children, ages thirteen to fifteen) were conducted in Israel; the last (31 children, age thirteen) was conducted in the USA in order experimentally to obtain NS–TL baseline data. All seven were similar in purpose; in each, an attempt was made experimentally to obtain large numbers of specific types of sentences that would be countable in the statistical frequency analysis. A *countable sentence* contains a verb string followed by:

Experiment and school	Total sentences		Counted sentences		Subjects		Major variables
	NL	IL	NL	IL	Male	Female	
I (Tel Aviv)	536	536	161	201	16	18	Sabras* 8th grade Hebrew at home
II (Jerusalem)	279	247	116	118	9	10	Sabras 8th grade Hebrew at home
III (Tel Aviv)	162	185	66	97	9	15	Sabras 8th grade Hebrew at home
IV (Ramat Gan)	332	314	132	158	14	12	Sabras 10th grade Hebrew at home
V (Jerusalem)	305	236	98	103	7	12	Sabras 8th grade Many languages at home
VI (Naham)	97	24	41	10	2	8	Sabras 8th grade Yemenite Arabic at home
VII Private homes (Silver Spring, Maryland)	–	902	–	339	16	15	Americans 8th grade English at home

*Sabra' is the accepted term signifying a Jew born in Israel.

TABLE 7.1 Characteristics of the seven experiments

(a) an object string (Ob) plus a time string (Ti), or
(b) an object string (Ob) plus a place string (Pl), or
(c) an object string (Ob) plus an adverb string (Ab), or finally
(d) a place string (Pl) plus a time string (Ti).

Any other type of sentence was not counted in the results reported.

Experiment I, considered to be the basic experiment, attempted to test the following two hypotheses.

(1) In the IH speaker's production of NL sentences, there will be a statistically significant trend towards one of the only two possible arrangements that can occur when two strings of combinations a–d follow the verb string.

(2) Significant trends discovered in the analysis of NL sentences produced by IH speakers will appear in an analysis of IL sentences produced by these same Hebrew speakers under the same experimental conditions.

Operationally, non-chance arrangements identified in terms of hypothesis (1) will be defined as an NL norm in each syntactic domain, and parallel non-chance arrangements identified in terms of hypothesis (2) will be defined as syntactic transfer, i.e. *relative frequency* in the NL and IL will be the determining factor as to whether or not language transfer occurs. These hypotheses are confirmed below with some important deviances.

Experiments II and III were conducted for the purpose of replicating the essential conditions of the basic experiment by keeping all major variables as constant as possible (see Table 7.1 for details). This was done in the belief that if the results of Experiment I were to be considered valid, these results should consistently be repeatable. Replication of empirical results has proven quite intractable in SLA research since it is not always easy to be sure what is repeatable across studies. It is something that must be attempted, however, to discover what is and is not fact in SLA. (This issue of replicability in SLA is discussed in Selinker 1985/6, a review article of the *Field Manual* (Perdue 1984) for the six-country European Science Foundation study of 'guest-worker' IL in northern Europe.)

For these reasons, an attempt was made to keep the major variables constant during the course of Experiments IV, V and VI, with the exception that one major variable was isolated in the design and purposely varied per experiment so that effect of this shift in variables upon the previously established results could be systematically studied: for Experiment IV the *grade*, and for Experiments V and VI the *language spoken at home*.

Experiment VII was conducted to establish an NS–TL *baseline*. In

188   *Rediscovering Interlanguage*

Interview for Experiment I

Card 1

(the interviewer lifts 2 books)

(1) Where are the books?	(1) eyfo hasfarim nimcaim?
(2) Where are the books now?	(2) eyfo hem axšav?

(the interview puts the books on the table)

(3) Where did I put the books?	(3) eyfo samti et hasfarim?
(4) When did I put them on the table?	(4) matay samti otam al hašulxan?
(5) Once again now, where are the books?	(5) od pam, eyfo hasfarim?

(the interviewer lifts them again)

(6) Again, where are the books?	(6) od pam, eyfo hasfarim?

Card 2

(1) What singers do you like?	(1) eyze zamarim ata ohev?
(2) Have you heard ____ this year?	(2) ata šamata et ____ hašana?
(3) Did you hear him last year?	(3) šamata oto lifney šana?
(4) What singer do you like best?	(4) eyze zamar ata ohev yoter?
(5) What is his best song?	(5) ma hašir haxi yafe šelo?
(6) When did you hear him sing it last?	(6) matay šamata et hašir haze bepam haaxrona?

Card 3

(1) Do you ever go to /kupat xolim/*?	(1) ata holex lekupat xolim?
(2) Where is it?	(2) eyfo ze?
(3) Which doctor do you see?	(3) eyze rofe ata roe?
(4) When did you first see Dr ____ ?	(4) matay raita bepam harišona et doktor ____ ?
(5) Did you see him again?	(5) raita oto od pam?
(6) When did you last see him?	(6) matay raita oto bepam haaxrona?

Card 4

(1) Where did you buy that watch (sweater)?	(1) eyfo kanita et hašaon haze (haxulca hazot)?
(2) When did you buy (receive) it?	(2) matay kanita (kibalta) oto (ota)?

Card 5

(1) Do you like English very much?	(1) ata ohev meod anglit?
(2) Do you understand (speak, read, write) English (Hebrew) very well?	(2) ata mevin (medaber, kore, kotev) tov anglit (ivrit)?
(3) Do you speak (read) English (Hebrew) very often?	(3) ata medaber (kore) letim krovot anglit (ivrit letim krovot)?

Card 6

(1) What subjects do you study in school?	(1) eyze mikcoot ata lomed?
(2) Which subject do you like best?	(2) eyze ata ohev yoter (haxi harbe)?
(3) Which do you like least?	(3) eyze ata ohev paxot (paxot mikol)?
(4) Do you like mathematics (physics) very much?	(4) ata ohev meod matematika (fizika)?
(5) What is your English (mathematics) teacher's name?	(5) eyx korim lamore laanglit (lamatematika) šelxa?
(6) When did you meet Mr (Mrs) ____?	(6) matay nifgašta im mar (im gveret) ____ ?

Card 7

(1) Do you like movies very much?	(1) ata ohev meod sratim?
(2) Do you go to the movies very often?	(2) ata roe otam harbe?
(3) What was the last movie you saw?	(3) ma haya haseret haaxaron šeraita?
(4) Do you want to see that picture again?	(4) ata roce lirot et haseret haze od pam?
(5) Where did you see ____?	(5) eyfo raita et ____?
(6) When did you see that movie at ____?	(6) matay raita et haseret haze be-____?

Card 8

(1) Do you want to go to the university (Technion)?	(1) ata roce lilmod bauniversita (batexnion)?
(2) Why do you want to go there?	(2) lama ata roce lilmod šam?
(3) When will you go to the university (Technion)?	(3) matay tilmad bauniversita (batexnion)?
(4) What will you study there?	(4) ma tilmad sam?

Card 9

(1) Where do you live now?	(1) eyfo ata gar axšav?
(2) Where did you live five (ten) years ago?	(2) eyfo garta lifney xameš (eser) šanim?
(3) Where would you like to live ten years from now?	(3) eyfo tagur beod eser šanim?

Card 10

(1) Do you bring friends home?	(1) ata mevi yedidim habayta?
(2) Do you bring them home very often?	(2) ata mevi otam letim krovot habayta?
(3) Whom have you recently brought home?	(3) bizman haaxaron mi heveta habayta?
(4) When did you last bring ____ home?	(4) matay heveta et ____ habayta bepam haaxrona?

* National Health Service

TABLE 7.2 The interviews

addition to testing these variables, it was felt that the experimental design should also include possible isolation and control of other potentially relevant variables. In all experiments, the role of the *sex variable* was tested; in Experiments I to VI the *language proficiency variable* was tested; and in Experiments I and III the *IQ variable* was tested.

Prior to Experiment I, an interview was prepared containing approximately fifty questions in Hebrew and fifty in English and the questions were placed on twelve 5 × 7 cards (see Table 7.2). The purpose of the interview was to achieve a similar framework in the two languages to serve the interviewer as a guide in his attempt to elicit countable sentences from the subjects, i.e. sentences with the above string combinations. A technical distinction is in order here:

Arrangement is used to mean the specific order or sequence of syntactic strings, and is symbolized by an en dash, e.g. Ob–Pl.
Combination is used to mean occurrence of strings in either arrangement and is symbolized by a plus sign, e.g. Ob+Pl equals Ob–Pl and Pl–Ob.
This distinction relates to the questions first brought up in Chapter 2:
 –   What does language transfer consist of?
 –   What actually is transferred?
 –   What types of language transfer occur?
The theoretical claim is that in syntactic transfer, arrangements for particular combinations are what get transferred and this is what *no* general linguistic theory has been able to cover. (The types of language transfer will be discussed below.)

The abstractness of categories, shown by the technical distinction arrangement/combination (such as Ob–Pl and Ob+Pl) parallels Nemser's use of capital letters for sets of phonetic productions that fall into attempted TL productions and perceptions. The abstract syntactic categories, i.e. *what actually is transferred*, are for NL and IL productions, the latter being attempted TL surface syntactic strings. In both cases, there is more than one possible production for a particular targeted category and this is why we need this technical distinction in IL syntax. Recall also that this sort of abstractness matches what we found in several of the CA models discussed in Chapter 4.

Note that the interview questions in Table 7.2 are grouped around semantic areas within the subjects' range of experience and, one hopes, within their range of interest. Two types of questions are included in the interview; questions which are specifically designed to elicit countable sentences are interspersed with questions whose function is to keep the conversation moving and to make certain that the important questions designed to gain exemplars of the relevant syntactic combinations do not appear conspicuous. Experience gained through the analysis of Experiment I revealed several sources of potential bias and inefficiency that had appeared in the design. Thus, a revised form of the interview was prepared and placed on nine 5 × 7 cards (see Table 7.3). The reduced interview containing approximately forty questions in Hebrew and in English, had the same purpose as the original. Three types of changes were included:

(1) Elimination of yes/no questions which contained two countable strings following the verb string, e.g. Do you like movies / very much?

(2) Substitution for (1) of sequence questions, e.g. Do you like movies? . . . (subject's hopefully affirmative response) . . . very much? – the aim being to elicit exchanges such as the following:
Do you like movies?
Yes I like movies.   (Recall that the subject has to answer in 'complete sentences'.)
Very much?
Yes, I like movies / very much.   *or*
Yes, I like very much / movies.

(3) Elimination of questions with two countable strings which tended to elicit three strings in succession after the verb, e.g.: 'When did you hear them / the last time?' 'I heard them / the last time / yesterday'. The same interview that was revised for Experiment II was used in Experiments III to VI, with the exception of the additional question for Experiments V and VI in the NL which related to the purpose of that experiment (see Table 7.3, Card 5). For Experiment VII the interview used for the other experiments was slightly revised to adjust to US conditions.

The common characteristics of the 132 subjects (57 boys and 75 girls) used in the first six experiments are that they were all born in Israel and had never lived in an English-speaking country. A deliberate shift of one major variable, the age variable, in Experiment IV produced the following differences: subjects used in this experiment were fifteen years old, in the tenth grade, and had five years of English instruction, whereas subjects used in the other five experiments were thirteen years old, in the eighth grade, and had

Card 1

(the interviewer lifts 2 books)

(1) Where are the books?   (1) eyfo hasfarim nimcaim?
(2) Where are the books now?   (2) eyfo hem axšav?

(the interview puts the books on the table)

(3) Where did I put the books?   (3) eyfo samti et hasfarim?
(4) When did I put them on the table?   (4) matay samti otam al hašulxan?
(5) Once again now, where are the   (5) od pam, eyfo hasfarim?
books?

(the interviewer lifts them again)

(6) Again, where are the books?   (6) od pam, eyfo hasfarim?

Card 2

(1) What subjects do you study in   (1) eyze mikcoot ata lomed bebet sefer?
school?
(2) Which subject do you like best?   (2) eyze ata ohev yoter (haxi harbe)?
(3) Which do you like least?   (3) eyze ata ohev paxot mikol?
(4) What is your English teacher's   (4) eyx korim lamore laanglit šelxa?
name?
(5) When did you meet Mr (Mrs) ___?   (5) matay nifgašta im mar (gveret) ___?

Card 3

(1) Where did you buy that watch   (1) eyfo kanita et hašaon (hasveder,
(sweater, jacket, shirt)?   hažaket, haxulca) haze (hazot)?
(2) When did you buy (receive) it?   (2) matay kanita (kibalta) oto (ota)?

Card 4

(1) Do you like movies   (1) ata ohev meod sratim?
(2) Very much?   (2) meod?
(3) What type of movies do like best?   (3) eyze min sratim ata ohev beyoter?
(4) What was the last movie you saw?   (4) ma haya haseret haaxaron šeraita?
(5) Where did you see ___?   (5) eyfo raita et ___?
(6) When did you see ___?   (6) matay raita et ___?

Card 5

(1) Where do you live now?
(2) Where did you live five (ten) years ago?

(1) eyfo ata gar axšav?
(2) eyfo garta lifney xameš (eser) šanim?
(3) (Experiments V & VI only: eyze safa medabrim babait? *)

Card 6

(1) Do you like English?
(2) Very much?
(3) Can you understand English?
(4) Very well?
(5) Can you speak English?
(6) Very well?

(1) ata ohev anglit?
(2) meod (bemiyuxad)?
(3) ata mevin anglit?
(4) tov (hetev)?
(5) ata medaber anglit?
(6) tov (hetev)?

Card 7

(1) Which Israeli singer do you like best?
(2) Which Israeli singer do you like least?
(3) Which foreign singer do you like best?
(4) What is his best song?
(5) When did you hear ____?

(1) eyze zamar israeli ata ohev haxi harbe?
(2) eyze zamar israeli ata ohev paxot mikol?
(3) eyze zamar mixuc laarec ata ohev haxi harbe?
(4) ma hašir haxi yafe šelo?
(5) matay šamata et ____ ?

Card 8

(1) What is your doctor's name?
(2) When did you see Dr ____?
(3) Where did you see him?

(1) mi harofe šelxa?
(2) matay bikarta ecel doktor ____?
(3) eyfo bikarta eclo?

Card 9

(1) Do you want to go to the university (the Technion, trade school)?
(2) Why do you want to go there?
(3) When will you go to the university (etc.)?
(4) What will you study there?

(1) ata roce lilmod bauniversita (batexnion, bebet sefer mikcoi)?
(2) lama ata roce lilmod šam?
(3) matay tilmad bauniversita (etc.?
(4) ma tilmad sam?

* What language do you speak at home?

TABLE 7.3 Revised interview for experiments II, III, IV, V and VI

three years of English instruction. A further deliberate shift in variables in Experiments V and VI accounted for differences among subjects regarding the language spoken at home. In the basic experiment and its two replications (Experiments I to III), the language was IH. This variable was kept constant for Experiment IV, where the age variable was tested. In Experiment V the subjects did not primarily speak IH at home but rather a wide variety of Middle Eastern languages, excluding Yemenite Arabic. The tapes in this experiment were tested informally on several adult Israelis who all stated that the Hebrew of these 19 subjects, though clearly the Hebrew of NSs, constituted a different dialect (Sephardic) from the IH of the subjects recorded during the course of the first four experiments. The major distinguishing feature, in the opinions of these judges, was of a phonetic sort in almost every case. Subjects in Experiment VI all spoke one language at home – Yemenite Arabic. For Experiment VII, 31 US eighth-graders (16 boys and 15 girls) who spoke only English at home and had never lived in a foreign country were interviewed to establish empirically an NS–TL baseline for the syntactic structures being studied.

The procedure used in the first six experiments was essentially the same. Before the interview session, the subjects to be used in that particular experiment were divided, without their knowledge, into small groups by their English teacher on the basis of his or her estimate of their English proficiency, with each group being homogeneous as to sex. The resultant groups had from two to five subjects per group, depending on the subjects' availability and the teachers' assignments to groups. Order was balanced in two ways: (1) male group first, female group first; female group first, male group first; (2) Hebrew portion first, English portion first. The latter condition was felt to be essential so that prompting in Hebrew could not account for the IL results, which indeed might have been the case if the Hebrew portion of the interview had always been presented to the subjects first. All interviews were conducted in their entirety by the author, who has no trouble communicating in Hebrew, although an NS would have been more desirable for the NL parts of I–VI.

The only instruction given to the subjects was to 'speak in complete sentences' and it is interesting that it took but a few seconds for most subjects to learn to speak in such units, even in IL. It has always seemed to me that the experimental technique of asking subjects to speak in complete sentences is a very useful one if the purpose is to gain large numbers of exemplars of particular NL and

IL structures. For obvious reasons, this purpose cannot be accomplished just by listening to large stretches of naturally occurring discourse. Given that the subjects needed no explicit instruction in order to be able to consistently produce complete sentences, not only in the NL but also in IL, I believe that some sort of basic language intuition is being tapped, probably more towards the formal end of the style continuum described by Tarone (1983). I have often wondered why this technique has not been used more often when the goal is as stated: to gain large numbers of exemplars of particular NL and IL structures (see Chapter 8 below).

I will now present four types of results: those from the data of the three linguistic systems experimented with (NL, TL and IL), and that of the role played by potentially relevant non-linguistic variables. For the sake of simplicity of presentation, the NL results of the six experiments conducted in Israel are presented here and described in pooled form, as are the IL results. Though it seems as if only one experiment is being reported, the results of the pooled data are in essence no different from those of the six experiments, except in the one case reported. The use of pooled data here parallels that of Nemser and Briere already reported above in this chapter. (The breakdown of the pooled frequencies for these studies is presented in Selinker 1966, Appendix D.) Since these pooled results prove to be repeatable in these experimental conditions, they are considered all the more valid. That is, one general result here is that the specific results of the basic experiment proved to be repeatable in the replication of the basic experiment's conditions at that particular point in time.

A general methodological result is also worth reporting here. In the course of the analysis of the data obtained in Experiment I, it was noticed that certain questions, which had unwillingly given two desired strings after the verb string, were consistently producing the same order in the subject's responses, e.g.:

> at mevina tov / anglit?   Do you understand English well?
> well English

produced the same order in the answer:

> ani xoševet šeani mevina tov / anglit. I think I understand English well.

The next full exchange on the tape also produced a repetition of the order given, but this time the order of strings was reversed:

at kora ivrit / tov? Do you read Hebrew well?
    Hebrew well
ken ani kora ivrit / tov. Yes, I read Hebrew well.

In fact, this sort of thing proved so troublesome that a total of 175 previously counted sentences (92 NL and 83 IL) had to be disqualified from statistical counts on the basis of being prompted by such questions, and the entire interview was revised before Experiment II was undertaken. The result of this revision was that the sequence type of question described above worked as predicted; not one sentence of the countable type had to be disqualified in the analysis of Experiments II to VI. (Concerning tying things together through time in terms of the teaching of SLA, we believed that this was an important enough methodological point to include it as a question in the *Workbook in Second Language Acquisition* (Selinker and Gass 1984, Problem 4.9, Question 3).

We will now look at the *specific results* of the pooled data:

(I) *NL (IH) data*: Several significant trends were discovered in the countable NL sentences produced by the subjects. As is apparent from the frequency counts (Table 7.4), two absolutes and one near absolute appeared in the NL data. Whenever an Ob and a Ti string occur after the verb, in 179 occurrences the order was Ob–Ti in 178 occurrences, while only once did the order Ti–Ob occur. (Sample NL and IL language examples are presented in Table 7.5 with extensive examples of IL and NS TL sentences presented in Appendix A.) The result establishing Ob–Ti as an NL norm, even though it was nearly absolute, was completely unexpected by the author and by an Israeli linguist consulted. It was felt, *before experimentation*, that the combination Ob–Ti would parallel the combination Ob+Pl where it was known that the order Pl–Ob occurred in the NL (and in the IL; recall that the frequent observation of the order Pl–Ob in naturally occurring interaction was what originally led to the formulation of the project, e.g. the sentence 'I bought downtown / the postcard').

Furthermore, it was soon apparent that another absolute would be established in the NL data if in the analysis of the combination Ob+Pl, noun objects (Obn) were distinguished from substitute or pronoun objects (Obs) and the frequencies for each were tabulated separately. Table 7.4 shows that where NL Obn+Pl were tabulated, no significant trend (p<.10) towards the unexpectedly dominant sequence occurs. In fact, NL Obn+Pl had proved exceedingly

Combination	Arrangement	NL		IL	
Ob + Ti	Ob – Ti	178		194	
			p < .001*		p < .001
	Ti – Ob	1		0	
Ob$_s$ + Pl	Ob$_s$ – Pl	77		58	
			p < .001		p < .001
	Pl – Ob$_s$	0		0	
Ob$_n$ + Pl	Ob$_n$ – Pl	73		85	
			p < .10		p < .20
	Pl – Ob$_n$	51		67	
Ob + Ad	Ob – Ad	25		70	
			p < .001		p < .001
	Ad – Ob	131		143	
Pl + Ti	Pl – Ti	34		24	
			p < .30		p < .01
	Ti – Pl	44		46	
Ob$_s$ + X	Ob$_s$ – X	164		170	
			p < .001		p < .001
	X – Ob$_s$	0		0	

* All probability values were calculated according to the quantity chi square (df = 1) as defined by McNemar (1962, p.209).

TABLE 7.4 String arrangement frequencies: pooled data

puzzling throughout the analysis, until the data for all six experiments were re-examined from an entirely different point of view, one that was not really in accord with the linguistics of the time. This new analysis began to reveal some promising trends. Table 7.6 shows a division of the pooled NL and IL Obn+Pl frequencies into major categories, each category being determined by the discourse/semantic content of the subject's responses. (Three minor categories, where frequencies do not occur for five of the six experiments, were not considered here; for details see Selinker 1966, Section 3.4.) Reanalysing the NL data at the bottom of the table, the pooled

		NL (Hebrew)	IL (Hebrew–English)
Ob + Ti	Obₛ – Ti	raite *et ze/lifney švuaun* 'I saw it two weeks ago'	I met *her/this morning*
	Obₙ – Ti	raiti *et haseret haze/lifney švuaun* 'I saw that movie two weeks ago'	I met *Mrs Cosman/today*
Ob + Pl	Obₛ – Pl	raiti *et ze/bekolnoa orgil* 'I saw it at the Orgil theatre'	I bought *it/in Tel Aviv*
	Obₙ – Pl	kaniti *et hašaon/baxanut* 'I bought the watch in a store'	I bought *my watch/in Tel Aviv*
	Pl – Obₙ	ani roca lilmod *bauniversita/biologia* 'I want to study biology at the university'	I will study *in the university/biology*
Ad + Ob	Ad – Ob	ani ohev *meod/sratim* 'I like movies very much'	I like *very much/movies*
	Ob – Ad	ani ohev *sratim/meod* 'I like movies very much'	I like *movies/very much*
Pl + Ti	Pl – Ti	ani gar *began yehuda/axšav* 'I live in Gan Yehudah now'	I live *in Tel Aviv/now*
	Ti – Pl	ani gara *axšav/beramat gan* 'I (fem.) live in Ramat Gan now'	I live *now/in Tel Aviv*

TABLE 7.5 Illustrative language examples

frequencies for (1), (2) and (3) are totalled on the one hand, and those for (4) on the other. The resulting tabulations show that when the responses concern 'subjects studied at school' (category 4), an almost absolute NL trend towards the order Pl–Obn occurs. But when the responses concern any of the other three categories the near absolute trend is, on the other hand, towards the order Obn–Pl. It appears that this result is one of the first in the literature showing discourse/semantic effects on surface syntax.

The next combination under study in Table 7.4, Ob+Ad, shows a highly significant trend towards the dominant arrangement Ad-Ob, though minimal grammatical pairs do occur and can be seen in Table 7.5. It is important to note that in such a situation, probabilistic controls of the type not usually set in classical CA (see Chapter 1 above) are necessary to establish NL (and IL) norms.

For the combination Pl+Ti, the frequencies of 34 and 44 fail to establish a significant trend (p < .30) towards either sequence. This result is also unexpected as it runs counter to the hypothesis stated above that a statistically significant trend would be discovered for

Responses concerning:		Ob_n–Pl	Pl–Ob_n
(1) buying and receiving	Hebrew (NL)	15	1
things	Hebrew–English (IL)	28	0
(2) seeing movies and	Hebrew (NL)	25	0
parades	Hebrew–English (IL)	14	0
(3) books on the table	Hebrew (NL)	24	0
	Hebrew–English (IL)	35	0
(4) subjects studied at	Hebrew (NL)	1	48
school	Hebrew–English (IL)	1	60

	Hebrew (NL)			*Hebrew–English (IL)*		
	Ob_n–Pl	Pl–Ob_n	P values	Ob_n–Pl	Pl–Ob_n	P values
Σ (1) (2) (3)	64	1	< .001	77	0	< .001
Σ (4)	1	48	< .001	1	60	< .001

Probability values were calculated according to the quantity chi square (df = 1) as defined by McNemar (1962, p.209).

TABLE 7.6 Semantic breakdown of Ob_n+Pl for pooled data in four categories

each combination. It seems reasonable to posit another new type of norm; the norm for NL Pl+Ti is not mandatorily one of the two possible arrangements but the *choice* of either arrangement since the possible arrangements are more or less equiprobable.

Finally, splitting the data another way produced another absolute. Noun objects are again separated from the substitute or pronoun objects; this time Ob+Ti and Ob+Pl are included. (No examples of a substitute object occur in the NL sentence with an Ad string.) The combination Obs+X is said to equal the total occurrences of Obs+Ti and Obs+Pl. Now the order Obs–X occurs 164 times while the reverse order does not occur.

Thus, results of looking at the NL data in Experiments I–VI appear generally to have upheld the first hypothesis presented above. There is a statistically significant trend towards one of two possible arrangements in almost every case. Exceptions parallel Nemser and Briere results.

(II) *IL (IH–English) Data*: The absolute and near-absolute norms established in the analysis of the NL data reappear in an analysis of the corresponding IL data obtained from these same subjects in the same experiments. According to Hypothesis 2, the parallel statistical trend is what *operationally* establishes language transfer in each case. As is apparent from the frequencies listed in Table 7.4, no counter examples occur to the absolutes Ob–Ti and Obs–Pl. (Sample IL language examples are presented in Table 7.5, with extensive examples of IL and NS TL sentences presented in Appendix A.) In these cases, then, statistically significant (in fact, absolute) parallel NL and IL trends are discovered. Thus, as with the Nemser and Briere studies, parallel frequencies in NL and learner behaviour provide a possible requirement to show language transfer.

A third IL trend which was statistically parallel to an NL norm occurs in the case of IL Ad–Ob, with both NL and IL significant at a <.001 level. As with NL Ob+Ad, minimal grammatical pairs occur. These can be seen in Table 7.5, with the former type enjoying a much larger frequency of occurrence. Another absolute was created in IL data when all object strings were divided into Obn and Obs. IL Obs–X (as defined above) occurs 170 times while the reverse order does not occur.

Concerning language transfer in light of Hypothesis 2, the conclusion to be drawn concerning Ob–Ti, Obs–Pl, Ad–Ob and Obs–X is that when *parallel non-chance* arrangements of this type result from the statistical operations performed, syntactic transfer is identified. Thus, 'syntactic transfer' in the experimental circumstances of these studies is operationally defined as a process which occurs whenever a statistically significant arrangement in the NL sentences reappears in IL behaviour.

In the case of NL Ob+Ti, we can speak of the transfer of a particular NL arrangement (Ob–Ti) to an IL combination (Ob+Ti), with the resultant IL arrangement (Ob–Ti) being measured the same as the NL one in every physical occurrence in the data of the abstract combination. The same is also true of Obs+Pl and Obs+X. The case is slightly different, however, for Ob+Ad, whose dominant arrangement, though highly significant, is far from being absolute. In this latter case, we can speak of the transfer of a particular NL arrangement (Ad–Ob) to an IL combination (Ob+Ad), with the resultant IL arrangement (Ad–Ob) being measured the same as the dominant one with much greater than chance frequency of occurrence.

The new type of norm described for NL Obn+Pl, where surface syntactic order is affected if not determined by discourse/semantic considerations, is paralleled by these frequencies registered from a semantic division of IL Obn+Pl (Table 7.6). Once again, semantic categories (1), (2) and (3) are totalled on the one hand, and category (4) on the other. The resulting tabulations show an absolute trend towards IL Obn–Pl for categories (1), (2) and (3) and a near-absolute trend towards Pl–Obn for category (4). Most importantly, the situation regarding syntactic transfer in the case of Obn+Pl is the same *after* the discourse/semantic breakdown described above is carried out. The pooled frequencies shown at the bottom of Table 7.6 indicate that the IL split is exactly the same as the NL one: categories (1) (2) (3) on the one hand and (4) on the other. As far as Obn+Pl (categories (1), (2) and (3)) is concerned, then, the transfer is of a particular NL arrangement (Obn–Pl) to an IL combination (Obn+Pl), with the resultant IL arrangement (Obn–Pl) being measured the same as the NL one in every occurrence of the combination in the data. Note that the transfer of NL Obn+Pl (category (4)) is almost exactly identical, but in reverse. Thus, we have demonstrated some sort of semanto-syntactic (and perhaps discourse-based) language transfer here.

For the reasons reported above, the fact that NL Pl+Ti shows no significant trend towards either possible arrangement is an unexpected result. In light of this, the significant trend that appears in IL Pl+Ti towards Ti–Pl (Table 7.4) is similarly unexpected. But the significance here is at the <.01 level, which is not as conclusive a result as that reported for other dominant trends in these experiments. One reasonable possibility is that a dialect difference is at work here (see result IV below) because when the frequencies registered for Experiments V and VI are removed, the new IL frequencies total 24 for Pl–Ti and 39 for Ti–Pl, a *non-significant combination* (p <.10). This last result is indeed credible since it parallels, though at a lower level, the non-significance (p <.95) created by the new NL frequencies of 32 for Pl–Ti and 33 for Ti–Pl. The conclusion to be drawn is that, with the limiting assumption of a dialect difference, the *choice* of either arrangement, found to be the NL Pl+Ti norm, *re*appears in an analysis of the IL sentences produced by the same learners whose sentences determine the NL norm. Thus, as regards NL Pl+Ti, no significant trend towards either of the two possible arrangements occurs and the conclusion is drawn that the choice of either arrangement is the NL norm. A non-significant NL result is also obtained when the data of Experiments V and VI are omitted from consideration on the grounds that they reflect a potential dialect difference. This latter move does, however, *change the IL result* from one of non-parallel significance to one of parallel non-significance. An extension of the criterion for identification and measurement of syntactic transfer would in this case be parallel non-significance. That is, the Israeli whose home language is IH, dialect A, has a choice as regards NL Pl+Ti and he *transfers this choice* to the production of IL Pl+Ti, and the resulting arrangement in the IL is either Pl–Ti or Ti–Pl, with more or less equal probability of occurrence. The Israeli whose home language is something other than or something in addition to this dialect, i.e. IH, dialect B, seems to have no choice. His dominant NL arrangement is Ti–Pl and he transfers this arrangement to his attempted production of English sentences containing these elements.

Thus, in considering language transfer, once more as with Nemser and Briere, relative frequency is seen to be a significant variable. In considering the parallel NL and IL data, the results of Experiments I–VI, then, appear to have upheld the second hypothesis concerning the identification of language transfer.

(III) *NS–TL (American–English) Data*: In order to gain some empirical idea as to what learners of English might be attempting to approximate in the syntactic domains studied in the above experiments, NL–TL baseline data were gathered in the manner described above in Experiment VI. All trends discovered in a statistical frequency analysis of the countable sentences obtained in this

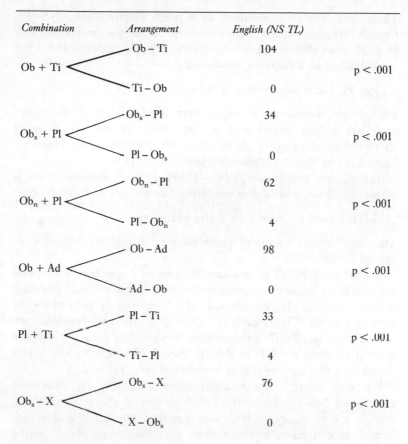

Combination	Arrangement	English (NS TL)	
Ob + Ti	Ob – Ti	104	p < .001
	Ti – Ob	0	
Obs + Pl	Obs – Pl	34	p < .001
	Pl – Obs	0	
Obn + Pl	Obn – Pl	62	p < .001
	Pl – Obn	4	
Ob + Ad	Ob – Ad	98	p < .001
	Ad – Ob	0	
Pl + Ti	Pl – Ti	33	p < .001
	Ti – Pl	4	
Obs – X	Obs – X	76	p < .001
	X – Obs	0	

Probability values were calculated according to the quantity chi square (df = 1) as defined by McNemar (1962, p.209).

TABLE 7.7 String arrangement frequencies: Experiment VII

experiment were highly significant. In fact, as is apparent from the frequency count in Table 7.7, no counter examples occur to the following absolutes: Ob–Ti, Obs–Pl, Obs–X and Ob–Ad. Examples are:

Obn–Ti:	I met Sister Leon / last year.
Obs–Ti (and Obs–X):	I met her / at the beginning of last year.
Obs–Pl (and Obs–X):	I met her / in school.
Obs–Ad (and Obs–X):	I like them / very much.
Obn–Ad:	I like movies / very much.

Therefore, each is established as a norm empirically of NS–TL English syntactic string behaviour. Although the trend towards Obn–Pl is not absolute, it is nevertheless highly significant and it too is established as a norm of English, e.g.:

Obn–Pl: I study English / in school.

Interestingly, the counter examples were all of category (4) above, but each has a long object and a long object is not the defining characteristic of category (4) in either NL Hebrew or IL Hebrew–English. (The Appendix provides several examples.)

Although the trend towards NS–TL Pl–Ti is not absolute, it too is highly significant and is also established as a norm of English, e.g.:

Pl–Ti: I lived in New York / five years ago.

The four counter examples show no pattern and are regarded as chance occurrences.

Use of these NS–TL data can be seen as *a new type of CA*, one quite different from those discussed earlier in this volume, this time between empirically established IL behaviour and empirically established NS–TL behaviour. Of eight syntactic combinations tested, seven specific IL arrangements produced by these subjects are transferred from the NL to the IL. And in the eighth case, it is a choice of arrangements that is transferred (see Table 7.8).

We now contrast these eight cases with the experimentally established NS–TL norm of English described above. First of all, though, it is necessary to clarify two concepts: 'non-error' and 'error'. A non-error is taken to mean those occasions when the IL string behaviour is *concurrent with* what is discovered in the NS–TL string behaviour, and error is taken to mean those occasions when the IL string behaviour is *deviant from* the NS–TL string behaviour. This is using CA thinking in an empirical manner.

In Table 7.8 the IL syntactic combinations are shown in terms of the arrangements transferred from the NL; these arrangements are contrasted with the arrangements established as norms of English. Numbers 1–6 in the table apply to all IH speakers interviewed in the first six experiments, while 7 and 8 apply respectively to the two groups of IH NSs isolated and labelled dialects A and B, respectively. These consistent concurrences with and deviations from an empirically established TL norm make it possible to identify three types of syntactic transfer – positive, negative and neutral:

Positive transfer occurs when the IL string arrangements are non-errors.

Hebrew (NL) and Hebrew–English (IL)	English (NS–TL)	Error classification	Possible transfer classification
(1) Ob – Ti	Ob – Ti	non-error	positive
(2) Ob_s – Pl	Ob_s – Pl	non-error	positive
(3) Ob_s – X	Ob_s – X	non-error	positive
(4) Ob_n – Pl (categories 1, 2 and 3)	Ob_n – Pl	non-error	positive
(5) Ad – Ob	Ob – Ad	error	negative
(6) Pl – Ob_n (category 7)	Ob_r – Pl	error	negative
(7) Ti – Pl (dialect 2)	Pl – Ti	error	negative
(8) Pl – Ti (dialect 1)	Pl – Ti	non-error	neutral
Ti – Pl	Pl – Ti	error	

TABLE 7.8 Contrastive string arrangements

Negative transfer occurs when the IL string arrangements are errors. *Neutral transfer* occurs when the IL string arrangements are either non-errors or errors, neither dominating significantly.

It is concluded that speakers belonging to dialect A show three types of transfer in their speech behaviour: positive, negative and neutral; speakers belonging to dialect B show only two: positive and negative.

The reader should be aware that there have been serious qualms about this sort of classification. It has been claimed that this analysis confuses product with process. That is, are the types of transfer identified here only an artifact of our methodology, a product of an IL/NS–TL CA and not indicative of internal learner SLA process? The argument against this analysis is presented in summary form in the Introduction to Gass and Selinker (1983a) and is formulated as follows:

> In the learning situation, learners use previous linguistic knowledge in interacting with the [TL]. Based on present information, we feel that there is only one process of transfer. . . . Hence, we now believe that there is no need to attribute separate processes (for example, positive, negative or neutral) to the learner. Our view is that the learner is transferring prior linguistic knowledge resulting in IL forms which, *when compared by* the researcher to the [TL] norms, can be termed 'positive', 'negative' or 'neutral'.
> (Gass and Selinker 1983a, p.6, emphasis in the original).

Truthfully, I have vacillated on both sides of this argument over the years, seeing merit in each. In teaching ESL, it seems to me that many learners do in fact regard errors that they know are caused by NL as 'negative'. One has to ask: (1) To what extent do learners regularly compare their IL productions with actual and perceived TL output and input to the learner? (2) To what extent are these comparisons used as the basis both for permanently setting their IL and for further learning? In Chapter 6 we saw that early on, Corder (1967) called the making of errors a crucial learning strategy. Also, Nickel (1970, 1973) in directing the important PAKS EA project came to the same conclusion. Nickel points out that there are two ways to look at errors, and this is discussed in Chapter 5 above. Taking this Corder/Nickel position seriously, in the framework developed here, the recognition of negative, or even neutral, language transfer on the part of the learner, by whatever means, could be a mechanism whereby the recognition of error becomes a strategy for learners to help promote their SLA, *necessary* 'in-between stations'.

As pointed out in Chapter 5, this position has not been seriously tested in second language research.

(IV) *Non-linguistic variables.* In an analysis of the data of all seven experiments, it is concluded that sex is not a significant variable. In only one case was a significant trend discovered, IL Ob–Ad towards a female domination, but it was at the unconvincing level of <.05. This one case is regarded as a freak sample obtained by chance. Experiment IV was conducted for the sole purpose of measuring the effect of a deliberate variation in the age-complex variable, i.e. age, grade in school, and amount of English instruction. It was found that the two-year age difference involved in this experiment has no effect on any of the results already reported. Thus, it can be assumed that these IL forms have stabilized and are good candidates for possible permanent fossilization.

Experiments V and VI were conducted for the sole purpose of measuring the effect of two deliberate variations of the variable labelled 'language spoken at home'. Only one difference in the results obtained in Experiment V from those of I–IV is discernible and that concerns Pl+Ti, which was explained above in terms of dialect A vs dialect B. Concerning 'language proficiency', no conclusions could be reached due to the inability of determining the equivalence of proficiency levels in the different schools.

The role of language transfer in creating interlanguage

In concluding this chapter I wish to provide my current view on the role of language transfer in creating IL, integrating results and insights which I believe remain valid from the three studies discussed in this chapter. The phenomenon of NL influence on the learning of a second language has been recognized for centuries and is a most substantial influence. The consensus view is that language transfer is *not* an 'all or nothing' phenomenon as was thought in the earlier days of CA (cf. initial chapters of this volume). The use of NL information in the formation and structure of ILs is, it is now clear, a selection process, i.e. there are some NL structures and processes more likely to be transferred than others, and the three studies presented in this chapter all conclude that this is so. All three studies attempt to discover experimentally what the transferred structures are in the limited domains studied. If language transfer is a selection process, then the term 'transfer' has to be defined most carefully each time it is used in an empirical study. It is this point that is struggled with in terms of the data presented in these studies.

After looking in detail at these three studies, as well as more recent ones (e.g. those presented in Gass and Selinker 1983 and Kellerman and Sharwood Smith 1986, as well as those summarized in Davies, Criper and Howatt 1984), and after contemplating the multiplicity of variables considered in this complex topic, I conclude that:

> Language transfer is best thought of as a *cover term* for a whole class of behaviours, processes and constraints, each of which has to do with CLI, i.e. the influence and use of prior linguistic knowledge, usually but not exclusively NL knowledge. This knowledge intersects with input from the TL and with universal properties of various sorts in a selective way to help build IL. (Cf. also Selinker 1984.)

In the studies presented here, only experimental data are considered, but results obtained fit in with studies where more naturalistic input to the learner is taken into account (cf. e.g. studies presented in Gass and Madden 1985).

A key question raised in these early studies which remains current is:

> – How does the analyst unambiguously show that language transfer has occurred?

These three early studies each choose the experimental answer of operational definitions, i.e. statistically based reasoning. This question has led directly to the very current concern of:

> – How does the analyst constrain a theory of language transfer, since use of the NL in the formation of IL is a selection process of some sort?

These studies empirically demonstrate – something revolutionary in the early 1960s – that NL and TL structural congruence is not enough to identify transfer. Language transfer seems to be predictable in a probabilistic sense if other than purely linguistic factors are taken into account, and the references cited above discuss such factors in detail.

As these three studies attest, and more recent studies confirm, the behaviour of an individual learner is never as predictable as that of a group of learners of a particular NL attempting to learn a particular TL. But all three conclude, along with most current studies, that CA is the best place to begin language transfer studies since structural congruence (or at the least, partial structural similarity) is most probably necessary, though not sufficient, for many of the claims regarding CLI. One conclusion is that the NL can serve a facilitative role in creating IL, especially where some property of NL and TL is perceived by the learner to match, this perception leading to interlingual identifications as discussed throughout the earlier chapters. One caveat is that there is evidence in the literature that, at least in the lexical domain, learners may, on occasion and apparently under probabilistic constraints, reject TL structures even if found in the NL. Another caveat is that all of this presupposes a 'process' view of transfer, but there is another alternative: a 'constraint' view of transfer. See Kellerman (1983) on the first point and J. Schachter (1983) on the second.

In doing language transfer studies, the analyst, in addition, must leave room for abstract organizing principles on the part of the learner. For example, in the word-order study above it was claimed that what is transferred is a particular arrangement for particular combinations. In the second phonological study, the unit of transfer in many cases was claimed to be the syllable, in essence another abstract unit. One would expect the growing literature on rhetorical and discourse transfer (e.g. Bartelt 1983) to show that abstract principles of organizing NL information would be candidates for sources of transfer, but even in the phonological domain such organizing principles can not be discounted, as for example the apparent case of Thai learners transferring organizing principles of NL tonality but not the actual tones of Thai to their Thai–English IL, as described above in Chapter 4.

Language transfer intersects with other processes and constraints throughout the IL experience (cf. Arabski 1979 and Kellerman 1986), the research task being to discover empirically the what, when, how and why of this all-pervasive phenomenon. In all three studies presented here there is, at least implicitly, the spectre of fossilization, i.e. the cessation of IL learning, often far from TL norms, often shown by the failure of learners to acquire a feature where a particular TL feature is expected. Such features in the Nemser, Briere and Selinker studies which were 'unexpected' appear to be good candidates for permanent fossilization.

Zobl (1983) and Andersen (1983) point out that non-learning can occur in areas where there is congruence of a feature of NL with a developmental feature as shown by the fact that the latter type of feature occurs frequently in various ILs no matter what the NL. It appears that such congruence may prolong the restructuring of a particular rule, leading eventually to a fossilized form. Kellerman (1983) relates fossilization to the language transfer concept of 'psychotypology', which involves the learner's perception of L1/L2 distance in some central way. He assumes cross-linguistic identification in a way that is compatible with the concept of interlingual identifications as presented throughout this volume, and argues that this form of perception is one of the bases for language transfer, speculating that it may also form one of the bases for the temporary (or even permanent) cessation of learning.

From these experimental studies to more recent ones in discourse, all evidence points to the conclusion that it is the learner's view of what is interlingually (or, perhaps, universally) the same that must be tapped. It is my view that phenomena such as avoidance strategies, learning and communication strategies, fossilization and backsliding, over-production of elements, additional attention paid to the TL (which often results in more rapid learning) and the transfer or application of typological organization must all be related to a basic learner strategy – the contrastive one of setting up interlingual identifications. All three studies presented here support this view and certainly do not contradict it.

An unanswered question considering the particularities discussed in these studies remains: What is the (IL) universality of the cross-linguistic phonological and syntactic units discussed in these studies? It is not clear how much this is tied to methodology (on research methodology cf. Chapter 8). For example, the Selinker results were described in a theoretical 'two-choice schema', e.g. Ob–Ti occurs or Ti–Ob occurs in the combination Ob+Ti studied; Ob–Ad occurs or Ad–Ob occurs in the combination Ob+Ad and nothing else. Language transfer is clearly defined in these contexts as parallel statistical dominance or non-dominance. However, as was pointed out, in the limited empirical domain, three relevant units appeared with autonomous linguistic material but were discounted in the artificial boundaries of the experimental design. It is my view that working within the framework of a two-choice schema should permit analysts to cover large areas of surface structure language transfer, and perhaps other IL, behaviour. But how much of language and IL behaviour is like that? Tarone *et al.* (1976) argue that as one moves more and more into syntax and semantics, the choice is less and less clear and more is open and unpredictable. What this means is that where there are *binary choices* for the learner statistical reasoning works well, but that there are important limits to this and that qualitative analysis becomes the prime research tool at times. (Cf.

Van Buren 1988, discussed in the last chapter, where binary choices for the learner take on a central theoretical role.)

Summary

These three early attempts to study language transfer experimentally, to test empirically the claims of technical CA, provide an empirical and intellectual foundation upon which more recent SLA studies can stand. They have influenced the strong current position of constraining empirically a theory of language transfer, with the NL not the either/or proposition conceived of in classical CA. Out of this comes a continuing frontier area of studying how this central complex of language transfer variables intersects with other known strategies and processes in the creation of IL.

From the Nemser study we learn that, regarding phonology learning at least, perception and production have to be looked at differentially in some cases, a result presaged by Lado (see Chapter 1 above). Structural congruence of some sort is still regarded as a necessary condition for some types of transfer to occur. Nemser's work confirms the use of CA as a technology, the most reasonable place to begin a language transfer study. His conclusions remind us of a Corder position, described in the last chapter, that of the learner identifying items and structures as same across systems with NL as facilitative in IL creation. This is so because the main effect of transfer is that the learner looks in the TL for items and structures that are 'NL-like', facilitating learning.

We learn empirically from Nemser, who draws heavily upon Weinreich and Haugen (cf. Chapter 2 above), that the results of interlingual identifications are different in some way from total NL/TL results, producing a large number of 'unexpected blends' in the IL with 'autonomous' approximative systems material repeatedly occurring. He points out (in my rephrasing) that blends and autonomous phenomena occur in both developing and highly fossilized ILs. He also concludes that, in language transfer terms, when the learner already has a category in the NL (e.g. 'stops' vs 'interdental fricatives'), there are fewer errors, also facilitating transfer and here language learning, a result we can relate to Corder's thinking (Chapter 6).

This result also relates closely to the psychotypology concerns of Kellerman's referenced above. Also related to current approaches is that Nemser may have been the first to recognize that frequency in the NL is a possible requirement for transfer, though Briere and

Selinker seem to have discovered that fact independently. In order to study the frequency variable, large numbers of exemplars of particular structures are required and there is no doubt that experimental methods are required since this phenomenon does not occur in more naturally occurring discourse. Nemser does not seem to list his total responses, but I total 5270 and both Briere and Selinker have similar totals. So we are in each case dealing with a respectable number of exemplars upon which to base our conclusions.

From Briere we learn similar lessons. First, there are significant perceptual/production differences, especially that production can precede perception, a result not overturned in the empirical literature. Second, frequency is a crucial criterion in determining what is and is not transferred. Third, replicating the Nemser result, there are occurrences of new substitutions for expected TL sounds. Briere does not call these new forms 'blends' as Nemser does, but given some of Corder's conclusions of Chapter 6, blends is most probably an inappropriate term for IL forms, though it does link us up with the bilingualism literature discussed in Chapter 2. Fourth, Briere also finds autonomous material in IL production, i.e. sounds not occurring in NL or TL, another result which still holds up. Note that doing this experimental work, Briere also provides substantial data with some 6720 responses considered. This is paralleled by Selinker's 4155 sentences. However, Selinker does not test perception so there is no parallel result to report here.

The importance of the variable of relative frequency for demonstrating language transfer found in Nemser, Briere and Selinker leads to a positive conclusion for importing the methodology of experimental psychology into SLA studies, and our relationship to this latter field is explored in the next chapter.

Updating the Selinker study, Andersen (1983) makes a particular point of the most important frequency variable. He contrasts the Selinker result of 'relative frequency in the L1 and IL' with other more recent results which show that relative frequency in TL speech is a prerequisite for the incorporation of at least some forms into the IL. Andersen discusses the Selinker result discussed above of Ob+Ad, where:

	NL(IH)	IL(Hebrew–English)	NS–TL(English)
Ob–Ad	25	70	98
Ad–Ob	131	143	0

Andersen points out that the English required order is Ob–Ad (I like cats/very much), whereas Hebrew, while 'permitting this order', uses the opposite order (Ad–Ob) more often, and states that: 'It is clear from the table that the order of these elements in the English IL of the Israeli children corresponds qualitatively and quantitatively to the [NL] and not the [TL] order' (Andersen 1983, p.187). Andersen concludes that this result provides a counter example to other empirical results since 'the order Ad–Ob seems not to have an independent source in the input or in [psychological] operating principles'. Thus, we can say that it is a well-established empirical result that relative frequency is a crucial determining factor of language transfer for the learner. It remains, however, unclear in every case exactly where that frequency has to lie in terms of psychological principles such as those of Slobin (1973), upon which Andersen draws, or the typological principles of Kellerman's discussed above.

Andersen makes an important point related to the Schachter (1983) view that the learner's developing knowledge of the L2, i.e. earlier IL stages, has to be considered a source of language transfer, whether transfer is considered as a process or as a constraint. Andersen speculates that given universal understanding of early ILs, for the learners studied by Selinker, earlier IL forms than those captured in this study might be:

I like.   *and*   I bought downtown.

where object pronouns are not expressed and which would 'provide an IL form to which [NL] word order can transfer (I like very much / cats; I bought downtown / the postcard) (Andersen 1983, pp.187–8). This would be the 'somewhere' in the Andersen principle of 'transfer to somewhere'. Recall in Chapter 2 and in this chapter the significance attached to the Weinreich observed German–English sentences of the type: 'He comes tomorrow / home.' Based on observations of the above type in the grammatical area, and parallel ones in the phonological area, Weinreich establishes the concept that is important to the development of IL as presented here: interlingual identifications. I find Andersen's suggestions not an alternative explanation but a possible step on the way towards learner fossilized interlingual identifications. But so far these ideas remain untested.

In all three studies, some items predicted for language transfer do occur and some do not. The large amounts of data in each case are essential to resolving some of the ambiguity, thus arguing for some importation of methodology from experimental psychology (cf. next chapter). An unexpected result in the Selinker study, which proved repeatable, was that topic of conversation, a semantic/discourse variable, can affect surface syntactic order in both the NL and the IL, and thus in the language transfer process. This is a current position, where it is widely believed that discourse constraints affect syntax (e.g. Givon 1979 and Lakoff 1987, in general linguistics) and where for many researchers in SLA, IL syntax, at least partially, is developed out of discoursal interaction (see Hatch 1984; Ellis 1985a and b; Selinker and Douglas 1985).

For reasons beyond the scope of this chapter but hinted at earlier, questions and insights raised in the Nemser, Briere and Selinker studies were obscured for a decade. Conflicts creating this situation appear to me to have been resolved for most colleagues. Thus, it is now possible to view the creation of IL as a process reflecting (universal) hypotheses about the L2 input, as well as a process of selectively using NL knowledge, as well as that of other ILs known to the learner. These general sorts of processes must intersect in some as yet unknown way, UG scholars seeing universal processes as prime; but arguments that see language transfer as prime were presented above. This issue is far from settled.

Finally, the Selinker study described here also replicates Nemser and Briere in finding autonomous material in IL, but this time primarily within three- (and four-) choice schemas, as opposed to the two-choice schema which was the main focus of the study. This result shows that too narrow a methodological focus, here focusing on experimentation with a two-choice schema alone, may tune us out to significant SLA results and may be a drawback to too large a dependence on research methodology borrowed from experimental psychology. This two/three-schema result leading to important IL fact, in this case autonomous IL word-order material, leads us in Chapter 8 into reflection on how we do research in SLA relating to the continual discovery of IL. And leading to these matters is a deep concern with language transfer. In this chapter we have linked language transfer through time from bilingualism, CA and EA to three early experimental studies which attempt to test CA predictions, and to the most recent work. We begin the next chapter with consideration of how IL gets continually discovered from this deep concern with language transfer. Hints have appeared above. It is a story that now deserves telling.

Points for discussion

(1) Consider Nemser's result that 'intermediate phones' exist in Hungarian–English interlanguage. Evaluate this in light of Briere's data. Then re-evaluate your conclusions based on the

finding of interlanguage 'autonomous material' in all three studies discussed in this chapter. How might such linguistic material relate to fossilization?

(2) Continuing to link concerns through time, trace the bilingualism, contrastive analysis, error analysis and experimental interlanguage connection in terms of language transfer as a 'selection' process.

(3) Given the data in this chapter, question the classical contrastive analysis assumptions as described in Chapter 1. Specifically, note the phenomena of blends and intermediate phones and the asymmetry between perception and production data as presented in both the Nemser and the Briere data. Consider how contrastive analysis can sometimes lead to correct predictions and sometimes to incorrect predictions when interlanguage behaviour is actually tested.

(4) With the data from this chapter in mind, think through the notion of cross-linguistic identification (called interlingual identification by Weinreich, Chapter 2 above) in terms of the following statement from this chapter: 'Reinterpreting Nemser, we can say that learners in creating IL sometimes make NL/TL categories equivalent and sometimes do not'.

(5) With the data from this chapter in mind, think through the notion of interlingual identification in terms of the Corder position in the last chapter. Recall that the position states that language transfer is facilitative because learners identify items and structures as same across languages as they are seeking, in the target language input, native-language-like structures. How solid is the conclusion that the native language performs primarily a facilitative role?

(6) In this chapter there is much discussion of the research methodologies of these three studies. Compare these with error analysis/interlanguage methodology suggested by Corder in the last chapter.

(7) It was suggested in the previous chapter that the procedures demonstrated for the study of language transfer in this chapter meet the criteria Corder set out for the empirical study of interlanguage. Argue either the positive or the negative side of this proposition.

(8) Choose a current language transfer study (see Larsen-Freeman and Long, 1991) and examine it in terms of the link through time from bilingualism to error analysis to contrastive analysis to the experimental interlanguage studies discussed in this chapter.

(9) Consider the problem of relevant units of second language acquisition. Outline what these units might be according to the evidence presented in this chapter.

(10) What do you think of the claim, made at several points in the chapter, that what actually gets transferred are abstract categories, such as Nemser's /T/ or Selinker's 'arrangement/ combination'? Discuss how this sort of abstractness matches what we found in several of the contrastive analysis models described in Chapter 4.

(11) We continue to focus on the paradox first brought up in Chapter 2 and summarized in the first paragraph of Chapter 3, how cross-linguistically learners make the same what 'cannot be the same'. One central concern in this chapter is: How can the learner 'tolerate' the 'disjunction' observed in the developing interlanguage and between the native language and the target language input? Do you have any ideas?

(12) Finally, it is clear that a key issue from the discussion on language transfer to date is the following: How does the analyst constrain a theory of language transfer, since use of the NL in the formation of IL is a selection process of some sort? What ideas do you have?

8 The continual discovery of IL

Purposeful ambiguity

The title of this chapter is meant to be ambiguous in several ways: first, the intellectual discovery and naming of the concept 'interlanguage'; next, the continual discovery by researchers and teachers of IL structure, processes and constraints; and last, the continual discovery of their own IL by individual learners attempting to communicate and negotiate meaning in an L2. A goal of classical CA and EA was to discover and explain L2 interference and learning problems. What was discovered was interlanguage, a clearer understanding of what is and is not IL fact, and the related substantive issue of how we do research and set up such facts in the various applied linguistics fields. A number of dictionaries define 'fact' as 'something that actually exists'. The content of this chapter concerns how we establish what actually exists in interlanguage. What sorts of evidence do we use to discover whether a hypothesized IL phenomenon actually exists? Do we, and should we, use the same sorts of evidence as those used in neighbouring fields?

I was moved to the content of this chapter initially by a careful rereading of the interesting interview conducted by Peter Shaw with Dick Allwright, Dave Eskey, Bill Rutherford and John Schumann which appeared in *English Language Teaching Journal* ('Talking Shop', April 1983, 37.2, pp.129–137). This rereading reminded me that the discovery and naming of the IL concept fits into Susanne Langer's view that: 'Most new discoveries are suddenly-seen things that were always there' (Langer 1942, p.1). That is, if 'interlanguage' is a correct concept that names a 'real-life' phenomenon, then in some serious sense it was 'always there'. Regarding IL, this view is backed up by what we have seen throughout this volume, from Lado through Martinet to Weinreich and to most of the contrastivists. One can read into their work some sort of 'in-between' language or grammar, and, as a result of this, create interesting SLA hypotheses as we have done, allowing us to see the wisdom of the 'purposeful misreading' suggested by Garfinkel (see Introduction above). It is important to recall that this notion of in-between language or grammar is explicit in the work of Harris, Van Buren, Nemser, Briere and Corder.

I would like to begin this chapter by structuring my comments around a significant portion of the aforementioned interview, providing what I hope will be useful background to the discovery of IL, explicitly linking things together through time. This interview leads to the substantive issues mentioned in the last paragraph. We have to face the problem of the relationship between underlying concepts and empirical research, especially since we have seen several times in this volume that deep-structure transfer is possible and may relate to fossilization. In the latter part of this chapter we move to consideration of what is and is not fact in IL and how we set up research frameworks, studying these by using the technique used throughout this book: comparison, but this time with other fields.

It is most important for those issues that concern us to look at other fields, especially those that on the surface appear similar, either in terms of subject matter or in terms of empirical methodology recommended by some of our colleagues. In my view no other subject matter presents the unique combination of language transfer and fossilization, of change (i.e. possible acquisition) and non-change (i.e. possible fossilization) over time, that we encounter in the analytical as well as in the learner discovery of IL. No other subject matter needs to integrate pedagogical concerns as we do, i.e. in ways that we seem to have to. No other subject matter combines serious consideration of these variables as they interact with concepts associated with the IL hypothesis: language transfer, backsliding, avoidance strategies, learning and communication strategies, simplification and complexification processes, permeability, and so on. For comparative research methodological purposes, I have chosen to look at mathematical psychology since, on the surface, its subject matter seems similar to ours and there are SLA colleagues who would have us emulate its empirical methods. If we do, as we did in the last chapter, we must be clear as to how our subject matter is and is not like theirs.

A seminal interview

Let us begin by quoting the relevant passages in Table 8.1.

Peter: What you seem to be saying, John, is that, if there was a breakthrough, it was getting going; that was the breakthrough. Otherwise, rather than talking about breakthroughs, we seem to prefer to talk about 'current best shots', and things like that. But Dave nominated Lambert and Gardner's work on motivation. I wonder if you could just briefly nominate two or three pieces of work in the 1970s that we might look back on in a few years and say, 'Well, those are the things that gave us impetus and provided useful directions in which to work', whatever the situation may be in terms of practical application?

Bill: In terms of frequency of citation, Selinker's interlanguage work would be a strong candidate. If nothing else, the term itself has filled a semantic gap, and certainly what lies behind it is very significant.

Dave: That's an example of what I meant earlier; I think that interlanguage itself is not a product of research, but rather that it is a concept that Corder and Selinker (I'm not quite sure who is responsible for it) have investigated through empirical research. But the concept didn't just spring out of the research. Rather, the research followed from the hypothesis.

John: Yes, all we needed was the term. Selinker seemed to have provided the term, with some description of it. The description was reinforced almost simultaneously by Corder's articles, and also by Nemser's. And then we have it all together, and then it just became a matter of getting samples of interlanguage and analysing it.

Dick: Have we disposed of the big bogies? If we haven't broken through into new territory, have we actually got rid of some bad old bits of territory that we ought to have abandoned long ago, and now have, because we have done research that tells us we were right to do so? Contrastive analysis has not been abandoned, though; it's coming back, isn't it?

John: I'm glad you mentioned that, because I think that's another big issue that has had a little bit of history in the 1970s. In the early seventies, people were trying to ignore interference. I'm not sure contrastive analysis is coming back, but certainly there is an interest in interference, which had been on the wane from, say, 1970 to 1975. Last year it was given a big impetus at the Michigan conference on language transfer, and now it's a fascinating and very vital area of research, and it's being looked at quite differently. We have seen it become unpopular, and now become popular again but on a very different basis, where it's extremely valuable and interesting, I think.

Bill: I think 'language contact' would be a better rubric for that kind of thing.

John: So what have we identified, then?

Peter: Well, we have now got Lambert and Gardner, and we've got Selinker's introduction to interlanguage . . .

John: And a new interest in language transfer and contrastive analysis, language contact.

Dave: And I would want to add the tremendous variety in the work on discourse analysis which seems much more directly relevant to the concerns of language teachers. I think all that you have just been discussing is an example of what to me has been the real gain in the last ten years: there is a much stronger sense now of the complexity of the problems we are dealing with, of the dimensions of the problems, so that simplistic theories

are not now being proposed as capable of covering everything. So people
now see contrastive analysis as part of a much larger network of things,
involving error analysis and all the problems involved in language transfer.
We now have a much richer conception of what language is, and what
language learning is, and I think that's a net gain, no doubt about it.

John: I think we also have to mention that morpheme studies have been valuable
in second language acquisition research. They are not popular right now,
but there's an awful lot of information that we have gained from them.

Bill: It was the first step.

John: Yes, it was the first step. It was easy to do. We had some instruments, like
the Bilingual Syntax Measure and so on, that made it possible to do it on
large numbers of people. People objected to the instruments. The attitude
towards it – people keep saying, 'I'm sick of morpheme studies' – is
probably like the position ten years ago when people were saying, 'I'm sick
of contrastive analysis', and it may just re-emerge in 1987 as being
tremendously valuable, if it hooks up with other similar developments in
the field, so I don't think we can forget about it.

TABLE 8.1   Relevant Dialogue

To initiate the discussion, I would like to perform a text analysis of
the content of the discussion in Table 8.1. I find:

(1) that one of the main values of the research mentioned in the
passage is in the 'getting going', i.e. that this body of research
has given us 'impetus and provided useful directions in which to
work', viz the setting up of a context or a world in which to work;

(2) that the term 'interlanguage' has 'filled a semantic gap';

(3) that 'what lies behind [the term "interlanguage"] is very
significant', an investigation of which is the central theme of this
volume;

(4) that the statement that IL 'itself is not a product of research' is
problematical. This statement is questioned by the bilingualism,
CA, EA and experimental research gone through in this volume.
'Interlanguage' was, in fact, a concept discovered *after* looking at
empirical data in these fields for many years. One of the goals of
this volume is to show that the concept does in fact 'spring out
of the research' and how that knowledge enriches us today in
terms of studiable hypotheses as shown throughout this volume;

(5) that given (1), it is also true that 'research followed from the
hypothesis'; in truth this was, and continues to be, its strength;

(6) that although I 'provided the term' the concept is surely evident
in the material in the original empirical study;

(7) that in fact 'some description of' IL was provided early on, in
terms of some IL data, arguing for its partial autonomy from
NL and TL data, in addition to some description of the

processes, strategies and constraints going into its creation (language transfer, learning and communication strategies, fossilization and backsliding), as well as an extended discussion of possible units of IL learning and production. Also, it was argued that such units cannot be covered by any known theory of linguistics, and, as argued above, this situation has not changed;

(8) that one can disagree with one widespread interpretation (though, as Sue Gass points out (pc), it is not a necessary interpretation) of the statement that my description of IL 'was reinforced . . . by Corder's articles and also by Nemser's'. One must disagree with the widespread conclusion that there is synonymy of the three concepts 'transitional competence', 'approximative systems' and IL. This is a widely held interpretation (e.g. Corder 1981). What I hope to show below is that, on the other hand, each of the three makes *different theoretical claims* about the nature of the SLA process;

(9) that '. . . then it just became a matter of getting samples of interlanguage and analysing it'. This follows from (1), is a process that has a strong momentum of its own and is what empirical SLA is all about (cf. Preston 1989);

(10) that language transfer study was temporarily 'on the wane'. As often happens with important intellectual trends, the 'revival' of interest in language transfer began independently in several parts of the world. This development is discussed in Chapter 7;

(11) that 'language contact' is a useful concept with a good and important focus. Its reintroduction, as we have shown, emphasizes continuing careful study of one of our intellectual roots, bilingualism;

(12) that 'the tremendous variety in the work on discourse analysis' is of great value;

(13) that a 'real gain' has been the 'much stronger sense now of the complexity of the problems we are dealing with, of the dimensions of the problems . . .' and that, as a result, we have now the hope that 'simplistic theories . . . capable of covering everything' are truly a thing of the past;

(14) that the morpheme studies were most valuable, in my view, primarily as training, because a large number of ELT practitioners were exposed through these studies to the idea of actually looking at second language data. This was a great step forward;

(15) that CA 'may just re-emerge as being tremendously valuable, if

it hooks up with other similar developments in the field'. CA is beginning to 'come back, but with safeguards', as Pete Becker (pc) so eloquently puts it. In some sense this volume is a response to that need.

Let me next comment on several of the above points – first, on the idea that the term 'interlanguage' filled a semantic gap. That is certainly true and is more important than meets the eye. As described above in this volume, CA is the tradition where most early SLA and IL researchers received their training. In my view, one of the major faults of CA as a predictor of learning problems was that *two* linguistic systems were talked about, NL and TL (as in the many quotes by Lado, Chapter 1 above), but *three* systems, with the third unnamed, seemed to me always to be implied; this is one of the direct links in the discovery of IL between CA and SLA. As has been noted, several researchers (e.g. Corder, Nemser, James, Selinker) came to this conclusion independently at about the same time in the early to mid 1960s. The research began to gain solid direction with the naming of the phenomenon as interlanguage, along with five sets of developments:

First, the ready acceptance of IL as 'reality', as showing that learner language has structure. Lightbown (1984) has pointed out that one of the most important accomplishments in SLA has been that we have shown that learner language does in fact have structure.

Second, the merging of two groups of scholars, those from adult second language teaching, especially from ELT, and those from child language acquisition, hence the name 'second language acquisition' to parallel it with first. The group from language teaching awkwardly called it (following Lado?) 'the psychology of second language learning'.

Third, the teaching of SLA courses in some linguistics departments and in some teacher training programmes. This was not always easy. One colleague told me that it was necessary to go through a progression of names over the years to get the subject matter accepted, from CA to EA to SLA. In some linguistics departments where SLA courses were beginning to appear, often in answer to student demand, there were unfortunately influential colleagues in theoretical linguistics who kept insisting that there was no place for this in a linguistics department. (This stage will, it is to be hoped, soon be behind us.) My answer to that, by the way, has always been as given in this volume: linguistics, to be a general theory of language, must realize that the world is not a set of monolingual language situations; there is no known theory of language that can handle IL units that are established in terms of language transfer and interlingual identifications.

Fourth, the gathering of IL data in an empirical way by more and more members of several groups of scholars, those groups named above, as well as by students in the new courses in SLA. An ever-increasing body of empirically derived data helped us to focus in a principled way on the strategies, processes and constraints underlying these data.

Fifth, the development of special interest SLA group meetings at TESOL, AILA LSA. At the annual and semi-annual meetings of these organizations (and perhaps several others, such as MLA and ACTFL), paper sessions were devoted to the topic, and, equally important, private meetings of interested colleagues began to occur. Often these meetings were devoted to questions of research methodology, especially problems of data collection. At one of them, the *SLANT Newsletter* (*Second Language Acquisition Notes and Topics: A Newsletter for Researchers*) was born. (The name was created by Dick Weist.) *SLANT*, which lasted about a decade into the 1980s, served as a focal point for information necessary to get the systematic study of learner language going. For example, important contacts were established when Uli Frauenfelder did a special issue on SLA research in France in 1976 (*SLANT* 3.2). *SLANT* was co-edited for years by Nancy Backman and then edited by Judi Chun but folded, like others of its kind, for financial reasons, although only after specialized journals had appeared. Contacts established by these means remain strong to this day.

These developments began to lend credence to an independent subject matter, but a curious one – one with its own type of data, its own theories and methodologies and, importantly, its own ways of relating to 'facts', but one that could not leave the contrastive perspective embodied in CA, bilingualism and EA. We have need to incorporate this perspective in the way stated in the interview: it must 'hook up with other similar developments in the field'. The empirically testable claim is: learners *compare* what they do with a perceived target, setting up interlingual identifications (which was earlier in this volume called a basic SLA learning strategy).

Let me now comment on the idea presented in the interview that once the semantic gap was filled, all one had to do was to go out and collect samples of IL and analyse them. Second *language* data began to be perceived as not just a random collection of 'errors', of 'deviances' from some other system, but as data which relate to the creation of some sort of language system (which may account for acceptance of the term 'inter*language*'). Then it became easier to find instances of IL everywhere one looked. However, as we have found from painful experience, unambiguous transcriptions of IL data (never mind unambiguous analyses) are not always possible. Hence, the conclusion that (IL) data are always ambiguous.

Herein lies a tale. On the issue of ambiguity of data, a rude shock occurred *after* publication of the morpheme gender results from the Toronto French-immersion situation (Tarone *et al.*, 1976). In that paper we presented careful statistical statements relating to, among other things, whether the learners said 'le' or 'la' in their English–French IL, relating the results in turn to the operationally defined concepts 'systematicity/variability' and 'stability/instability' in IL systems. This distinction appears related to the 'junky data' theory (Wong Fillmore, pc), namely that input to the learner is the input created by other immersion children and that these junky data affect the resultant IL drastically. Of the dozen or so people who eventually listened to those tapes and checked the transcripts, someone said: 'They are not saying "le" or "la" clearly on all these occasions. Sometimes they are saying [lə],' a strategy which in retrospect makes sense for NSs of English learning French. We were never able to sort out the facts, and the conclusions presented in print may thus not be valid. This tale gives credence to Tarone's view (1984) that research 'products', especially printed articles and books, should be regarded *not* as sacred product but as part of the 'process' of doing SLA.

Let me next comment on what I think is a very plausible implication in the interview regarding the relationship between Corder's, Nemser's and Selinker's early work, a common view that is still regularly brought up at conferences: that the terms 'transitional competence' and 'approximative systems' are synonyms for 'inter-language'. Corder has dealt with this topic several times (cf. Corder 1981, *passim*), but to my knowledge Nemser has not. If I understand Corder's position correctly, it is that all three terms refer to the same phenomenon, the first term emphasizing the 'transitional' nature of the learner's language, the second emphasizing that the learner is 'approximating' ever closer the TL, and the third emphasizing the 'language' aspect of SLA.

I wish to take a view diametrically opposed to that summarized in the last paragraph. The view I wish to defend is that we are here dealing with three different theoretical approaches to the nature of SLA, each of which makes significantly different claims and predictions about IL. First, and perhaps most significantly, a strong form of the transitional competence hypothesis would claim that learner languages are *always* transitional in nature. I believe that this strong claim is false and that it ignores the reality of entirely fossilized competences (cf. Coulter 1968 as presented in Chapter 5 above, and Jain 1974). It also ignores the reality of early fossilization in some sociopolitical situations (cf. Perdue 1984, discussed in Selinker 1985/6). The IL hypothesis, in contrast, while not denying the transitional nature of *some* subsystems of learner language, claims that even from day one of exposure to TL data, stabilization and fossilization of IL subsystems is possible and common. As pointed out in Chapter 7, Nemser makes quite explicit statements about the possibility of fossilization, and, of course, Corder does as well.

Second, we have already dealt briefly with distinctions between the 'approximative systems hypothesis' and the 'IL hypothesis' (Tarone *et al.*, 1976). In that paper, we interpreted from Nemser two assumptions that are derivable from his published work. Assumption (a) is that the learner's language is *directional* in that it evolves in stages which closer and closer approximate (Nemser, 1971b) the norm of the TL. Assumption (b) is that these stages are necessarily *discrete* (*ibid.*). We noted in Tarone *et al.* (1976) that assumptions (a) and (b) are in fact separable claims and are crucial assumptions which distinguish the two hypotheses.

In considering these assumptions, the empirical literature, as I read it, does *not* suggest that learners of an L2 'closer and closer approximate' the TL until such learners become indistinguishable from NSs of the TL. In fact, it seems to me that all evidence is to the contrary: fossilization names the real phenomenon of the permanent non-learning of TL structures, of the cessation of IL learning (in most cases) far from expected TL norms. (An extensive discussion of fossilization related to this point is presented in Selinker and Lamendella 1978 and Scovel 1988.) What seems to confuse the issue is that there are some learners who appear very TL-like in some subsystems of IL in some IL genres and discourse domains. It is my experience that such learners can fake it quite well by conversation-ally controlling the domain of talk and by avoiding certain inherently difficult areas of TL grammar, such as phrasal verbs and modals in English.

This impression is borne out by a well-structured empirical study by Dagut and Laufer (1985) who look at a 'genuine avoidance' phenomenon in Hebrew–English, where learners who are 'passively familiar' with certain forms tend to avoid using these forms while expressing themselves, arguing that (following Schachter 1974) 'such avoidance can be properly understood only by an interlingual (i.e. contrastive) approach'. This ability selectively to avoid TL material under conditions of control, in my view, can make learners appear very TL-like when in fact they are not. What appears to happen is that the basic learning strategy, discussed throughout this volume, of interlingual identifications, in the face of what Dagut and Laufer call 'systemic incongruity' between L1 and L2, dominates the learning process indirectly by appeal to avoidance strategies. (The central issue of 'control' in IL development and non-development is discussed in Ellis 1985a, Ard 1985, and Bialystok and Sharwood Smith 1985.)

Concerning assumption (b) of Nemser (1971a), as we indicate above, Selinker and Lamendella (1978) argue that this is indeed a reasonable claim. Though IL 'discreteness' is very difficult to show empirically, it is necessary to posit this view to account for the phenomenon of 'backsliding', i.e. the sudden, dramatic re-emergence of an IL system long absent from the learner's speech performance. (Cf. Kellerman's (1987) discussion of 'U-shaped' behaviour in SLA.) In Selinker and Lamendella (1978) we argue that IL learning is best viewed as a 'cline progression' from stable plateau to stable plateau; as Corder puts it (cf. Chapter 7 above), the learner is operating with a system at each point, with some subsystems fossilizable at an early stage. Given this view, the temporary stable configurations that one sees in IL learning are more readily accounted for. This would be opposed to the 'dynamic continuum' of Bickerton (1975) that has IL learning looking like 'a more or less regular gradient of change', which we argue the empirical evidence does not support.

The move towards interlanguage

Concerning the conclusion that the concept 'interlanguage' came first and then empirical research followed, I would deny the claim that IL 'itself is not a product of research'. Sufficient evidence from several fields has already been presented in this volume to deny the claim. However, in this discussion I would like readers to keep in mind the substantive background issues of what is and is not fact in IL and how we do research in our field. These issues I will return to later in the chapter when explicitly comparing what we do with a neighbouring field. First, we develop some steps in the intellectual discovery

Sheffield Hallam University
Adsetts Learning Centre (3)

Issue receipt

Title: Materials and methods in ELT : a teacher's
guide / Jo McDonough and Christopher Shaw.
ID: 1017345252
Due: 26-01-12

Total items: 1
19/01/2012 03:40 PM

Don't forget to renew items online at
http://catalogue.shu.ac.uk/patroninfo or
telephone 0114 225 2116

and naming of the IL concept after much empirical work.

Doing CA, the first study discussed in detail in Chapter 5 above originally had the excruciating but revealing title of: 'Preliminary Analysis of Potential Phonological Problems (and Procedures for their Eradication) Involved in the Teaching of American English to Native Speakers of Israeli Hebrew'. As we saw in Chapter 5, this material shows that its approach is structurally contrastivist. Phonemes are compared, predictive IL data and hypothetical learning problems are set up and procedures suggested for their 'eradication'. This work is primarily ELT based, one case where theory and practice are intricately interwoven. It is significant that this volume begins with the pedagogically oriented work of C.C. Fries. The notion IL came out of research and practical experience, including the difficult daily experience of helping NNSs struggle with expressing and negotiating meanings in English. This experience, gained in several settings, produced in essence *observational data* (see below) which was (and still is) central to the conceptualization of SLA as initially IL learning through interlingual identifications. For example, data mentioned in Chapter 2 and developed in Chapter 7 above were initially discovered by noticing that an advanced Israeli learner of English regularly produced sentences of the type:

I bought downtown / the postcard.

I like best / movies.

I lived five years ago / in Tel Aviv.

which looked like language transfer from the native language, Hebrew. This observation linked up two notions: (1) From the IH 'habit' (as it was called then) of putting adverbs before object phrases after verbs, an error occurs if transferred into English. The reasonableness of this notion was reinforced by (2) recalling Weinreich's research conclusion (1953, pp.30, 37; Chapter 2 above) that the sentence: 'He comes tomorrow / home,' produced by a German speaker of English, is 'an example of the application of a grammatical relation of word order from one language (German) to the morphemes of another (English)'. This insight and the empirical work which followed it led to the production of one of the first experimental studies on language transfer (Selinker 1969, described in the previous chapter) and eventually to the notion IL. This notion first appears in print, *after* much experimental work, as a footnote (fn5) to the paper just referenced.

Since beginning this volume with C.C. Fries, it is important to re-emphasize the relationship of practice to theory, the order of events being:

Observation of a phenomenon in a language class → Hypotheses
→ Empirical work → Theoretical conceptualization → Further
observation either in a language class or in interactional settings →
Further empirical, theoretical work → etc.

This experience of the importance to *SLA theory* of observation in a
practical language class is by no means unique. Kellerman, in the
introduction of his talk to the 1984 Milwaukee linguistics conference,
reported such an experience; the insights leading to his transferability
and psychotypology work came from first observing Dutch learners of
English, whom he teaches regularly, producing (or avoiding) certain
structures in their Dutch–English. The next empirical experience
with CA (as opposed to observing regularities in spontaneous and
classroom speech of NNSs) was in a CA course at Georgetown. CA
was taught as a technology based on linguistic discovery procedures.
One took Lado's dictum seriously when he stated: 'individuals tend
to transfer . . .', the quote that appears on p.1 of this volume. Lado
produced a second dictum that was also taken seriously, which
appears at the end of Chapter 1 above:

The list of problems resulting from the comparison of the foreign
language with the native language . . . must be considered a list of
hypothetical problems until final validation is achieved by checking
it against the actual speech of students.
(Lado 1957, p.72)

The third experimental study in Chapter 7 in essence was an attempt
to put these CA dicta into practice. The fact is that it was a long time
and after much CA and experimental empirical work that it was
realized that these dicta were in fact leading out of classical CA and
into IL and psycholinguistics.

In reading the vast CA literature it is easy to recall trying to look
carefully at each contrastivist's data and not just the conclusions
about errors and learning problems claimed. One result of looking at
CA colleagues struggling with technical CA and putting Lado's dicta
into practice proved striking: lacunae or 'residue' to expected CA
predictions kept appearing in the literature, and these are discussed
in Chapter 4 above. A second factor that was striking was that certain
key terms were not being carefully differentiated: 'error', 'interference', 'transfer', 'learning problem', 'difficulty', and perhaps
others. This is documented in Chapter 1 above.

A third notable factor regarding the classical CA literature is the
realization on the part of many authors that individual differences

were affecting the results being obtained, but that these authors could not seem to integrate this observation with their CA predictions as to how the L2 data would turn out. As pointed out in Chapter 1, this phenomenon was termed 'statistical predictions without statistical controls'. This appeared everywhere in the classical CA literature, from Lado's 'tend' to other scholars' uses of 'may', 'is likely to', etc. This is discussed in several chapters above.

A related phenomenon that is striking about classical CA is a lack of clarity as to what a CA was supposed to do. One kept seeing multiple goals. Was it supposed to predict errors? Was it supposed to suggest procedures to eradicate these errors? Was it supposed to deal with difficulties NNSs have in perceiving TL messages, in producing TL comprehensible messages? In retrospect I believe that what we were trying to do was provide predictive IL data, as is discussed in earlier chapters.

One further interesting phenomenon in the classical CA literature is that even in domains where predictions are possible, more than one possibility could erode the theoretical power of the prediction. A well-known example is Di Pietro (1964) where for Italian [zb] the English-speaking learner could apparently produce one of two choices – either insert a 'support' vowel or unvoice both members of the cluster – but the analyst in the CA framework seemed incapable of showing which one of the two possibilities is in fact chosen by the learner under which conditions. We owe a debt to Di Pietro here for his rare clarity in these matters (cf. Selinker 1966, pp.20–1) for he was ahead of his time here; the centrality of binary choice in SLA studies has been discussed by Bley-Vroman (1983) and Van Buren (1988).

By the mid 1960s it was clear to many that there were serious problems with CA: its lack of clarity and its inability to find in the data what it attempted to predict just seemed to be 'in the air'. Empirical SLA, particularly what has become the IL Hypothesis, began in the attempts to do 'rigorous' CA (Lado 1957, Preface), as Lado suggested we do. When Lado said that CA predictions must be considered 'hypothetical' and must be 'checked' by the analyst 'against the actual speech of students', one took this as an empirical challenge. Notice how practical concerns enter into this with Lado's emphasis on 'students'. This is the direct link from Fries to current work in SLA, which is referred to in Chapter 1. Without Fries's contrastive insights, careful CA studies might never have happened. Lado took Fries's insights a major step forward into the challenge of checking CA statements against the actual speech of L2 learners.

Lado's students took this challenge directly into IL and SLA.

The CA research plan behind the third experimental study in Chapter 7 began with:

(a) the observed data referred to above, i.e. where Israelis regularly said English sentences such as: 'I bought downtown / the postcard,' 'I like best / movies,' and 'I lived five years ago / in Tel Aviv'; and

(b) A belief in the CA claim of language transfer which sentences like these seemed to bear out.

These two were merged with:

(c) The experimental psychologist Donald S. Boomer's insistent query: 'But, operationally speaking, *exactly* how do you define "language transfer" so that you can identify an exemplar when you see one?'

All of this provided an early operational constraint on studying the phenomenon of language transfer empirically. An additional constraint was provided by a second query by Boomer: '*Exactly* how is the concept of language transfer related to the psychological concept of "transfer-of-training" with all its rich conceptualization?' This constant probing by Boomer of the fundamentals of our discipline and the detailed reading of highly valued texts in his discipline led to looking at language transfer empirically in a new way, one detailed in the last chapter. I thus consider mathematical experimental psychology as a set of founding texts, and a little later in the chapter I look at a 'highly valued' text in that field.

Thus, in summarizing this section, we have identified five streams in the move towards IL: working with descriptive CA and bilingualism data; working on large linguistics texts; the contrastive insights of Fries, Lado, Harris, Weinreich, Haugen and Corder; observational and then empirical insights into how Israeli learners were learning English; and, finally, being tantalized with the methodology of mathematical psychology to solve the problems of CA and bilingualism, hinted at here but described in detail in earlier chapters. All these led to an attempt to identify several fundamental research questions regarding language transfer in a CA framework. It also led to an attempt to discover an operational and experimental procedure that would gain many exemplars of data relevant to the Israeli's production of sentences like those quoted above. In the research plan, questions were asked such as those outlined in Chapter 2 above: What is language transfer? What does language transfer consist of? How does language occur? What actually is transferred? What types of language transfer occur? An attempt to answer these appears in the work described in Chapter 7, work which follows the experimental psychology paradigm as laid out by Boomer. Now here is the crux of coming to the concept of IL. It emerged from years of experience discussing the experimental language transfer results with colleagues in two universities, Edinburgh and Washington, and these colleagues are thanked in the general Acknowledgements section.

The term 'interlanguage', with the meaning from second language acquisition, appears for the first time in print in *General Linguistics* as the write-up of the experimental portions of the language transfer study:

> An 'interlanguage' may be linguistically described using as data the observable output resulting from a speaker's attempt to produce a foreign norm, i.e., both his errors and non-errors. It is assumed that such behavior is highly structured. In comprehensive language transfer work, it seems to me that recognition of the existence of an interlanguage cannot be avoided and that it must be dealt with as a system, not as an isolated collection of errors.
> (Selinker 1969, fn 5)

After twenty years of hundreds of empirical studies, one would not wish to say anything different. This quotation argues that one is compelled to the concept IL after carefully studying experimentally obtained language transfer data. The key idea is there, that the learner's 'observable output . . . is highly structured . . .' and that it '. . . must be dealt with as a system, not as an isolated collection of errors'. It also stated that:

> This notion of interlanguage may puzzle some readers and this is quite understandable. Especially with regard to individual differences the status of the interlanguage as an unambiguous system is not clear; this concept should be developed in the coming years.
> (*ibid.*)

Bley-Vroman (1983) develops the idea that IL as an unambiguous system is not entirely clear, arguing that through a 'comparative fallacy' we have got away from the original IL notion of dealing with IL 'as a system', halting progress in describing IL. This is true to some extent, and is surely true for the example Bley-Vroman dissects (from Tarone *et al.* 1976). However, in rebuttal, the framework presented by Bley-Vroman appears to provide no place for the TL in the learning mechanism. This is surely equally wrong, especially if we are right about (a) the centrality of interlingual identifications in IL learning and (b) about TL frequencies as a necessary condition for some types of language transfer to occur (cf Chapter 7 above).

As the interview in Table 8.1 points out, in Selinker (1969 and 1972) 'some description' of IL is provided, namely:

(1) Language transfer data in an IL format are presented (1972, p.226).
(2) An extensive discussion of possible units of IL phonology and word order is presented (*ibid.*, p.227).
(3) Evidence is presented concerning various strategies of learning and communication (pp.219–21).
(4) Evidence is presented (pp.218–19) that processes other than language transfer operate in Indian–English IL (from Jain 1969).
(5) An outline of 'entirely fossilized IL competence' is presented (p.217).

Points (4) and (5) reflect much of what is discussed in the various treatises on 'World Englishes' (e.g. Platt and Weber 1980; Platt, Weber and Ho 1984; Kachru 1982) though the conflict supposedly set up by the distinction nativization/fossilization has to be worked out empirically. In certain kinds of societies, the results of learner ILs are clearly stabilized NN varieties of the international language English used for specific purposes and learned to a large extent through the school system. Part of the future discovery of IL must be a more complete understanding of the relationships between learner ILs and these stabilized new varieties.

In this regard, the methods and results of research in Indian–English by Valentine (1985) are interesting to look at. Her conclusions are very close to those gained in SLA research in language transfer and IL:

> It is suggested that the linguistic skills particular to male and female speakers of Hindi ... are transferred to Indian English by creative authors. The Indianizing of the text reveals language features of male and female speakers typical in this non-native variety of English.
> (Valentine 1985, abstract)

She looks at communication and cultural strategies in the NL, Hindi, such as the way topics are initiated and maintained in discourse and the way organizational devices such as 'I see', 'I know', and 'I said' are used. She also looks at 'naming patterns' in discourse where there is a sharp division between male and female speakers, in that female speakers use 'no-naming' patterns, using kinship terms, whereas male speakers use personal naming patterns and more honorifics. There are also sex differences in strategies used for discourse topic initiation and topic flow. For the female speaker, the goal and strategies used are not necessarily 'to gain conversational control and to introduce new information, but to maintain an uninterrupted, friendly stream of discourse', whereas the male speaker is 'more successful in having his discourse topic acknowledged, secured, adopted, and developed by his listener' (*ibid.*, p.10) by adopting strategies Valentine describes. There is thus cultural and contextual transfer which Valentine (pc) believes will not change unless Hindi itself 'moves' in the direction of non-sexist language.

Valentine's conclusions on World English sound similar to those in SLA, but facing the issue of how one does research to establish what is fact, the methods used by Valentine appear different, something we should explore. She looks at 'cross-sex' conversations in novels by north Indian authors which 'artistically reflect' real-life conversation. I can recall especially during a stay at CIEFL in Hyderabad in February 1983, how strongly this type of research was criticized by Indian linguistics colleagues. However, in listening to it presented and after fruitful conversations, I have come to the conclusion that authors of this and similar studies feel that it represents a reality they know. If we in SLA accept such results as predictive IL data, as we did with the CA studies in Chapters 4 and 5, we can suspend negative judgements as some in SLA would proclaim and await results. In fact, some in this field arc ready to take the tools they have developed and check out the results against actual conversational data. Cultural and contextual transfer are quite important to developing ILs and we should jointly spend some empirical time looking at how these stable varieties get there, for they do so, partly at least, through developing and non-developing ILs. (Cf. Williams 1987, Zuengler 1989a and Davies 1989 for discussion of the problematic relation of World Englishes to interlanguage.)

Additionally, we should note that the concept of World English, like the IL concept, did not arise out of thin air but was in fact a product of research, much of it empirical like that of Platt and Weber (1980). In judging our concepts, we have to deal with several epistemologically opposed databases for evidential correctness, for evidential truth. Next I turn to the more general problem posed by the interview extracted at the beginning of the chapter: What is and is not fact in IL, and how do we research in our field? We need particularly to investigate the relationship between underlying concepts and SLA thought.

Establishing facts/setting up research frameworks

I find that these problems often resolve themselves into a conflicting series of claims regarding the establishment of what is 'fact'. And as I hear contending arguments, conflict may be often reducible to opposing databases for evidential correctness. I don't think this situation has been recognized sufficiently widely. In the applied linguistics disciplines I see three, and only three, epistemologically different databases in terms of our subject matter, a subject matter that has the unique combination of language transfer and change, or possible acquisition, with non-change, or possible fossilization, over time that we encounter in attempted learner discovery as well as in analyst discovery of IL:

(1) *Experiential evidence*: those data derived from an individual experience with language learning, which empirically may take the form of a diary study.

(2) *Observational evidence*: those data derived from observing learners in action, which *empirically* may take the form of a classroom log of events.

(3) *Empirical evidence*: those data derived from a carefully planned and well-executed study, qualitative/case study, quantitative/ experimental or a mixture.

Remember what we are trying to do here: we are trying to determine such questions as to how we in SLA continually discover, in the language learner phenomena we look at, underlying concepts such as 'interlanguage', 'language transfer', 'fossilization' and the rest. So we are first looking at types of evidence upon which people base such decisions. For example, we should try to understand on what basis various types of colleagues believe in the distinction learning/acqui- sition or do not believe in it.

Evidence type (1) concerns what one knows to be true about the processes of SLA and IL as a result of personal experience, i.e. *as a learner* of second and/or foreign languages, relating generalizations about the processes to what one knows and feels to be true about oneself in these roles. In my experience this is a powerful determinant of what one *knows* to be 'SLA fact'. People often argue from this basis, or at the least, veto and reject what one knows to be false on this basis. As noted above, Preston and I *know* that we are between us fossilized in a good number of languages, and Schumann *knows* that he learns more of a language when he feels closer to the speakers of that language.

In contrast, evidence type (2) concerns what one *knows* to be true about SLA processes and what is correct from personal experience, but this time from a different sort of personal experience, now as *an experienced observer* of learners of second and/or foreign languages. Experience as a language teacher is the experience *par excellence* here. There is no question that individuals argue from this basis. In further contrast, evidence type (3) concerns what one *knows* to be true about these processes from a different sort of personal experience, *as a consumer* of published research on TESOL, ELT, CA, EA, SLA, etc. I find type (3) particularly tricky, since in most cases the truth claim comes from secondary sources – e.g. 'The results of X's study show . . .' – and too often it is these *stylized conclusions* which become the stuff of truth as to the processes we are concerned with.

But of course, in the real world it is often a mixture of all three that determines what for us is the status of what we know to be true. For example, how do I know that the paradox written about in Chapter 2 and at the beginning of Chapter 3 is true? How do I know that learners, in Weinreich's phrase, 'make the same what cannot be the same'? Empirically, I believe that I have shown here that all the evidence bears out this conclusion; I am particularly thinking of Weinreich's (re-phrased) conclusion that *no* learner transfers the entire morphological system of the NL to the IL. Experientially, I know that I do not; for me language transfer is indeed a selection process. Observationally I continually attempt to discover IL in the learners I teach, and years of language teaching *observing* students makes me sure that this conclusion is correct. Thus, happily in this case, all three types of evidence here coalesce.

It is thus my position that, given the newness of our field and the inchoate state of our knowledge of SLA and IL, each of these three types of evidence should be kept separate and each be treated with respect. Much of the disagreement we see in the literature and hear at conferences results in talking at cross-purposes, in not keeping these three separable forms of evidence separate and not being able, perhaps, to be clear about which type of evidence is prime for the particular point under discussion. That is, part of the criteria for 'fact' in the applied linguistics fields must be that what we glean from empirical evidence does not stray too far from the experiential/observational.

How, then, do we as teachers and as researchers establish facts in our field? Specifically, what can we say that is correct about IL learning that will make sense to the continuum of practising language teacher and theoretician of SLA, whether primarily in ELT, foreign language learning, theoretical linguistics, psychology, cognitive science, etc.? As I have tried to argue in this volume, in the long run we need to ask these questions in some sort of contrastive framework, especially in light of the observational and experiential evidence that teachers constantly compare in contrasting the oral and written IL performances of their learners with some expected TL norm. Whether or not we are talking about classroom learners, some sort of contrastive framework is also strongly called for if it proves correct, as argued throughout this volume, that a basic learning strategy is one of interlingual identifications.

In a neighbouring applied linguistics field, that of language for specific purposes (LSP), Swales (1986) points out that what has happened historically in that field is that it has consistently enlarged the scope of what it attempts to cover. This is also true of SLA and IL studies, with – as was pointed out in the interview extract above – the current interest in discourse, pragmatics and various types of context. Positively speaking, perhaps because we demand that theoretical generalizations in SLA and IL not vary too far from experiential and observational evidence, we are better able to face the real-life SLA complexities we run across, such as those found in the complex English situation in India. We now can plan large-scale and more precise longitudinal studies, such as the European Science Foundation project (Perdue 1984; discussed in Selinker 1985/86 and summarized Perdue 1991). R. Vanikar (pc) points out that such a study would be an important one to do in India.

Exploring the question of 'fact' contrastively

Let us now contrastively explore the questions of what is and is not fact in IL and how we do research in SLA. For example, in Chapter 7 we noted the *fact* that, determined by experimental methodology, 'autonomous material' in IL exists. Namely, all three studies (Nemser, Briere and Selinker) using the experimental methodology of mathematical psychology empirically find such material. So, prototypical statistically based psychological texts must be considered 'founding texts' for CA and IL, as discussed in the Introduction to this volume. As noted above, the empirical result matches observational evidence as well. But there is a catch with the Selinker result: it occurs primarily within three- (and four-) choice schemas, as opposed to the two-choice schema which was the main focus of the study. The conclusion must be that this result also shows that too narrow a focus, here focusing on the two-choice schema alone, may force us to ignore significant SLA results and may be a drawback in creating too large a dependence on a research methodology borrowed from experimental psychology. This is so since it was argued there that a three- (or four-) choice schema looks to be impervious to experimental methodology. This leads us to reflect on how we do research in SLA relating to the continual discovery of IL and the founding texts we depend on for our setting up of frameworks to decide SLA fact.

In the spirit of contrastive thinking, the mainstay of this volume, we need to particularize these questions by considering the relationship of theoretical concepts and empirical research in the applied linguistics disciplines. Since experimental psychology continually forms one of our set of 'founding texts', we need to find a representative actual text from this field and comparatively investigate it in relation to what we/they study and how we/they study it. How do we find a 'highly valued' text (Bley-Vroman and Selinker 1984) in another discipline? We seek out an authority in that discipline who is familiar with language and language learning issues. Such a scholar is George Miller, who says, in regard to the text *Psychology and Mathematics: An Essay on Theory* (Coombs 1983): 'I want all my first year graduate students in experimental psychology to read it. No – to memorize it' (blurb to Coombs 1983). This is a good candidate for such a text; it is exactly how I feel about some of the founding texts discussed here, especially Weinreich (1953).

Coombs 1983 provides an interesting counterpoint to what we do. It attempts to relate theoretical systems, especially mathematical systems, to empirical generalizations in psychology, especially those concerning 'psychological judgement' and 'preferential choice behaviour', i.e. 'what to do next'. The latter is 'reflected in decisions' which the author claims is a 'ubiquitous' phenomenon (*ibid.*, p.17). In fact, just such decisions face second language learners regularly. Thinking through the relationship between empirical systems – in our case second language behaviour since we can never observe 'learning' – and theoretical systems in psychology is, after all, *where we began*. One only has to recall the psychological origin of the concept of 'transfer' to appreciate fully how much our theoretical conceptualization in SLA and IL has been tied up with this relationship – through either synthesis or antithesis (Chapter 1 above).

Another example of an older experimental psychology founding text with which we have been dialoguing is Osgood (1953, 1966) (see Kleinjans 1958, Selinker 1966, pp.17–18, 21–2 and Gass and Selinker 1983a, Introduction). There is a centrality to their notion of transfer and to their hypothesis-testing paradigm in our research. Many of our colleagues are still involved (often quite reasonably, I think) with statistical reasoning in the reducing of oral and written IL data to manageable proportions in the attempt to search for empirical regularities. In fact, as is shown in the last chapter and described in this one, this is where we began the background research which leads directly to the discovery of IL, i.e. the attempt to test experimentally the empirical claims of classical CA. I believed that if one could only show statistical dominate towards one choice in a 'two-choice schema' that was parallel in the NL and in attempted production of the TL norm, then 'language transfer' could unambiguously be shown; but the hitch is the phrase 'two-choice schema', which is discussed above.

Coombs' book concerns itself with what has been a goal since the earliest language transfer studies: 'the prediction of future observations, in situations not yet encountered' (Coombs 1983, p.8). What we should be after in the long run is a theory of SLA and IL learning, that no matter what the situation we would in principle be able to predict such phenomena as:
- when language transfer occurs
- what actually would be transferred
- which items or rules would fossilize and which would not
- when fossilization would onset
- what IL genres and discourse domains are affected by which language transfer factors and which fossilization phenomena
- what degree of backsliding is temporary and what permanent
We must continually ask why this sort of prediction has proved so intractable for us.

One problem is that it is impossible for us to restrict ourselves to the laboratory since conditions are always changing for people in the real world, and our generalizations, no matter how carefully arrived at, do not appear to be able to accommodate such change. After all, we want our SLA and IL generalizations to make sense to those involved in the difficult daily task of language teaching. I am reminded of the amount of variation (cf. Gass *et al.* 1989a and b), in linguistic terms as well as in other terms, of the ILs that we try to study. I think the AI people are probably right, namely that the best we can do in this regard is to derive as precise theories as we can in 'a world of imprecision' (Goguen 1978).

In his book Coombs comments elegantly on the problem of prediction, as he does on others, some of which have been raised (or should have been raised) in the SLA and IL literature – the distinction, for example, between 'model' and 'theory', one which we should maintain since, as Coombs points out, sometimes 'a theory can be false when a model is not' (Coombs 1983, p.10 and Section 4.3). In our case, what often passes for theory appears to be some sort of process flow chart which must account for a unique set of events but which has little predictive power.

Another issue of value to us that is discussed by Coombs in relation to mathematical psychology is that of 'necessary and sufficient conditions' (*ibid.*, Section 5.3). Necessary but *not* sufficient conditions abound in the SLA and IL universe. Consider 'language transfer' again. In a CA perspective, NL and TL congruence as to some subset of linguistic structures was both necessary *and* sufficient for language transfer to occur. Empirically the predictive power of CA proved to be false, but *only* on sufficiency grounds; congruence of some sort is still a necessary condition for transfer to occur, with many attempts in the empirical literature to constrain a too-powerful theory (cf. Gass and Selinker 1983a, *passim*). In fact, this is one of the major reasons why this 'look through time' is being undertaken. As pointed out in the Introduction and shown in Chapter 1 above, if one changes Lado's 'will' statements (i.e. the learner *will* do X or Y) to 'may' statements (i.e. the learner *may* do X or Y), one often has an important issue that can be looked at in current terms. Without this looking through time perspective, I believe that many of the important ideas in our founding texts are too easily overlooked because of the baby and bathwater syndrome discussed in Chapter 1.

In this regard, Weinreich (1953) points out that for language transfer to occur, 'interlingual identifications' must be presumed and for these it is necessary to presume structural congruence of some sort. As Weinreich recognized (see Chapter 2), none of this is sufficient to predict transfer. In an EFL situation (as opposed to an ESL situation), observational evidence shows that the oft-observed *homogeneity* of student errors in language classrooms makes the sufficiency condition that much stronger. As Levenston (1982) observes, this might be why CA has always been more attractive in the EFL situation, i.e. where observational evidence carries strongest weight. The ESL situation, having heterogeneous classes with regard to the NL of the students, masks the CA effect. There is a lot of truth to this argument, which follows from the hypothesis that interlingual identifications are a basic learning strategy.

Another background issue discussed by Coombs, and one we should keep in mind as background to our continual attempts to understand our theories as we try to discover IL, is that of over-generalization of theories. How one generalizes in SLA and IL studies is worthy of deep concern, since a necessary audience is that of the language teaching community. We must be clear that replication in our field is difficult, and this is discussed in Selinker 1985/6. A compounding factor is that one central way in which we have generalized historically is through analogy. An all too common method is to claim that one should believe something central about adult SLA because 'a child learns that way' (whether true or not), which supposedly provides a necessary condition for what one should do in language teaching. A classic example is that of Fries (1945, critiqued by Morley *et al.*, 1984). Another method of generalizing is rationalized argument, which is necessary but from a database in a different research domain. I have already described that situation with regard to Lado in Chapter 1 above. Widdowson's insightful LSP work is rightfully influential, but his method of generalizing (e.g. Widdowson 1978, 1983) has been to describe observationally NS behaviour and its relation, once again, to what adult SLA is about and then to what L2 teachers should do, with little empirical reasoning provided.

Another method of generalizing in the applied linguistics disciplines is the only one some colleagues think is appropriate, that of empirically based theorizing of the type used in Chapter 7. Here one looks at a (one hopes) well-controlled situation and generalizes on the basis of statistical reasoning. As should be clear by now, my view is that this is one important way to generalize, but only that. Statistical significance does *not* always equal theoretical significance.

A different approach entirely is that of case studies, from which it is very difficult to generalize. This is a type of study with which I am very sympathetic (cf. Selinker 1979 and Selinker and Douglas 1985). It has as its justification the notion that language learning is often too complex for clear hypothesis testing, where, as Lado long ago pointed out (cf. Chapter 1 above), the individual variation in which one is interested gets lost in pooled data. One has to remember that, as shown in this chapter and the last, quantitative study is one place where IL began and at times has returned to. But I find that that type of reasoning makes sense to me only in cases where the learner has limited IL choices and each of these choices is clear. There may be a depth of reality that is missing. With a controlled case study one finds out about something in depth that is relevant to learners as they struggle to learn, and that is quite insightful. Murphy O'Dwyer (1985) concludes her very interesting diary study of teacher trainees by stating that her analysis supports Gaies's conclusion that 'non-quantitative research, such as the diary studies, reveals the enormous variety and complexity of issues and attitudes involved in classroom interaction' (Murphy O'Dwyer 1985, p.123).

Allwright (1983, p.201) states the heart of the issue, which I see as a paradox, as: 'Can we test hypotheses in some way that meets any generally accepted criterion for any serious research or can we only illuminate?' Murphy O'Dwyer states in this regard: 'I do not consider that this study has done anything more than illuminate issues in classroom learning. I do not feel that any hypotheses arise for testing . . .' (*ibid.*). (She does see some implications for teachers revealed in her analysis, however.) The paradox is that we need to recognize that 'the enormous variety and complexity' found in IL and SLA, inside classrooms and without, can provide data which are too complicated to be totally resolved by the neat categories that are supposed to be the only ones for determining factual status for our concepts. To be clear, I am not here arguing against quantitative research, but only against its tyranny. This must be the case if it is true, and I believe that it is, that such non-quantitative research 'reveals universal aspects of learning and teaching processes' (Murphy O'Dwyer 1985, p.123). Such aspects as rhetorical strategies used in IL discourse, communicative effectiveness in a particular context, how the learner 'knows' that he or she has been successful in a particular context, are very difficult to study quantitatively with cross-sectional methodology. (For an extended discussion of a multi-layered research methodology for studying SLA in context, see Selinker and Douglas 1989.)

However, there is no doubt that a work such as Coombs' (1983) keeps us on our toes. He distinguishes between 'generality' of a theory and 'power' of a theory. The latter has particularly plagued us as regards CA; the theory was just too powerful and predicted behavioural events which simply did not occur. But a positive point about a too-powerful theory is that it aids understanding through strong predictions against which counter evidence, from a factual viewpoint, must be built up. From Coombs we learn that in order for a too-powerful theory to aid understanding, a field must have a *strong empirical base* to which one's theories can refer. This conclusion adds legitimacy to the gathering of IL data and especially possible IL universals, as was called for several times in the Corder Festschrift (Davies *et al.*, 1984).

In SLA, IL and language teaching studies we are beginning to develop an empirical base, but for some at too slow a pace. For example, one colleague, in reporting experiences at a recent TESOL, told of going to a paper about syllabus design and teaching methodology that the presenter was basing upon 'what Japanese businessmen do in an ESL classroom', which of course involves IL data. The inevitable 'How do you know?' questions came up and the audience was supposed to take as empirical what was obviously experiential, although not labelled as such. This important sort of teaching paper should, we can now surely agree, be backed up by empirical learning data (often IL but not exclusively), which can be combined with principles underlying one's proposed teaching suggestions (cf. Alderson 1985).

Concerning the central question of over-generalizing the result of empirical data analysis, one should consider studies such as the important one by Arabski (1979). Its importance is attested to in the review by Ard and Gass (1980), where this study is praised for, among other things, the wealth of well-organized data it contains and its marvellous introductory chapter, one of the finest in the literature. (Kellerman 1984 also discusses and integrates the detail of this study.) In that study, Arabski looks at the developing (and non-developing) Polish–English IL of three groups of Polish students: beginning high school, advanced high school, and beginning university. Data consist of compositions on: 'Why I wouldn't like to get married before I finish my studies'.

Different types of error are shown in Arabski by level in easily comparable percentage terms; errors are broken down into types, such as NL transfer, over-generalization, and simplification; transfer is shown to exist as 'the major source of errors in every level of our corpus' (p.102); and qualitative detail is presented in terms of lexical errors, errors in the use of prepositions, articles and pronouns, tense and mood, word order and morphology, a wide spectrum of IL use. We will ignore here the focus on 'errors' or forms that deviate from expected TL use. The difficulty with this study lies in its over-generalization of results to an entire IL without taking into account the problem of genre and discourse domains in IL learning (cf. Selinker and Douglas 1985, Gass 1988, Gass *et al.*, 1989a and 1989b, Preston 1989). Arabski's results, applying at the most to one domain of discourse, that of classroom written IL concerning a particular topic, are empirically valid, I would claim, only within that domain. Yet Arabski discusses the results, and the results are talked about in detail, *as if* they apply to the entire IL. (Arabski (pc) now agrees with this conclusion. Cf. Arabski and Selinker (in preparation), which discusses this limitation and how to correct it in the Polish context within IL theory by discourse domains.)

Such over-generalization of results that apply to at most one or two domains runs counter to the original spirit of the IL Hypothesis which hints at a strong contextual basis for IL use. For example, it is stated in the original 'IL' paper that 'fossilizable structures tend to remain as potential performance, re-emerging in the productive performance of an IL, even when seemingly eradicated. Many of these phenomena reappear in IL performance when the learner's attention is focused on new and difficult subject matter' (Selinker 1972, p.215). Fossilization, as discussed above, was first noticed contextually, but it was not realized how context-dependent IL learning is in the original formulation, though, as is shown in Chapter 7 above, language transfer effects in terms of surface-structure word order were shown in the earliest experimental studies to depend on such notions as 'topic talked about'. Thus, context dependency in IL as fact was empirically determined.

Importantly, given the practical motivation to study IL as discussed in Chapters 1 and 6, unless empirical results are carefully circumscribed as to applicable domain, language teachers will most probably not gain the advantage of being able to 'get round' the effects of stabilization and fossilization. Fossilization, it will be remembered, refers to a cessation of IL learning, often far from TL norms. But it must be remembered that fossilization seems to occur in a differential manner according to linguistic levels (Scovel 1977, 1988) and maybe according to discourse domains (Selinker and Lamendella 1978; Selinker and Douglas 1985; Zuengler 1989a, 1989c). On a practical level, if language teachers know (a) the domain-specific limits of an SLA study, and (b) those discourse domains of importance to their learners, then 'strategies of communication' applicable to those domains should be derivable which will make communication in those domains possible for most learners in spite of the effects of fossilization. It would then become an empirical question of a combined language teaching/IL theory – a type of theory we should cease to neglect – whether the particular strategies recommended do in fact get round which points of fossilization in which contexts for which types of exchanges of meaning for which types of learners.

Thus, relating to the continual attempt to discover IL, careful reading of Coombs on over-generalization of theories and domains of theories helps us to maintain healthy interaction between empirical systems and theoretical systems. Basic to all this is that the question of how we know what is 'fact' in IL learning and what is not becomes particularly important in a practical context since the notion IL and its attendant notions of language transfer, fossilization, backsliding, and various types of learning and communication strategies appear to be widely viewed as 'one of the starting points for communicative approaches to language teaching. The implied tolerance of L2 errors represented a radical break from all preceding approaches to language teaching, especially critical of the most prevailing attitudes to errors' (Programa to the 4th 'Seminario Nacional de Professores Universitarios de Ingles', Florianopolis, Brazil, July 1982). They add that the IL 'approach could also be closely connected to the "humanistic" schools of language teaching, as well as to teaching methodology which aims to develop successful learning and communication through the training of appropriate strategies' (*ibid.*). Is it fact that the IL approach is connected to these 'humanistic' approaches in language teaching, perhaps providing some 'factual' basis for them? Before I read that statement I would have said no. For us this conclusion arises on unknown grounds and there seem to be *no* 'decision-making procedures' such as one obtains in the laboratory science Coombs is talking about. Part of the reason is that for us there is the difficult task of replication in what we do, as alluded to above. We have been unsuccessful in thinking up 'critical experiments', as the work which Coombs describes *must* do to distinguish between various theoretical approaches. In fact, we have papers which describe the multitudinous theoretical approaches which we have (e.g. Schumann 1976, Rutherford 1984b), where what seems clear is that we do not really have theories in Coombs' sense, but an interesting series of *theoretical concepts*.

Is this situation particularly bad for us? It may be, since, as the interview at the beginning of the chapter points out, we are very susceptible in language teaching in particular, and applied linguistics in general, to fads and bandwagonism. This is one trend this book has tried to fight against by attempting to make clear some of the unsettled issues that underlie some of these fads. It is my perspective (see Introduction) that much of our problem lies in not making explicit the dialogue we must undergo as a field with our founding texts.

In this light, it is interesting that there are not only fads *for* particular perspectives but fads *against* particular perspectives as well. For example, one negative fad I find distressing is what has been called, in slogan terms, 'Krashen bashin''. But if one takes the perspective presented here, we would want to work through the various claims made by Krashen (Krashen 1982; Krashen and Terrell 1983, etc.) one by one, 'purposefully misreading' them in the positive way done for Lado in Chapter 1, and deciding in each case what reasonable formulation of the particular claim would hold up to experiential, observational or empirical evidence as we know and understand the relevant data, being as explicit as possible in each case. We would have to be very clear which domain of inquiry and which factual claims are being applied to. Then we would not be 'talking through each other'. One of the interesting things we would then notice about Krashen's work is that researchers by and large reject the learning/acquisition distinction, whereas teachers by and large seem to accept it. In a case like this, we should probably ask: What do teachers know (observationally) that we do not?

In trying to come to grips with various claimed facts in what we do, another factor that must be borne in mind is, as Sue Gass points out, that SLA, unlike the subject matter of many other fields, is something about which *everyone* seems to have an opinion. This has an effect on what we do and what we believe about what we do. (We have raised this point before in terms of teaching introductory SLA courses. See Selinker and Gass 1984, Introduction.)

In the final analysis, is it the case that I believe that language transfer is a significant factor in SLA and IL learning primarily because of the empirical evidence or because of the experiential, which in this case tells me that I consistently use my NL in my various attempts to express meanings in various L2s? Or is it the case that I believe in fossilization because of the empirical evidence or because I am a fossilized learner, *par excellence*, in a number of languages? But, getting more precise, is my belief that language transfer and fossilization occur within discourse domains based on empirical, experiential or observational evidence? This latter seems more technical somehow and harder to get experiential about. And what about the colleagues who promote humanistic approaches to language teaching, as mentioned favourably in the quote above? What is it about language learning that inspires them to believe what they do in spite of unanswered attacks on them in the literature (cf. e.g. Scovel, 1982 on suggestopedia)?

As we read Coombs (1983) we have to ask if we in language teaching and learning are *more susceptible to the personal* than colleagues in other fields in evaluating the truth claims and the factual status of the theoretical concepts we propose, and if so, why. I am not sure, but looking carefully at other fields through my experience in language for specific purposes, I do know that our work involves matters conceptually different from those, for example, of a geneticist who takes a certain type of plate and grows certain types of bacteria, getting certain consistent results 990 times out of 1000 (e.g.

Hanawalt 1972, discussed in Selinker 1979).

Thus, not without controversy I am sure, I want to claim that certainly at times our work involves conceptually different sorts of phenomena from those in other fields and we have to be very careful if we try to apply their methodology to our data. Another telling example of our subject matter being unique is that nowhere in our journals do we have anything to parallel what one regularly sees in some scientific journals, for example advertisements for slides which contain proteins. Closer to home, looking at the data which Coombs considers, we must ask: Does everyone seem to have an opinion about 'psychological preference behaviour' which affects the factual status of that behaviour and concepts which experimental psychologists working in this area propose when they study this phenomenon? I am not entirely sure, but from my reading of that literature, as well as from some informal subject-specialist informant work, I doubt it. The opinions of introductory students in that area do not seem to affect its teaching as happens in introductory SLA (cf. Selinker and Gass 1984, Introduction). Put another way, experiential and observational evidence count for much less in Coombs' field than in ours.

Summary

In the final analysis, then, how does one know that the IL Hypothesis is on the right track and will not be another fad? Perhaps it is because it has generated hundreds of studies and continues to do so. But linking things together through time, as is done in this volume, one sees that classical CA, after all, also generated hundreds of studies. One way I surely know that IL is reasonable is through experiential data: I have tried to learn many languages and have become fossilized in all of them. One also knows observationally, from observing and keeping track in many ESL classes over the years, especially in terms of EAP writing courses taught through the mechanisms of 'safe rules' and 'self-analysis' sheets; no matter what one does, one still sees non-native talk and writing.

Over the years, in addition, the SLA field has examined SLA data empirically for more than twenty-five years and has looked at such data from many different perspectives – bilingualism, CA, EA, IL, psycholinguistic, theoretical linguistic, neurofunctional, ethnographic, ethnomethodological. From all of this and from experiential/observational databases, we can conclude that the IL Hypothesis is *a reasonable theoretical story*. The IL Hypothesis, as I currently see it, states that in attempting to express meanings in an L2 and in attempting to interact verbally with native, as well as with other non-native, speakers of that L2, at least the following occur.

(1) People create a (partly) separate linguistic system.
(2) In that system interlingual identifications and language transfer are central.
(3) One selectively uses the NL by context.
(4) One fossilizes at least parts of the IL.
(5) One selectively fossilizes differentially according to linguistic level and discourse domain.
(6) The IL one is creating is susceptible to the force of several types of language universals, as well as interlanguage universals.
(7) The IL one is creating is susceptible to the training and learning strategies that are adopted.
(8) The IL one is creating is susceptible to simplification and complexification strategies.

It is my claim that each of these is factual not only because each one has some bit of empirical evidence to back it up, but because one can find experiential and observational evidence as well.

In order to see how difficult it is to come to truth in what we do, we present in the next chapter an allegory on a related substantive issue, which we derive from the interview at the beginning of the chapter: the substantive issue of how we know that the phenomenon of fossilization in IL should be given factual status. Is the permanent non-learning in L2, i.e. cessation of IL learning often far from expected TL norms, *a fact or not?* To see, we move to the allegorical account in Chapter 9 so that we as language teachers and researchers can participate as observers in a conversation which occurred among researchers from several fields concerning the factual status of this central concept of the IL Hypothesis: fossilization.

Points for discussion

(1) At the beginning of the chapter it was stated that the concept of 'interlanguage' was 'always there' in the work from Lado through Martinet to Weinreich and to most of the contrastivists. That is, that 'one can read into their work some sort of "in-between" language or grammar'. Do you think this a fair reading of the literature?
(2) Do you think the older view of learner forms as just a random collection of errors, of deviances from the target language, is still with us? On what do you base your response? Specifically,

look at the literature and see if there is any evidence that this view still has some validity.

(3) Do you agree with the arguments presented in this chapter, that each of the three concepts, 'transitional competence', 'approximative systems' and 'interlanguage', makes a different theoretical claim about the nature of the SLA process? Review the arguments and try to see both sides of the issue.

(4) Review the statement that unambiguous transcriptions of interlanguage data are not always possible and the conclusion made that interlanguage data are always ambiguous. Collect some interlanguage data and see if you can always transcribe what is said and if you can always make an unambiguous interpretation of these utterances. What sorts of problems do you in fact have?

(5) Consider the teaching angle in the discovery of interlanguage. It was claimed here that the notion 'interlanguage' arose from both research and practical experience, with several examples cited including that of Kellerman (1983), who noticed in a classroom setting that certain structures were and were not occurring in Dutch–English interlanguage. If you have been a language teacher, state how your own experience with the difficult daily task of helping NNSs struggle with expressing and negotiating meanings in a foreign or second language has produced *observational data* which are central to your conceptualization of what occurs in learner language.

(6) Evaluate the following statement, made several times throughout this volume and repeated in this chapter: 'linguistics, to be a general theory of language, must realize that the world is not a set of monolingual language situations; there is no known theory of language that can handle IL units that are established in terms of language transfer and interlingual identifications'. In terms of the setting up of research frameworks as discussed here, how might linguistics go about moving towards this goal? How might the discussion of Coombs' work in this chapter help in this regard?

(7) Are you convinced that second language acquisition and interlanguage studies 'cannot leave the contrastive perspective' embodied in the fields of CA, bilingualism and EA? How would we incorporate this perspective in the way stated in the interview in this chapter, that it must 'hook up with other similar developments in the field'? Do you agree that in retrospect it is wise to look at classical contrastive analysis as trying to provide

predictive interlanguage data, as is discussed in this and earlier chapters?

(8) Given the discussion in this chapter about the setting up of research frameworks, what is the best way to test empirically one of the basic claims of this volume, that 'learners *compare* what they do with a perceived target, setting up interlingual identifications'? How would you empirically try to decide whether or not this is 'a basic SLA learning strategy'?

(9) Consider the range of colleagues interested in interlanguage and second language acquisition, a continuum from practising language teacher to theoretician of second language acquisition. Consider the question asked in this chapter: What can we say that is factually correct about interlanguage learning that will make sense to each person along this continuum? Or is this an impossibility? Does the argument given here, that this question is resolvable in the long run by asking these questions in a sort of contrastive framework, resolve the issue satisfactorily?

(10) It is stated that the three types of evidence discussed in this chapter – the experiential, the observational and the empirical – should be kept separate and that each should be treated with respect. Does this whole discussion make sense? Can you find examples in the literature where this is and where this is not the case? Specifically, argue on either side of the following claim made in the chapter: 'Much of the disagreement we see in the literature and hear at conferences, results . . . in talking at cross-purposes, in not keeping these three separable forms of evidence in fact separate and not being able, perhaps, to be up-front about which type of evidence is prime for the particular point under discussion.' How do you feel about the notion that part of the criteria for fact in our field must be that what we glean from empirical evidence does not stray too far from experiential and observational data? Or does the following statement from Goguen (1978) make more sense: that the best we can do is to derive as precise theories as we can in 'a world of imprecision'?

(11) In this chapter we explored contrastively the questions of what is and is not fact in IL and how we do research in SLA, by looking at a 'highly valued' text in a neighbouring discipline, a field that researchers in interlanguage studies have depended on greatly: mathematical psychology. Recreate the argument for dealing with the fact noted in Chapter 7 that, determined by experimental methodology, 'autonomous material' in inter-

language exists. Are the arguments using material from Coombs convincing in this regard? Relate to the claim in this chapter that the empirical result leading to above 'fact' matches observational evidence as well. Are you comfortable with the conclusion presented above that prototypical statistically based psychological texts must be considered 'founding texts' for contrastive analysis, interlanguage and second language acquisition in general?

(12) Finally, using the three types of data we have discussed here – the experiential, the observational and the empirical – take each one of the following points and evaluate it both independently and in tandem with the rest:

– that the interlanguage hypothesis is a reasonable theoretical story
– that in attempting to express meanings in an L2 and in attempting to interact verbally with native (as well as with other NN) speakers of that L2, people create a (partly) separate linguistic system
– that interlingual identifications and language transfer, in a selective way, are central to the creation of that system
– that one selectively uses the NL by context
– that one fossilizes and selectively fossilizes differentially according to linguistic level and discourse domain
– that interlanguage systems as cognitive systems are uniquely permeable
– that the interlanguage one is creating is susceptible to the force of several types of universals, to the training and learning strategies that one adopts, to communication strategies, to simplification and complexification strategies and to backsliding.

9 The reality of fossilization: An allegorical account

So, we come to the factual status of fossilization. I know it exists. I also know that most teachers and researchers I've talked to know that *non*-learning is a persistent problem in SLA, that fossilization, or a cessation of IL learning often far from TL norms, is a reasonable way of looking at this non-learning. As reported above, Van Buren (1988) sees fossilization as one of two major binary choices facing a learner in determining whether the IL grammar should be a 'wide' one or a 'narrow' one. Also, Scovel (1988) makes the question of phonological fossilization central in his extended discussion of critical period issues, while Preston (1989) devotes a significant part of his volume to the fossilization issue, suggesting a model to account for two distinct types of fossilization. Zuengler (1989a, b and c), like Preston, concludes that social identity factors are prime causes.

In fact, though definitions of the phenomenon vary widely, there are literally hundreds of studies in the literature which claim to have shown a fossilized phenomenon, or speculate on a fossilizable phenomenon, or assume fossilization and speculate on its possible cause in the case under study. There have been several famous subjects in this literature, e.g. Alberto studied by Schumann (1976) and Wes studied by Schmidt (1983). The former argues for the importance of social and psychological distance from TL speakers, and the latter argues for factors 'which are specifically relevant to learning the grammatical code'. A study by Bean (1988) concentrates on personality factors; Sims (1988) relates fossilization to strategies of learning. An important series of arguments concerns what Davies (1984) calls 'partial knowledge' and J. Schachter (1990) terms the 'completeness issue'. Both focus on the fact that L2 learners appear to end up with 'incomplete knowledge' of the target language. For Schachter, incompleteness is 'an essential property of any adult L2 grammar', the corollary being that 'completeness' is *not* a possible property of L2 grammars. Her arguments for this principle are convincing, with the advanced learners of English she studied. By and large their knowledge of the parameter studied was insufficient and distinguishable from native-speaker knowledge.

Whatever the cause proposed, general acceptance of the reality of the phenomenon named by the concept is important. Yet there persists doubt among some colleagues as to the reasonableness of the central claim of fossilization, that there exist forms which will remain in learner speech permanently, *no matter what the learner does* to attempt their eradication. Certainly, language teachers have reason to be disturbed by this claim since, on the surface at least, it seems to undermine the language teaching process. However, language teaching colleagues, in my experience, do not persist in this view when it is realized that fossilization is ecologically reasonable, that Klein (1984, 1986) makes a good case for fossilization as beneficial to learners if the 'freezing' does not take place too early, because (a) fossilized systems are often simple, and (b) therefore, they are more easily learnable than mature TL systems, and (c) one can do many things with these limited means. In my view there is good evidence for each of these claims.

Teachers, in my experience, also begin to relax when one realizes that there is nothing in the SLA literature to suggest that some effects of fossilization cannot be bypassed in the learning/teaching process if emphasis is placed on communicative abilities in context. The learning/teaching process can continue as successfully as ever, the hypothesis being that one can 'get round' fossilization if one realizes that most, if not all, learners can be taught to express meanings in an L2 and to interact with L2 speakers in clearly specified discourse domains. A stronger hypothesis, yet to be tested, is that catching learners at the beginning of (academic) discourse domains (Selinker 1984) might lower the expected fossilization curve.

In spite of all these studies and discussions, there is another side. What I wish to come to grips with now is to try to understand the view which opposes the reasonableness of this fossilization claim. This opposing view, as I understand it, wishes to challenge the notion that people are programmed to fossilize when they attempt to express meanings in an L2, and it appears most unhappy with the implicit, and sometimes explicit, genetic claims (cf. e.g. the LPS claims in Chapter 2 above) entailed when one maintains that learners will fossilize 'no matter what' they do. The real arguments, then, are about its inevitability (cf. Selinker 1984).

We need to account for the agreed-on fact that most, if not all, learners find it very difficult at many points in their language learning careers to change IL forms to correspond to an expected TL norm, i.e., as stated above (and in Selinker 1984) that non-learning in SLA is a serious problem. Opposing colleagues appear to claim that 'it is just a matter of time', that 'the learner did not have the proper exposure to the TL', that 'the learner really did not want to be too target-like' in terms of group identity, and the like. Though these factors can affect the temporary stabilization of some IL forms, causing a plateau in a developing IL, they *cannot* account for the permanent cessation of IL learning often far from expected TL norms, which appears to occur for most, if not all, learners in most discourse domains, and these factors are discussed in detail in Selinker and Lamendella 1978.

But here we will try to illustrate the problem of deciding fact in SLA, a field where, as you may recall from the discussion in the last chapter, *everyone* has an opinion. We will illustrate the problem of deciding whether the fossilization notion should be considered fact by an allegorical account of a conversation which occurred at the home of a colleague in theoretical linguistics, since this conversation highlights the issue of how people decide what is factual and what is truth in *both* linguistics and SLA. I wish to recount my recall of this conversation since I have found that over the years I have been involved in several such puzzling conversations, usually late at night after a formal talk and, truth to tell, some imbibing.

The Cast (in no particular order)

A: a theoretical linguist, specializing in phonology
B: an anthropological linguist, widely published on many topics
C: a sociolinguist, specializing in pidgin and creole languages
D: a second sociolinguist, also specializing in pidgin and creole languages
E: a theoretical linguist, specializing in North American Indian languages
F: a psycholinguist, specializing in personality factors, originally from Eastern Europe, whose English is elegant but noticeably foreign
Me: an applied linguist, specializing in IL, SLA, LSP, ESL/EFL theory, and discourse analysis

All are native speakers of English except F. It is late, after a formal lecture by C followed by a big meal in a posh Italian restaurant. Most of us are drinking beer.

C: (*à propos of nothing I can remember*) You know, I really don't believe in this fossilization stuff (*to me*). In the final analysis, what makes *you* believe it?

F: (*to me*) You don't have to answer.

Me: Don't worry, I've had to do this a lot. I guess the reason is because I'm a fossilized learner *par excellence* in several languages.

D: No really, why do you believe in it?

Me: It's true, I'm a fossilized learner *par excellence* in several languages.

F: Don't do it.

Me: It's OK. This conversation has been coming a long time. I don't mind having it. I guess my answer is that I just don't see adults becoming native speakers of the next language.

B: What's a 'native speaker'?

Me: Yes. What Chomsky would say, I guess, someone with the full range of behaviours and intuitions that recognized native speakers of English have, for example.

F: That's clearly a side issue.

Me: Yes. In terms of the SLA literature, the attempts which failed at UCLA, you know, the attempted 'de-fossilization' experiments, where they took someone's old immigrant grandmother and tried to 'de-fossilize' her and got some change in behaviour in a tutored situation, but when they got her back to talking English in a relaxed way, back came the expected interlanguage forms. And there was Schumann's informant Alberto who . . .

C: There he goes, quoting Andersen 1984, etc., etc.

Me: OK, I won't do that. But the literature, as I read it, is important to why I believe . . .

C: I'll tell you a story. I read this in *Time* Magazine.

B: He's reduced to that.

C: (*clearly ignoring B*) The author of the piece tells about a Russian spy in Idaho who was caught after living for over ten years with the local people and being taken for a native. Now the *Time* correspondent who interviewed the spy was really clever. He asked him: 'How were you able to pass among those Americans for so long?'. And you know what the spy said?

Me: I can hardly wait.

B: Tell us, tell us.

C: He said: 'If you would have been shot, you would have been able to do it too.'

E: Did he learn English as a child?

C: No, man. He went to spy school in Moscow as an adult.

Me: OK, so he's an isolated case. You can't argue about the vast majority of learners and what they do based on a story like that.

C: Oh yes I can. It shows that *anyone* who must pass as a native speaker when he's in danger, man, can do it.

Me: I just don't believe it.

F: Undoubtedly there are such instances. . . . Rather, granting there are

such instances, do most of the learners we know about ... can they
become native speakers if they were faced with such a need?

Me: My claim is no, no matter what the need.

D: Come on, why do you say that?

Me: Take the European guest worker language situation.

A: How's that relevant?

Me: The people at Nijmegen who run the five-country project, who have
been looking at this for a long time ... the European Science
Foundation project ... they have built the reality of fossilization into
their project. The ones who wrote the second language acquisition
Field Manual [Perdue 1984]. They go even further than I've been
prepared to go. They claim that, in certain sociolinguistic situations,
from day 1, even before day 1, people will fossilize. In my terms that
they are pre-programmed to fossilize. They talk about Turks in
Germany, for example, where in 'gate-keeping' situations like
needing to get a job or to get an apartment, they come across
unsympathetic Germans and it's that kind of social situation which
...

B: Yeah, they just can't identify with such Germans and that's what does
it?

Me: Look, there's a body of carefully collected data, evidence which is
gathering, and I've seen nothing in the evidence these past fifteen
years to tell me that fossilization is wrong. Look, this European thing,
this *Field Manual*. This is perhaps the most important book in the
field I've read in the last five years ...

D: You mean more important than C's? (*much laughter*)

Me: Yeah, in the second language acquisition field. Sure.

A: What's this *Field Manual*?

Me: It's like the Slobin *Field Manual* in child language acquisition. In fact,
Slobin and Lyons are on the board, the overseeing board of the
European Science Foundation project. They're eventually going to
study six languages in five countries, in some sort of overlapping grid.

[Author's note: Actually, five NLs and six L2s, to make ten IL situations:
Punjabi–English, Italian–English, Italian–German, Turkish–German,
Turkish–Dutch, Arabic–Dutch, Arabic–French, Spanish–French, Spanish–
Swedish, Finnish–Swedish.]

The manual, a couple of hundred pages, gives the history of the
project to date, the results discovered, the country teams, suggested
methodologies, so that the results can be compared country by
country. For example, they're studying Pakistanis and Indians in
Britain and Swedes in Finland and so on.

C: I still don't see how this all gets you to the main point of your
fossilization.

Me: It's not just mine, any more.

C: OK, that they just can't do it, they *can't* change.

Me: OK, take the Toronto French-immersion children. They've been
       studied five years after the first studies and ten years after the first
       studies and people in that situation tell me – OK you don't want
       references – people in that situation tell me that those children
       definitely have an interlanguage, and it appears that they have
       definitely fossilized some of the structures that the original studies
       predicted they would.

[Author's note: To be fair to C's position, Harley and Swain (1984) report
that to date they have not discovered any 'positive evidence' to show
permanent fossilization of a particular IL structure, though NN structures
are visible in the English–French IL of immersion students after ten years of
exposure to French.]

F: The French-immersion children are an interesting case. Take the
       same kid and put him in France and he would become a native
       speaker.
Me: Probably.
F: That's the interesting point. They would not fossilize if they went to
       live in France.
Me: Yes, and played with native-speaking peers of the target language.
A: That only shows they don't identify with Quebec speakers of French.
C: Yes, that's my point. If they did identify, they could change what you
       call fossilization.
Me: I don't deny that group identification is a factor in setting up the
       sociolinguistic conditions that give rise to fossilization.
C: What a fudge.
Me: No, group identification does fit in. As near as we can figure, the
       crucial variable that triggers fossilization in these kids is sociolingu-
       istic, the absence of native-speaking peers of the target language.
A: That is, they don't identify with them.
Me: I think so, but in Toronto it's more than that. There are very few
       native speakers of French and they've tried to drive the immersion
       kids around to the few native speakers to form play groups, but I
       gather it's had limited success.
F: But if these immersion children had been taken to France . . .
Me: But they hadn't. The immersion children who are now no longer
       kids, say sixteen or seventeen, speak an English–French inter-
       language and my bet is that the stuff we've predicted has fossilized
       with these people and won't change.
C: How do you know?
Me: We (or rather they – the researchers in that situation) will certainly
       look.
C: Well, there you go again. If they don't change, it doesn't say they
       can't change, in some dangerous situation where they have to pass as
       native speakers.
Me: That so many all over the world seem fossilized and you're back to,

they can if they want.

C: Yes.

Me: OK, take F here, if it's OK. May I?

F: *(gracious nod)*

Me: We all agree that F is a very fluent speaker of English, even an elegant speaker of English, but is noticeably foreign, non-native, certainly on the phonetic level.

C: If he was in great danger, he could change.

Me: I say, he's a fossilized speaker of English and could not.

C: I say he could, if the danger was great enough.

Me: In all domains, I just don't believe it. In all contexts, no, no way.

C: Yes, definitely.

Me: No. *(to F)* Do you believe that you could change your English on the phonetic level to become indistinguishable from native speakers under conditions like C is talking about, with enough danger, in all domains and contexts?

F: *(not denying, providing a knowing smile)*

Curtain falls

How does one resolve such debates? In order to state where we are on these issues of facts and research, on temporary vs permanent non-learning, on units of interlingual identifications, on problems of CA, on in-between grammars, etc., we move to the final chapter, a brief summary of what we have learned from the long journey taken in this volume to link interlingual phenomena together through time.

Points for discussion

(1) Retell the allegory in this chapter to your colleagues. Do you all agree on the telling and the point the allegory is trying to make or are there important differences in a Rashomon-like way? And is 'allegory' in fact the right way to describe this tale?

(2) After contemplating this allegory, how do you think the factual status of fossilization is resolved? Integrate your response with the discussion of types of evidence in the last chapter.

(3) What language learning experiences have you had that could be described as 'non-learning' and 'plateau-like'? Have you ever been so stuck at a plateau in an L2 where you thought you would never progress beyond that point? Give an example. What happened? Has the experience varied by the oral language or written language involved? Has it varied by what domains of talk you were engaged in or to whom the talk was addressed? What strategies have worked to get you out of the problem? Are there cases where no matter what you do, you cannot change some

interlanguage behaviour? Does this make a difference? In your ability to communicate? In the social situation? Do you think you can 'outgrow' an interlanguage at some point and be as good as a native speaker? What would be the conditions for this to happen?

(4) Give an example where large numbers of speakers of your native language appear to fossilize in a particular L2. Do language teachers get frustrated here? If so, what do they try to do? Some colleagues (Sue Gass, for example) have 'operationalized' the definition of fossilization to a period of *five* years, i.e. they say that, if a form remains in learner speech or writing for five years we will call it 'fossilized'. Given the example you have just produced, does this time period make sense? Is this definition of fossilization reasonable for all occasions? Is it reasonable for most occasions? Please elaborate. How does this definition fit in with the one given in Selinker and Lamendella 1978: 'a cessation of interlanguage learning often far from target language norms'? If you have access to a copy of this article, you might like to consider their neurofunctional approach to fossilization and how you would account for the example you have given in this question.

(5) Seek out Selinker and Lamendella 1978 where it is argued that interlanguage learning is best viewed as a 'cline progression' from stable plateau to stable plateau and that from each plateau, the learner is operating with a system at each point, with some subsystems fossilizable at an early stage. Do you agree that the evidence supports this view, that the temporary stable configurations one sees in interlanguage learning are thus readily accounted for? Why or why not?

(6) Now seek out Bickerton 1975. This view of a 'dynamic continuum' that has interlanguage learning looking like 'a more or less regular gradient of change' is directly opposed to the view in the preceding question. How would a careful reading of Bickerton affect your answer to the previous question?

10 Reframing interlanguage: Where we are

In this volume we have aimed at linking current interlanguage research together through time with earlier work in several fields. This volume is not a history per se; one goal has been to show what we need to extract from earlier work in order to understand and place in perspective what is known today about IL and SLA.

We reframed the IL debate in terms of founding texts of our discipline. We have attempted here to make our dialogue with these texts more explicit than hitherto in the literature. We noted in the Introduction some dangers in not doing so. Rereading founding texts in the way suggested here provides IL hypotheses to be tested, many of which are not in the current literature. As we borrow theory and research methodology from other fields, we need more carefully to consider how we determine fact in IL. We need to ask: What types of evidence are called into play for what purposes?

A major point throughout this volume has been that, in some important sense, interlanguage has always been there. This conclusion is backed up by the detail of this book. From Lado in Chapter 1, through Martinet and Weinreich in Chapter 2, to the descriptive contrastivists and error analysts in Chapters 3 to 5, to the earliest experimental contrastivists, such as Briere, in Chapter 7 – one can read into their work some sort of 'in-between' language or grammar. We saw that this notion of in-between component exists more explicitly in the work of Harris (Chapter 5), the early work of Corder and Van Buren (Chapter 6) and of Nemser (Chapter 7). It is argued here that careful study of their data is needed to understand and enrich current work.

In re-examining these works, we found that there are certain needs that must be included in current IL thought, especially a richer language transfer perspective which would include translation phenomena. Translation equivalents are here regarded as an important strategy for learners as they look across linguistic systems; study of translation equivalents should be included in the research agenda of SLA studies. In language transfer work in general we need to research some basic assumptions. Throughout this volume it has been shown that language transfer statements in the literature can generally be reframed as 'if–then' statements. For example, in Chapter 6 I conclude that we need to build on Kellerman's suggested laws of language transfer by investigating what is taken as given in his formulation: that the learner 'establishes a correspondence' between surface forms across linguistic systems.

The data studied in this volume reinforce the IL notion of the existence of a *partially* separate linguistic system united by what Weinreich has called interlingual identifications. Surface-structure equivalences are not enough. We argue here for the plausible reality of interlingual identifications at the level of deep-structure grammatical transfer. A hypothesis then generated in Chapter 5 is that learners create partially separate *underlying* linguistic systems which they identify as same, a hypothesis that should be investigated in a UG framework.

Interlingual identifications is the suggested mechanism that unites units across linguistic systems. We argued that interlingual identifications are a basic, if not *the* basic, SLA learning strategy. A central claim is that learners regularly *compare* what they produce in IL with a perceived target, setting up interlingual identifications. Corder, for example (Chapter 6), concludes that the NL acts 'as a heuristic tool' as the learner attempts to discover the formal properties of the TL, facilitating especially the learning of those features which resemble features of the NL. If this is the case, and this volume discovers no empirical reason why it should not be so, then we are back again to some form of CA. The learner must have *a means to identify* which features of the TL 'resemble' features of NL. In Chapter 4 we explored those possible means in terms of the number of different CA models a learner might draw upon in forming IL.

It is a continuing SLA research task to discover what the comparative and contrastive units of interlingual identifications are and what their underlying causes might be. These pages should help give substance to this question. In this volume we present several detailed series of hypotheses which involve an ordering to interlingual identifications. For example, in the area of morphology, we hypothesized that learners look first for structural correspondence and then, when that does not entirely work, for translation correspondence. Furthermore, it is quite plausible that syntactic identifications, at least at times, work in reverse. Yet another testable hypothesis is that, given the necessity for some sort of universal linguistic processes in the creation of IL, ordering is involved in the following way: language transfer concerns at times are prime and universal principles are activated if the learner's attempt at interlingual identifications fails.

We also concluded (Chapters 2 and 3) that learners establish units of equivalence between stable and developing competence systems in the face of what Weinreich describes as the paradox or dilemma of language contact. The learner somehow must make the same what 'cannot be the same'. Many examples of this linguistic paradox are presented above. These examples suggest the need for a reframed general linguistics which, as Wode (1984) points out, would recognize the all-pervasiveness of language transfer as a linguistic phenomenon and would be able coherently to handle contrastive and interlanguage data. It is concluded in this volume that some parts of IL do not correspond well with a linguistics that has as a basic assumption that the world is a set of monolingual languages. Thus we see the need for a general linguistics which tests CA and SLA hypotheses.

This conclusion, based on a drawing together of over fifty years of literature, is not a new idea. The same general point has been made by Ferguson in a series of papers over many years (1963, 1968, 1985, 1989). Ferguson (1989), for example, lists a series of 'tentative' CA and IL findings for which . . . no theory of language, linguistic or otherwise, provides an explanation . . .'. Some of them were seen in this volume. For example, in the work of Nemser (Chapter 7) there are clear perceptual/production differences in cases where the linguistic facts would have predicted none. There is a linguistic answer which Nemser proposes that would be hard to fit into current theories: a dual phonemics. Additionally, in the work of both Nemser and Briere we saw a large set of linguistic productions for certain sounds which are unexplained to this day.

We saw in this volume scores of hypotheses about IL variation not handled in the current literature. We noted in Chapter 3 that the Fries and Pike (1949) notion of 'co-existent phonemic systems' could apply to IL in a consideration of lect-switching with borrowed forms and NL-like pronunciation in IL. Possible IL code-switching should be investigated, especially where multiple language acquisition is involved. Another series of variation hypotheses discussed here concerns the acquisition of morphology. The notion of language transfer as a selection process appears to have its first instantiation as a result of Weinreich's observation that no learner transfers the entire morphological system of the native language. Weinreich (1953) provides much more detail in this regard than we have space for in this volume. He presents a most important set of data (and theoretical speculation about them) concerning bound vs free morphemes and suggests there is a continuum involved. Odlin (1989) discusses the few IL studies where bound morphemes are involved, but the important concept 'degree of boundedness' seems not to have been integrated into current empirical and theoretical discussion.

Concerning linguistic theory, we propose in these pages the heretical view that issues long considered dead by theoretical linguists may not be so for SLA. An example is the case where widely applying phonological rules call into question the taxonomic phoneme. This issue should be important to us since one hypothesis presented here is that, *at times*, the taxonomic phoneme is the phonological unit of linguistic borrowing and language transfer. Since NL linguistic systems are also broken up by learners in interlingual identifications, it cannot be the *only* phonological unit of transfer. Another area of linguistic theory concerns discarded notions of grammatical structure. Given the importance of translation in interlingual identifications and its non-inclusion in linguistic theory, it is not impossible that (a) the old surface structure unit of kernel sentences (Chomsky 1957) combines with (b) translation equivalents and (c) Sebuktekin-like diaforms (Chapter 4, above) to form some part of core IL. We cannot close off such possibilities based on arguments derived solely from native-speaker intuition; we should not fear purposefully to misread linguistic theory as well.

In general, in researching the formation and fossilization of IL we should be looking for multiple effects such as the three suggested at the end of the last paragraph. Here we present our understanding to date of the *multiple effects principle*:

> It is a general law in SLA that when two processes work in tandem, there is a greater chance for stabilization of forms leading to possible fossilization.

It appears that the multiple effects phenomenon was first noticed (but not named) in the EA tradition by Jain (1969, 1974). Jain concluded that in Indian–English there are stronger stabilization tendencies when two processes work in tandem – in his case, language transfer and TL forms on signs that the learner regularly sees. Zobl (1980), Wode (1981) and Andersen (1983) all conclude that language transfer works in tandem with universal processes in stabilizing IL form, at the least in bringing about a delay where the learner gets stuck and stays at a plateau invoking potential fossilization (Chapter 6, above). Harley and Swain (1984) discover another factor working in tandem with language transfer: salience in the input. This appears to contribute to stabilizing interlingual identification of TL pronoun plus auxiliary with NL pronoun. In Chapter 5 we see another combination at work – particularized order of acquisition: what gets learned first, whether related to universals or not, works in tandem with language transfer. In that case, the forms concerned appear to be especially strongly fixed. In a specific-purpose acquisition context where consciousness-raising (C-R) strategies (Rutherford 1987) are a significant part of the input, Selinker and Lakshmanan (1990) find a multiple effect in non-native academic writing: language transfer and perceptual variables. Out of that work, a *corollary* is here suggested:

> Apparently fossilized IL structures will not become open to destabilization through C-R strategies when the multiple effects principle applies.

They then report on the discovery of a possible triple effect with language transfer, perceptual variables and the structure of the TL all working in tandem to get a particular IL outcome. The following theoretical prediction is made here:

> In every instance of the multiple effects principle, language transfer will be involved.

Should this prove to be true, it will reinforce the centrality of interlingual identifications.

As a result of the study of IL in context with literate subjects, we come to consideration of a set of uncontrolled variables in UG-based SLA research. In this research there is often a methodological dependence on written materials, often a grammatical judgement test. Such subjects are by definition literate and *some* subjects tested in these studies have learned English primarily from written language sources. With such literate subjects there is also IL variation in literate genres and domains (cf. for example Selinker and Douglas 1985, discussed in Gass 1988 and Selinker and Douglas 1989). Most UG-based SLA studies, certainly in the USA, have used foreign students whose IL, I strongly suspect, is determined, at least in part, by uncontrolled-for specific-purpose effects (both written and oral) interacting with language transfer effects. (Specific-purpose variables and the possible contextualization of the important pro-drop parameter are discussed in Selinker and Douglas 1989.)

Let me make a final comment regarding fossilization. It is a puzzling phenomenon with varying definitions in the literature, but it is widely agreed to be central to IL concerns (see Larsen-Freeman and Long, 1991). To make headway we need to focus some research effort on sorting out individual differences from group effects. Linking scholarship over time, we can see this need in Lado's work (Chapter 1, above), in the rich detail of Wong Fillmore's (1976) data, and in UG-based SLA accounts (e.g. Flynn and O'Neil 1988, p.19). Weinreich (Chapter 2) concentrated on the group and saw bilinguals and learners stabilizing forms. Nemser (Chapter 7) recognized permanently stabilized approximative systems; Nemser's data, especially, should be reviewed for individual differences. Looking beyond SLA, Thomason and Kaufman (1988) see the imperfect learning implied in fossilization as at times comparable to and effecting shift-induced language change. Also, Trudgill (1986) showed that, when dialects are in contact, stabilized group interdialects are formed. SLA work from a sociolinguistics and social psychology point of view (e.g. Preston 1989; Zuengler 1989a, b and c) makes it clear that some sort of group identity criterion is involved in stabilization of IL form, with effects being both individual and more general. This is also a result (Chapter 8) of contemplating the nativization data of World Englishes.

The sociolinguistically based SLA work rarely integrates concerns of UG, which must be included in any proposed general laws on SLA, given the reality of deep-structure grammatical transfer and the completeness arguments of J. Schachter (1988 and 1990), both argued for in these pages. In a parallel manner, the UG-based work in SLA rarely concerns itself with questions of group identity. Thus, we come back to a central argument presented in this volume: current conceptualization of theory in SLA is limited and limiting. In reframing the IL debate, we argue for researching the particularities of fossilization and language transfer in a broad conceptual/historical framework.

Appendix

Sample set of obtained English sentences

A sample set of 170 English sentences obtained under experimental conditions from American and Israeli school children appears in this appendix. The first three sentences in each group were recorded in Silver Spring, Maryland, the last seven in Israel.

(1) Where are the books now?

> the books are on the table
> your books are in your hand
> the books are on the table now
> the books are now in your hand
> the books are in your hand now
> the books the books are in your hands
> now the books are in your hand
> the books now are in your hand
> the books are now on the table
> the book is on the the table

(2) All right, where did I put the books?

> you put the books on the table
> you put the books on the chair
> you put them on the table
> you put the book in the desk
> you put the books on the the on the chair
> you put the books on the table now
> you you put the books on the table
> you put the books on the table
> you put the book the books on the table
> the books are on the table

(3) What subjects do you study in school?

I study English math geography
I study in school math science geography gym art
in school I study English math geography
I learn geography mathematic mathematic
I study in school mathematics history geography
I study at school mathematics Hebrew
in school I I learn English Hebrew
I studied at school historia mathematica and sport
I'm study in school the same subjects
we learn we learn in school Hebrew mathematics science

(4) OK, what subject do you like best?

subjects I like best are geography art and home arts
I like English and geography best
I like recess best
I like the mathematics
I like best history
I like best the the geo– Hebrew lessons
I like best geography history and Hebrew
I like mathematics best
best I like English and ma– mathematics
I like best mathematics

(5) All right. When did you meet your teacher?

I met Mrs Friedman on September 7th
I met Mrs Friedman two three days ago
I met Sister Leon last year
I met Mr Yanko two years ago
I meet Nomi three three years ago
I met him three years ago
I met Mr Margaliot two years ago
I met her at the beginning of the year
I met her a year before
I met my mathematics teacher before two years

(6) Where did you buy that watch?

I bought this watch in Lansburgh's
I got it from my sister
I bought my watch at a store

I got it for a present
I bought my watch in the town
I buy my watch in the shop
I get it from America
I bought it in Haifa
I bought my watch in Tel Aviv
my father bought it

(7) When did you buy it? Sentence now. When did you buy it?

I got the watch around four or five months ago
I got my watch when I came home from camp
I bought my watch four years ago
I bought this watch before one year
I get it before five year
I I get the watch when I was twelve year
I buy it three years ago
I bought my watch two years ago
I bought it three three years ago
my father bought it six or seven years ago

(8) How about you? Do you like movies?

yes I like movies
I like movies a little
yes I do like movies
yes I like them very much
yes I like very much movies
I like movies very much
I like it very much
yes I like movies
yes sure I like very much movies
I like very much films

(9) What type of movie do you like best?

I like war and murder stories best
I like any kind of movies
I like horror movies best
best I like movies about gangsters war
I like funny movies
I love movies of famous men
I like to see cowboys movies

I like best the Tarzan
I like best the the history movies
I like comic movies and some serious ones

(10) All right, when did you see that movie?

I saw the movie a couple of days ago
I saw it about about a month ago
I saw it about two weeks ago
I saw *My Fair Lady* last week
I see it yesterday
yesterday I saw America America
I saw it two days two days ago
I see the movies a few days ago
I saw this film last week
I saw it before two months

(11) Where do you live now?

right now I live in Washington
I live in Forest Park Apartments now
I live at 11013 Bucknell Drive
I live now at 61 Rambam Street
now I live in Jerusalem
I live in Jerusalem
I live now in Jerusalem
now I'm living in Tel Aviv
I live now in Ramat Gan
now I also live in Ramat Gan

(12) Where did you live five years ago?

I lived at 307 Oneida Street, Northwest Washington
I lived in Glenmont Hills, a suburb of Wheaton, five years ago
five years ago I lived in Pittsburgh, Pennsylvania
I live five years ago in Ramat Gan
I lived in Tel Aviv
I live in Jerusalem five years ago
I li– I I lived in Aliya Street
I li– I I lived also in Ramat Gan
five years ago I lived in Ramat Gan
I I have been living in Lud

(13) All right, what singer do you like best? Do you know?

I like Paul McCartney
I like Sonny and Cher the best
I like the Beatles best
the Israel singer I like best is Rivka Michaeli
the best I like the singer Elvis Presley
I like best the Beatles
I like Nehama Hendel best
I like be– the best Nehama Hendel
I like be– Benny Berman the best
I like Paul Anka, Elvis Presley

(14) When did you hear that singer?

I heard Frank Sinatra a couple day ago
I heard her today
I heard them a couple years ago
I I hear Rivka Michaeli yesterday
I hear them ye– yesterday
I heard them always in the radio
I heard her last yesterday
yesterday I heard the Beatles
one year ago I have I have heard her
I think yesterday I have heard her

(15) All right. When did you see your doctor?

I saw him about two months ago
I saw Dr Jacobs before I went to camp
I saw Dr Wolf today
I saw Dr Halevi last year
I saw Dr Drifus before one year
I saw him eight years ago
I see Dr Sneh two months ago
I saw her the last time two months ago
I see him a year ago
I saw him last before two month

(16) Where did you see him?

I saw my doctor at his office
I saw him at a doctor's office
I saw him at the Silver Spring Medical Hospital

I see Mr Lavon in Ben Yehuda Street
I saw him in his room
I saw him in my house
I saw him in his in his apartment
I saw him in his office
I saw him in his house
in Ramat Gan I saw him

(17) OK. How about you? What will you study in the university?
Sentence now. What will you study there?

I plan to study nursing in college
I'll study chemistry in college
I'd like to study chemistry
I want to study biologia
I will study there languages
I I want to study in the university law
I will study to be lawyer
I will study languages there
I will learn there English and French
I want to study in the university chemistry and biochemistry

References

Adjemian, C. 1976. On the nature of interlanguage systems. *Language Learning* **26**, 2: 297–230.

Adjemian, C. 1983. The transferability of lexical properties. In Gass, S. and Selinker, L. 1983a.

Adjemian, C. and Liceras, J. 1984. Accounting for adult acquisition of relative clauses: universal grammar, L1, and structuring the intake. In Eckman, F., Bell, L. and Nelson, D. (eds) *Universals of Second Language Acquisition*. Newbury House, Rowley, Massachusetts.

Alderson, J. C. (ed.), 1985. *Evaluation. Lancaster Practical Papers in English Language Education*, v.6. Pergamon, Oxford.

Allwright, R. L. 1983. Classroom-centred research: a brief historical overview. *TESOL Quarterly*, **17**: 191–204.

Andersen, R. W. 1983. Transfer to somewhere. In Gass and Selinker 1983a.

Andersen, R. W. 1984a. What's gender good for, anyway? In Andersen 1984b.

Andersen, R. W. 1984b. *Second Languages: A Cross-Linguistic Perspective*. Newbury House, Rowley, Massachusetts.

Arabski, J. 1979. *Errors as Indications of the Development of Interlanguage*. Universytet Slaski, Katowice.

Ard, J. W. 1984. Prospects of differential linguistics. Talk given at the University of Michigan.

Ard, J. W. 1985. Vantage points for the analysis of scientific discourse. *English for Specific Purposes* **4**: 3–20.

Ard, J. W. 1989. A constructionist perspective on non-native phonology. In Gass and Schachter 1989.

Ard, J. W. and Gass, S. 1980. Review of Arabski 1979. *Language Learning* **30**: 505–8.

Armagost, J. 1970. Primary questions formation in English and Spanish. Unpublished paper. University of Washington.

Asher, J. 1982. *Learning Another Language through Actions: The Complete Teacher's Guidebook*, 2nd ed. Sky Oaks Productions, Los Gatos, California.

Atai, P. 1964. A contrastive study of English and Persian question signals. Unpublished PhD dissertation. University of Michigan.

Bar Adon, A. 1959. *Lesonam ha-meduberet sel ha-yeladim be-yisrael* (Children's Hebrew in Israel). Section 0.5. Unpublished PhD dissertation. Hebrew University of Jerusalem.

Bartelt, H. G. 1983. Transfer and the variability of rhetorical redundancy in Apachean English interlanguage. In Gass and Selinker 1983a.

Basham, C. 1989. Deixis as a clue to distinctness in L2 production. Paper presented at the 'Second Language Research Forum' UCLA.

Bean, M. S. 1988. Personal identity and the pragmatic personality: case study of a fossilized adult. Unpublished manuscript. University of Southern California, Los Angeles.

Beck, A. and Foster, S. 1989. Navajo–English as a nativized dialect. Paper presented at the 'Second Language Research Forum' UCLA.

Beck, A., Foster, S. and Selinker, L. 1989. Acquiring markers of coherence in non-native written English. Paper presented at the 'Second Language Research Forum' UCLA.

Becker, A. L. 1988. Language in Particular: a lecture. In Tanner, D. (ed.), *Linguistics in Context*. Ablex. Nornood, N.J.

Bialystok, E. and Kellerman, E. 1987. Language strategies in the classroom. In Das, B. K. (ed.) *Communication and Learning in the Classroom Community*. Regional Language Centre, Singapore.

Bialystok, E. and Sharwood Smith, M. 1985. Interlanguage is not a state of mind: an evaluation of the construct for second language acquisition. *Applied Linguistics* 6: 101–7.

Bickerton, D. 1975. *Dynamics of a Creole System*. Cambridge University Press.

Binda, J. 1960. Introduction to Blanc 1960.

Blanc, H. 1953. Review of Weiman 1950. *Word* 9: 87–90.

Blanc, H. 1954. Israeli Hebrew. *Middle Eastern Affairs* 5: 385–91.

Blanc, H. 1956. Review of Rosén 1955. *Language* 32: 794–802.

Blanc, H. 1957. Hebrew in Israel: trends and problems. *Middle East Journal* 11: 397–409.

Blanc, H. 1960. Intensive spoken Hebrew. *English Language Services*, Book 1, Section 2.5. Washington, DC.

Bley-Vroman, R. 1983. The comparative fallacy in interlanguage studies: the case of systematicity. *Language Learning* 33: 1–17.

Bley-Vroman, R. 1989. What is the logical problem of foreign language learning? In Gass and Schachter 1989.

Bley-Vroman, R. and Chaudron, C. Forthcoming. A critique of Flynn's parameter setting model of second language acquisition. Manuscript. University of Hawaii.

Bley-Vroman, R. and Selinker, L. 1984. Research design in rhetorical/grammatical studies: a proposed optimal research strategy. *English for Specific Purposes* 82/83: 1–4, and 84: 1–5.

Bloomfield, L. 1933. *Language*. Chapter 5. New York.

Borer, H. 1983. *Parametric Syntax: Case Studies in Semitic and Romance Languages*. Foris, Dordrecht.

Briere, E. J. 1964. On defining a hierarchy of difficulty in learning phonological categories. Unpublished PhD dissertation. University of Washington.

Briere, E. J. 1966. An investigation of phonological interference. *Language* 42: 768–96.

Briere, E. J. 1968. *A Psycholinguistic Study of Phonological Interference*. Mouton, The Hague.

Briere, E. J., Campbell, R. N. and Soemarmo. 1968. A need for the syllable in contrastive analysis. *JVL&VB* 7: 384–9.

Cancino, E., Rosansky, E. and Schumann, J. 1974. Testing hypotheses about second language acquisition: the copula and negative in three subjects.

Working Papers on Bilingualism 88–96.

Candlin, C. N. 1966. Unpublished PhD dissertation. Yale University.

Carstens, V. 1984. ECP effects in Yoruba. Paper presented to NELS XV. Brown University, Providence.

Chomsky, N. 1965. *Aspects of the Theory of Syntax*. MIT Press, Cambridge.

Chomsky, N. 1981. *Lectures on Government and Binding*. Floris, Dordrecht.

Chomsky, N. 1986. *Knowledge of Language: Its Nature, Origin, and Use*. Praeger, New York.

Chomsky, W. 1958. *Hebrew, the Eternal Language*. Chapter 10. Philadelphia.

Clahsen, H. 1980. Psycholinguistic aspects of L2 acquisition: word order phenomena in foreign workers' interlanguage. In Felix, S. (ed.) *Second Language Development Trends and Issues*. Narr, Tübingen.

Clahsen, H., Meisel, J. and Pienemann, M. 1983. *Deutsch als Zweitsprache. Der Spracherwerb ausländerischer Arbeiter*. Narr, Tübingen.

Cohen, A. D. 1967. The grammar and constituent structure of the noun phrase in Spanish and English. Unpublished PhD dissertation. University of Texas.

Cohen, A. D. 1991. *Second Language Learning: Insights for Learners, Teachers and Researchers*. Newbury House/Harper and Row, New York.

Coombs, C. H. 1983. *Psychology and Mathematics: An Essay on Theory*. University of Michigan Press.

Corder, S. P. 1967. The significance of learners' errors. *International Review of Applied Linguistics*. V, no.4.

Corder, S. P. 1971a. Idiosyncratic dialects and error analysis. In Svartvik, J. (ed.) (1973) *Errata: Papers in Error Analysis* and in the *International Review of Applied Linguistics*, IX, no.2, 1971, University of Upsalla Press.

Corder, S. P. 1971b. Describing the language learner's language. *CILT Reports and Papers*, no.6.

Corder, S. P. 1971c. The elicitation of interlanguage. *IRAL*: special issue for Bertol Malmberg's sixtieth birthday. Julius Groos, Heidelberg.

Corder, S. P. 1972. Die Rolle der Interpretation bei der Untersuchung von Schulfehlern (The role of interpretation in the study of learners' errors). In Nickel, G. (ed.) *Fehlerkunde*.

Corder, S. P. 1976. The study of interlanguage. *Proceedings of the Fourth International Congress of Applied Linguistics*, v.2.

Corder, S. P. 1977a. Simple codes and the source of the second language learner's initial heuristic hypothesis. In *Studies in Second Language Acquisition*, vol.1, no.1.

Corder, S. P. 1977b. Language continua and the interlanguage hypothesis. *Proceedings of the Fifth Neuchatel Colloquium*.

Corder, S. P. 1978a. Language distance and the magnitude of the language learning task. *Studies in Second Language Acquisition*, II, no.1.

Corder, S. P. 1978b. Strategies of communication. *Association Finlandaise de Linguistique Appliquée*, no.23.

Corder, S. P. 1980. Formal simplicity and functional simplification in second language acquisition. In Anderson, R. (ed.) *New Dimensions in Second Language Acquisition Research*. Newbury House, Rowley, Mass.

Corder, S. P. 1981. *Error Analysis and Interlanguage*. Oxford University Press.

Corder, S. P. 1983. A role for the mother tongue. In Gass and Selinker 1983a.

Coulter, K. 1968. Linguistic error analysis of the spoken English of two native Russians. Unpublished thesis. University of Washington.
Cowper, E. 1984. Parasitic gaps and coordinate structures: a unified account. Paper presented to NELS XV. Brown University, Providence.
Cushing, S., Taylor, H., Webster, C. and Shumann, J. Forthcoming. A lexical method for language learning.
Dagut, M. and Laufer, B. 1985. Avoidance of phrasal verbs – a case for constrastive analysis. *SSLA* 7: 73–80.
Davies, A. 1989. Is international English an interlanguage? *TESOL Quarterly* 23: 447–67.
Davies, A., Criper, C. and Howatt, A. P. R. 1984. *Interlanguage*. Edinburgh University Press.
De Geest, W., Dirven, R. and Putseys, Y. 1969. Reflexive inchoatives revisted. *Le Langage et l'Homme* II: 31–3.
Di Pietro, R. J. 1961. Borrowing: its effect as a mechanism of linguistic change in American Sicilian. *General Linguistics* 5: 30–6.
Di Pietro, R. J. 1964. Learning problems involving Italian [s], [z] and English /s/, /z/. *Proceedings of the Ninth International Congress of Linguists*, 1962. Mouton, The Hague.
Diebold, A. R. 1961. Incipient bilingualism. *Language* 37: 97–112.
Diebold, A. R. 1964. Incipient bilingualism. In Hymes, D. (ed.) *Language in Culture and Society*. Harper and Row, New York.
Dingwall, W. O. 1964. Diaglossic grammar. Unpublished PhD dissertation. Georgetown University.
Drubig, B. 1970. Fehlleranalyse im Bereich der Morphologie und Syntax (Error analysis in the domain of morphology and syntax). In PAKS 1970, no.5.
Dulay, H. and Burt, M. 1973. Should we teach children syntax? *Language Learning* 23: 245–57.
Dulay, H. and Burt, M. 1974. Natural sequences in child second language acquisition. *Language Learning* 24: 37–53.
Eckman, F. R., Bell, L. W. and Nelson, D. 1984. *Universals of Second Language Acquisition*. Newbury House, Rowley, Massachusetts.
Eisenstein, M. R. (ed.) 1989. *The Dynamic Interlanguage: Empirical Studies in Second Language Variation*. Plenum, New York.
Ellis, R. 1982. The origins of interlanguage. *Applied Linguistics* 3: 207–23.
Ellis, R. 1985a. Sources of variability in interlanguage. *Applied Linguistics* 6: 118–31.
Ellis, R. 1985b. Teacher–pupil interaction in second-language development. In Gass and Madden 1985.
Eubank, L. (ed.) Forthcoming. *Proceedings of the Special Session on Universal Grammar, 1989 Second Language Research Forum*. University of California, Los Angeles.
Eubank, L. 1989. Parameters in L2 learning: Flynn revisited. *Second Language Research* 5.1: 43–73.
Faerch, C., Haastrup, K. and Phillipson, R. 1984. *Learner Language and Language Learning*. Gyldendalske Boghandel, Denmark.
Faerch, C. and Kasper, G. (eds) 1983. *Strategies in Interlanguage Communication*. Longman, London.
Felix, S. W. 1985. More evidence on competing cognitive systems. *Second*

Language Research 1: 47–72.

Ferguson, C. A. 1963. Linguistic theory and language learning. In *Georgetown University Round Table on Languages and Linguistics*, 1983. Georgetown University Press, Washington, DC.

Ferguson, C. A. 1968. Contrastive analysis and language development. In *Georgetown University Round Table on Languages and Linguistics*, 1968. Georgetown University Press, Washington, DC.

Ferguson, C. A. 1985. Contrastive analysis: a linguistic hypothesis. In *Scientific and Humanistic Directions of Language: Festschrift for Robert Lado*. Janowsky. K. R. (ed.). John Benjamin's, Amsterdam.

Ferguson, C. A. 1989. Language teaching and theories of language. In *Georgetown University Round Table on Languages and Linguistics*, 1989. Georgetown University Press, Washington, DC.

Ferguson, C. A. and Slobin, D. I. 1973. *Studies of Child Language Development*. Holt, Rinehart and Winston, New York.

Fisiak, J. (ed.) 1980. *Theoretical Issues in Contrastive Linguistics*. John Benjamin's, Amsterdam.

Flynn, S. 1987a. *A Parameter-Setting Model of Linguistic Acquisition: Experimental Studies in Anaphora*. D. Reibel, Dordrecht.

Flynn, S. 1987b. Contrast and construction in a parameter-setting model of second language acquisition. *Language Learning* 37: 19–62.

Flynn, S. 1989. The role of head-initial/head-final parameter in the acquisition of English relative clauses by adult Spanish and Japanese speakers. In Gass and Schachter 1989.

Flynn, S. and O'Neil, W. (eds) 1988. Linguistic theory in second language acquisition. Kluwer, Dordrecht.

Fox, R. P. 1968. A transformational treatment of Indian English syntax. Unpublished PhD dissertation. University of Illinois.

Frank, M. Z. 1961. Hebrew as she is spoke. *Jewish Heritage* 3: 16–22.

Fries, C. C. 1945. *Teaching and Learning English as a Foreign Language*. University of Michigan Press.

Fries, C. C. 1952. *The Structure of English: An Introduction to the Construction of English Sentences*. Harcourt, Brace and Company, New York.

Fries, C. C. and Fries, A. 1961. *Foundations of English*, Kenkyusha, Tokyo.

Fries, C. C. and Pike, K. L. 1949. Coexistent phonemic systems. *Language* 25: 25–50.

Garfinkel, H. 1967. *Studies in Ethnomethodology*. Prentice Hall, Englewood Cliffs.

Gass, S. (ed.) 1987. Special issue on lexical acquisition. *Studies in Second Language Acquisition* 9: 2.

Gass, S. 1979. Language transfer and universal grammatical relations. *Language Learning* 29: 327–44.

Gass, S. 1982. Review of Fisiak 1980. *SSLA* 5: 131–4.

Gass, S. 1984. The empirical basis for the universal hypothesis in interlanguage studies. In Davies *et al.* 1984.

Gass, S. 1988. Integrating research areas: a framework for second language studies. *Applied Linguistics* 9: 198–217.

Gass, S. and J. Ard. 1984. *Second Language Acquisition and the Ontology of Language Universals*. John Benjamin's, Amsterdam.

Gass, S. and C. Madden. 1985. *Input in Second Language Acquisition*. Newbury

House Publishers. Rowley, Massachusetts.
Gass, S. and Schachter, J. (eds) 1989. *Linguistic Perspectives on Second Language Acquisition*. Cambridge University Press.
Gass, S. and Selinker, L. (eds) 1983a. *Language Transfer in Language Learning*. Newbury House, Rowley, Massachusetts.
Gass, S. and Selinker, L. 1983b. Language transfer: a conference report. In Eppert, F. (ed.) *Transfer and Translation in Language Learning and Teaching (Anthology Series, Number 12)*. Singapore University Press.
Gass, S., Madden, C., Preston, D. and Selinker, L. 1989a. *Variation in Second Language Acquisition: Psycholinguistic Issues*. Multilingual Matters, Clevedon.
Gass, S., Madden, C., Preston, D. and Selinker, L. 1989b. *Variation in Second Language Acquisition: Discourse and Pragmatics*. Multilingual Matters, Clevedon.
Gimson, A. C. 1964. *An Introduction to the Pronunciation of English*. London.
Givon, T. 1979. *On Understanding Grammar*. Academic Press, New York.
Gleason, H. A. 1955. *An Introduction to Descriptive Linguistics*. Holt, Rinehart and Winston, New York.
Gnutzmann, C. 1970. Zur Analyse Lexicalischer Fehler (On the analysis of lexical errors). In PAKS 1970, no.5.
Goffman, E. 1974. *Frame Analysis*. Northeastern University Press, Boston.
Goguen, J. 1978. *Lectures on Artificial Intelligence*. Xerox, UCLA.
Gruber, R. 1950. Hebrew as she is spoke. *Commentary* 10: 466–9.
Haggard, M. Models and data in speech perception. In Wathen-Dunn 1967.
Hakuta, K. 1974. Prefabricated patterns and the emergence of structure in second language acquisition. *Language Learning* 24: 287–97.
Halle, M. 1963a. Phonology in generative grammar. In Fodor, J. A. and Katz, J. J. (eds) *The Structure of Language: Readings in the Philosophy of Language*. Prentice Hall, Englewood Cliffs.
Halle, M. 1963b. On cyclically ordered rules in Russian. *American Contributions to the 5th International Congress of Slavists:* 113–32. Mouton, The Hague.
Halliday, M. A. K. 1973. *Language as a Social Semeotic*. Edward Arnold, London.
Halliday, M. A. K. 1979. *Explorations in the Function of Language*. Edward Arnold, London.
Hanawalt, P. C. 1972. Repair of genetic material in living cells. *Endeavor* 31: 83–97.
Harley, B. 1984. Age as a factor in the acquisition of French as a second language in an immersion setting. In Andersen 1984.
Harley, B. and Swain, M. 1984. The interlanguage of immersion students and its implications for second language teaching. In Davies *et al.* 1984.
Harris, Z. 1954. Transfer grammar. *IJAL* 20: 259–70.
Hatch, E. 1984. Theoretical review of discourse and interlanguage. In Davies *et al.* 1984.
Haugen, E. 1950. The analysis of linguistic borrowing. *Language* 26: 210–31.
Haugen, E. 1953. *The Norwegian Language in America*. University of Pennsylvania Press, Philadelphia.
Haugen, E. 1954. Problems of Bilingual Description. In Report of the Fifth

Annual Round Table meeting on Linguistics and Language Teaching.
Haugen, J. 1983. Item analysis of the errors in a dictation test. Unpublished paper. University of Michigan.
Hawkins, B. 1985. Is an 'appropriate response' always so appropriate? In Gass and Madden 1985.
Henning C. (ed.) 1977. *Proceedings of the Los Angeles Second Language Research Forum.* University of California, Los Angeles.
Hockett, C. F. 1958. *A Course of Modern Linguistics.* Macmillan, New York.
Hoekstra, T. 1984. Parasitic gaps in Dutch and adjacency of case assignment. Paper presented to NELS XV. Brown University, Providence.
Hoi, D. T. 1965. Representation of time and time-relationship in English and in Vietnamese. Unpublished PhD dissertation. University of Columbia.
Huebner, T. 1983. *A Longitudinal Analysis of the Acquisition of English.* Karoma, Ann Arbor.
Huybregts, R. and van Riemsdijk, H. 1984. Parasitic gaps and across-the-board rules application. Paper presented to NELS XV. Brown University, Providence.
Jain, M. P. 1969. Error analysis of an Indian English corpus. Unpublished paper, University of Edinburgh.
Jain, M. P. 1974. Error analysis: source, cause and significance. In Richards 1984.
Jakobovits, L. A. 1970. *Foreign Language Learning: A Psycholinguistic Analysis of the Issues.* Newbury House, Rowley, Massachusetts.
James, C. 1980. *Contrastive Analysis.* Longman. London.
Kachru, B. 1982. *The Other Tongue: English Across Cultures.* University of Illinois Press, Urbana.
Kellerman, E. 1977. Toward a characterization of the strategy of transfer in second language learning. *Interlanguage Studies Bulletin* 2: 58–145.
Kellerman, E. 1983. Now you see it, now you don't. In Gass and Selinker 1983a.
Kellerman, E. 1987. Aspects of transferability in second language acquisition. Unpublished PhD dissertation. University of Nijmegen.
Kellerman, E. and Sharwood Smith, M. (eds) 1986. *Crosslinguistic Influence in Second Language Acquisition.* Pergamon Press, New York.
Klein, W. 1984. Some remarks on the syntax of learner varieties. Unpublished paper. Nijmegen.
Klein, W. 1986. *Second Language Acquisition.* Cambridge University Press.
Kleinjans, E. 1958. A descriptive-comparative study predicting interference for Japanese in learning English noun-head modification patterns. Unpublished PhD dissertation. University of Michigan.
Konig, E. 1970. Tranformational grammar and contrastive analysis. In PAKS 1970, no.6.
Krashen, S. 1982. *Principles and Practice in Second Language Acquisition.* Pergamon Press, Oxford.
Krashen, S. and Terrell, T. 1983. *The Natural Approach.* Pergamon Press, Oxford.
Kuhlwein, W. 1970. Intra- und Interstrukturale Fehlleistungen auf der Phonemishch-Graphemischen Ebene (Intra- and interstructural errors in the realm of phonemics-graphemics). In PAKS 1970, no.5.

278   *Rediscovering Interlanguage*

Labov, W. 1969. Contraction, deletion and inherent variability of the English copula. *Language* **45**: 715–62.
Lado, R. 1957. *Linguistics across Cultures*. University of Michigan Press.
Lakoff, G. 1987. *Women, Fire, and Dangerous Things: What Categories Reveal about the Mind*. University of Chicago Press.
Langacker, R. W. 1969. An analysis of English questions. Unpublished paper. University of California, San Diego.
Langer, S. 1942. *Philosophy in a New Key: A Study in the Symbolism of Reason, Rite and Art*. Harvard University Press, Cambridge.
Larsen-Freeman, D. and M. Long. 1991. *An Introduction to Second Language Acquisition Research*. Longman, London and New York.
Lattey, E. 1982. What is the 'same thing' in interlinguistic comparison? In Lohnes and Hopkins 1982.
Lees, R. B. 1959. The Grammar of English Nominalizations. M.I.T. Ph.d. dissertation. Published as Lees 1963.
Lees, R.B. 1963. *The Grammar of English Nominalizations*. Mouton and Co, The Hague.
Lehn, W. and Slager, W. R. 1959. A contrastive study of Egyptian Arabic and American English: the segmental phonemes. *Language Learning* **9**.
Levenston, E. 1971. Over-indulgence and under-representation, aspects of mother-tongue interference, in Nickel 1971.
Levenston, E. A. 1982. Review of Carl James. Contrastive Analysis. (Applied Linguistics and Language Study Series). Longman Group. Harlow, 1980. *Applied Linguistics* **3**: 174–5.
Lightbown, P. 1984. The relationship between theory and method in second language acquisition research. In Davies *et al*. 1984.
Lohnes, W. F. W. and Hopkins, E. A. 1982. *The Contrastive Grammar of English and German*. Karoma, Ann Arbor.
Long, M. 1985. Input and second language acquisition theory. In Gass and Madden 1985.
Long, M. and Sato, C. 1984. Methodological issues in interlanguage studies: an interactionist perspective. In Davies *et al*. 1984.
McNemar, Q. 1962. Psychological Statistics. (3rd edition) John Wiley & Sons, London.
Meara, P. 1984. *The Study of Lexis in Interlanguage*. In Davies *et al*. 1984.
Meisel, J., Clahsen, H. and Pienemann, M. 1981. On determining developmental stages in second language acquisition. *Studies in Second Language Acquisition* **3/2**: 109–35.
Morag, S. 1959. Planned and unplanned developments in modern Hebrew. *Lingua* **8**: 247.
Morley, J., Robinett, B. W., Selinker, L. and Woods, D. 1984. ESL theory and the Fries legacy. *JALT Journal* **6**: 171–207.
Mueller, H. J. (ed.) 1954. Report of the Fifth Annual Georgetown University Round Table Meeting. *Monograph Series in Languages and Linguistics* no.7. Georgetown University Press, Washington, DC.
Murphy O'Dwyer, L. 1985. Diary studies as a method for evaluating teacher training. In Alderson 1985.
Myint Su 1971. Analysis of lexical errors. Unpublished M. Lit. dissertation. University of Edinburgh.
Nemser, W. 1961a. The interpretation of English stops and interdental

fricatives by native speakers of Hungarian. Unpublished PhD dissertation. Columbia University.

Nemser, W. 1961b. Hungarian phonetic experiments. Xerox form. New York.

Nemser, W. 1971a. *An Experimental study of Phonological Interference in the English of Hungarians*. Indiana University, Bloomington, and Mouton, the Hague.

Nemser, W. 1971b. Approximative systems of foreign language learners. *IRAL* 9: 115–23.

Newmeyer, F. J. 1969. English aspectual verbs. *Studies in Linguistics and Language Learning* 6. University of Washington, Seattle.

Nickel, G. 1970. Introduction to PAKS 1970, no.5.

Nickel, G. 1971. *Papers in Contrastive Linguistics*. Cambridge University Press, Cambridge.

Nickel, G. 1973. Grundsatzliches zur Fehleranalyse und Fehlerbewertung. In Nickel, G. (ed.) *Fehlerkunde*, 2nd ed. Cornelsen-Velhagen & Klasing.

Nickel, G. 1979. Some controversies in present-day error analysis: 'contrastive' vs 'non-contrastive' errors. *IRAL* 27: 293–306.

Nickel, G. 1988. Recent Trends in Contrastive Linguistics and Error Analysis. *Journal of Applied Linguistics* 4: 75–80.

Nida, E. 1949. *Morphology: The Descriptive Analysis of Words*. 2nd ed. The University of Michigan Press, Ann Arbor.

Odlin, T. 1985. *Input and Second Language Acquisition Theory*. In Gass and Madden 1985.

Odlin, T. 1989. *Language Transfer: Cross-Linguistic Influence in Language Learning*. Cambridge University Press.

Osgood, E. 1953. *Method and Theory in Experimental Psychology*. Oxford University Press.

Osgood, E. 1966. Meaning cannot be R? *Journal of Verbal Learning and Verbal Behavior* 5: 402–7.

Otanes, F. T. 1966. *A Contrastive Analysis of English and Tagolog Verb Complementation*. University of California, Los Angeles. Oxford University Press.

Oxford, R. 1990. *Language Learning Strategies: What Every Teacher should Know*. Newbury House/Harper & Row, New York.

PAKS (*Project für angewandte kontrastive sprachwissenschaft*, 'Project on Applied Contrastive Linguistics') 1970 Institut für literatur- und sprach-wissenschaft, Lehrstuhl Anglistik: Linguistik. University of Stuttgart.

Palmer, H. E. 1921. *The Principles of Language Study*. Reprinted, Oxford University Press 1964.

Pankhurst, J., Sharwood Smith, M. and van Buren, P. Forthcoming. *Readings in Second Language Research*. Reidel, Dordrecht.

Perdue, C. (ed.) 1984. *Second Language Acquisition by Adult Immigrants: A Field Manual*. Newbury House, Rowley, Massachusetts.

Perdue, C. 1991. The European Science Foundation project on adult language acquisition. In Ferguson, C. A. and Huebner, T. (eds) *Second Language Acquisition: Contributions and Challenges to Linguistic Theory*. Multilingual Matters, Clevedon.

Perlmutter, D. M. 1968. Deep and surface structure constraints in syntax. Unpublished PhD dissertation, Massachusetts Institute of Technology.

Pienemann, M. 1989. Is language teachable? Psycholinguistic experiments and hypotheses. *Applied Linguistics* 10: 52–79.

Pienemann, M. and Johnson, M. 1986. An acquisition-based procedure for second language assessment. *Australian Review of Applied Linguistics* 9/1.

Pike, K. 1944. *Phoenetics*. University of Michigan Press.

Platt, J. and Weber, H. 1980. *English in Singapore and Malaysia*. Oxford.

Platt, J., Weber, H. and Ho, M. 1984. *The New Englishes.* Routledge & Kegan Paul, London.

Preston, D. R. 1989. *Sociolinguistics and Second Language Acquisition*. Blackwell, Oxford.

Radaravanija, P. 1965. An analysis of the elements in Thai that correspond to the basic intonation patterns of English. Unpublished PhD dissertation. Columbia University.

Reed, D. W., Lado, R. and Y Shen 1948. The importance of the native language in foreign language learning. *Language Learning* 1: 17–28.

Richards, J. C. 1984. *Error Analysis: Perspectives of Second Language Acquisition*. Longman, London.

Rizzi, L. 1982. *Issues in Italian syntax*. Foris, Dordrecht.

Romaine, S. 1989. *Bilingualism*. Blackwell, Oxford.

Rosén, H. B. 1955. *Haivrit selanu: dmutah be-or sitot ha-balsanut* (Our Hebrew language: viewed by linguistic methods). Chapters 2 and 3. Tel Aviv.

Rosén, H. B. 1962. *A Textbook of Israeli Hebrew*. University of Chicago Press.

Ross, J. R. 1969. Adjectives as nominal phrases. In Reibel, D. A. and Schane, S. (eds) *Modern Studies in English: Readings in Transformational Grammar*. Prentice Hall, Englewood Cliffs.

Rutherford, W. 1984a. *Universals in Second Language Acquisition*. John Benjamin's, Amsterdam.

Rutherford, W. 1984b. Description and explanation in interlanguage syntax: state of the art. *Language Learning* 34:127–55.

Rutherford, W. 1987. *Second Language Grammar: Learning and Teaching*. Longman, London and New York.

Rutherford, W. 1989. Interlanguage and pragmatic word order. In Gass and Schachter 1989.

Sapir, E. 1927. *Language*. Harcourt Brace, New York.

Sato, C. J. 1985. Task variation in interlanguage phonology. In Gass and Madden 1985.

Sauer, K. 1970. (Untitled contrastive analysis paper on Spanish/English syntax). Unpublished paper. University of Washington; described in Selinker 1971.

Saussure, F. de 1922. *Cours de Linguistique Générale*. 2nd ed. Payot, Paris.

Schachter, J. 1974. An error in error analysis. *Language Learning* 24: 205–14.

Schachter, J. 1983. A new account of language transfer. In Gass and Selinker 1983a.

Schachter, J. 1988. Second language acquisition and universal grammar. *Applied Linguistics* 9: 219–235.

Schachter, J. 1989a. Testing a proposed universal. In Gass and Schachter 1989.

Schachter, J. 1989b. A new look at an old classic. *Second Language Research* 5: 30–42.

Schachter, J. and Rutherford, W. 1979. Discourse function and language transfer. *Working Papers in Bilingualism* 19. Ontario Institute for Studies in Education, Toronto.

Schachter, J. 1990. On the issue of completeness in second language acquisition. *Second Language Research* 6: 93–124.

Schachter, J. and W. Rutherford. 1979. Discourse function and language transfer. *Working Papers in Bilingualism* 19.

Schachter, J., Tyson, A. and Diffley, F. 1976. Learner intuitions of grammaticality. *Language Learning* 26: 67–76.

Schachter, P. 1966. Transformational grammar and contrastive analysis. In Kaplan, R. (ed.) *Selected Conference Papers of the Association of Teachers of English as a Second Language. NAFSA Studies and Papers, English Language Series 12.*

Schmidt, R. W. 1983. Interaction, acculturation, and the acquisition of communicative competence: a case study of an adult. In Wolfson and Judd 1983.

Schumann, J. 1976. Second language acquisition research: getting a more global look at the learner. *Language Learning*, Special Issue 4: 15–28.

Schumann, J. 1978. *The Pidginization Process: A Model for Second Language Acquisition.* Newbury House, Rowley, Massachusetts.

Scovel, T. 1977. *The ontogeny of the ability to recognize foreign accents.* In Henning 1977.

Scovel, T. 1982. Questions concerning the application of neurolinguistic research to second language learning/teaching. *TESOL Quarterly* 16: 323–31.

Scovel, T. 1988. *A Time to Speak: A Psycholinguistic Inquiry into the Critical Period for Human Speech.* Newbury House/Harper and Row, New York.

Sebuktekin, H. I. 1964. Turkish–English contrastive analysis: Turkish morphology and corresponding English structures. Unpublished PhD dissertation. University of California, Berkeley.

Seliger, H. W. 1977. Does practice make perfect? A study of interaction patterns and L2 competence. *Language Learning* 27: 263–78.

Selinker, L. 1960. Preliminary analysis of potential phonological problems (and procedures for their eradication) involved in the teaching of american English to native speakers of Israeli Hebrew. Unpublished M.A. Thesis. Washington D.C.: The American University.

Selinker, L. 1966. A psycholinguistic study of language transfer. Unpublished PhD dissertation. Georgetown University.

Selinker, L. 1967. Language contact: resultant semantic categories in Israeli Hebrew. In Stuart, D. G. (ed.) *Linguistic Studies in memory of Richard Slade Harrell.* Georgetown University Press, Washington.

Selinker, L. 1969. Language transfer. *General Linguistics* 9 (2): 67–92.

Selinker, L. 1970. Basic clause types in Israeli Hebrew. *Word* 26: 373–85.

Selinker, L. 1971. A brief reappraisal of contrastive linguistics. In Whitman, R. and Jackson, K. (eds) Proceedings of the Pacific Conference on Contrastive Linguistics and Language Universals. University of Hawaii Press, Honolulu.

Selinker, L. 1972. Interlanguage. *International Review of Applied Linguistics* 10: 209–31.

Selinker, L. 1979. On the use of informants in discourse analysis and

282   *Rediscovering Interlanguage*

language for specific purposes. *International Review of Applied Linguistics.* 17: 189–215.

Selinker, L. 1980. Les domaines de reference dans une theorie de l'interlangue. *Encrages–Acquisition d'Une Langue Etrangere.* N. Speciale, Automne, 1980.

Selinker, L. 1984. The current state of interlanguage studies: an attempted critical summary. In Davies *et al.* 332–43.

Selinker, L. 1985–6. Review (Article) of Perdue 1984. Language Learning 35: 567–84 and 36: 83–100.

Selinker, L. and Douglas D. 1985. Wrestling with 'context' in interlanguage theory. *Applied Linguistics* 6.2: 190–204.

Selinker, L. and Douglas, D. 1989. Research methodology in contextually-based second language research. *Second Language Research* 5.1: 1–34.

Selinker, L. and S. Gass. 1984. *Workbook in Second Language Acquisition.* Newbury House Publishers, Inc. Massachussetts.

Selinker, L. and Lakshmanan, U. 1990. Consciousness-raising strategies in the rhetoric of writing development. Paper presented to the 1990 TESOL Annual Meeting. San Francisco.

Selinker, L. and Lamendella, J. 1978. Two perspectives on fossilization in interlanguage learning. *Interlanguage Studies Bulletin* 3.2: 144–91.

Selinker, L., Swain, M. and Dumas, G. 1975. The interlanguage hypothesis extended to children. *Language Learning* 25: 139–52.

Sharwood Smith, M. 1982. Crosslinguistic aspects of second language acquisition. *Applied Linguistics* 3: 192–99.

Sharwood Smith, M. 1983. On first language loss in the second language acquirer: problems of transfer. In Gass and Selinker 1983a.

Sharwood Smith, M. 1984. Review of Corder 1981. *Applied Linguistics.*

Sharwood Smith, M. and Rutherford, W. 1984. Proposal for interlanguage core grammar. Unpublished MS.

Sims, W. 1988. Fossilization and language learning strategies. PhD preliminaries, University of Minnesota.

Slobin, D. I. 1973. Cognitive prerequisites for the development of grammar. In Ferguson and Slobin 1973.

Stockwell, R. P. and Bowen, J. D. 1965. *The Sounds of English and Spanish.* Chicago University Press.

Swain, M. 1985. Communicative competence: some roles of comprehensible input and comprehensible output in its development. In Gass and Madden 1985.

Swales, J. 1986. Current developments and future prospects. *Annual Review of Applied Linguistics*, vol.7. Cambridge University Press.

Tarone, E. 1979. Interlanguage as chameleon. *Language Learning* 29: 181–91.

Tarone, E. 1983. On the variability of interlanguage systems. *Applied Linguistics* 4: 143–63.

Tarone, E. 1984. Forward to Selinker, L. and S. Gass. 1984. *Workbook in Second Language Acquisition.*

Tarone, E. 1988. *Variation in interlanguage.* Edward Arnold, London.

Tarone, E., Frauenfelder, U. and Selinker, L. 1976. Systematicity/variability and stability/instability in interlanguage systems: more data from Toronto French immersion. In Brown, H. D. (ed.) *Language Learning* Special Issue

4: 93–134.

Thomason, S. G. and Kaufman, T. 1988. *Language Contact, Creolization and Genetic Linguistics.* Berkeley, University of California Press.

Trudgill, P. 1986. *Dialects in Contact.* Blackwell, Oxford.

Valentine, T. 1985. Gender differentiation in conversational style in Indian English. Paper presented to the annual South Asian Linguistics Association conference. Ann Arbor.

Valentine, T. 1986. Aspects of linguistic interaction and gender in South Asia. Unpublished PhD dissertation. University of Illinois.

Van Buren, P. 1972. Contrastive analysis. In Allen, J. P. B. and Corder, S. P. (eds) *The Edinburgh Course in Applied Linguistics,* vol.3.

Van Buren, P. 1988. Some remarks on the subset principle in second language acquisition. *Second Language Research* 4: 33–40.

van den Berg, M. 1988. The creation of an artificial pidgin and its subsequent depidginization. Unpublished manuscript. Catholic University, Nijmegen.

Verma, M. K. 1966. A synchronic comparative study of the structure of the noun phrase in English and Hindi. Unpublished PhD dissertation. University of Michigan.

Wagner, K. H. 1969. A proposal on nominalizations I, PAKS 3/4: 27–58.

Watkin, K. 1970. Fossilization and the interlanguage hypothesis. Unpublished MS. University of Washington.

Weiman, R. W. 1950. *Native and Foreign Elements in a Language: A Study in General Linguistics Applied to Modern Hebrew.* Chapter 6. Russell Press, Philadelphia.

Weinreich, U. 1951. Research problems in bilingualism with special reference to Switzerland. Unpublished dissertation. Columbia University.

Weinreich, U. 1953. *Languages in Contact.* Publication of the Linguistic Circle of New York, No.1.

Weinreich, U. 1954. Linguistic convergence in immigrant America. In Mueller 1954.

White, L. 1985. The acquisition of parameterized grammars: subadjacency in second language acquisition. *Second Language Research* 1: 1–17.

White, L. 1989. The adjacency condition on case assignment: do L2 learners observe the Subset Principle? In Gass and Schachter 1989.

Whitney, W. D. 1881. On mixing in language. *Transactions of the American Philological Association* 12: 1–26.

Widdowson, H. G. 1978. *Teaching Language as Communication.* Oxford University Press 1964.

Widdowson, H. G. 1983. *Language Purpose and Language Use.* Oxford University Press.

Williams, J. 1987. Non-native varieties of English: a special case of language acquisition. *English World-Wide* 8: 161–99.

Wode, H. (ed.) 1983. Papers on language acquisition, language learning and language teaching.

Wode, H. 1977. *On the Systematicity of L1 Transfer in L2 Acquisition.* In Henning 1977.

Wode, H. 1978. Developmental sequences in naturalistic L2 acquisition. In Hatch, E. (ed.) *Second Language Acquisition.* Newbury House, Rowley, Massachusetts.

Wode, H. 1981. *Learning a Second Language*. Narr, Tübingen.
Wode, H. 1984. Some theoretical implications of L2 acquisition research and the grammar of interlanguages. In Davies *et al.* 1984.
Wolfson, N. and Judd, E. 1983. *Sociolinguistics and Second Language Acquisition*.
Wong Fillmore, L. 1976. The second time around: cognitive and social strategies in language acquisition. Unpublished PhD dissertation. Stanford University.
Yang, D.-W. 1984. On the integrity of control theory. Paper presented to NELS XV. Brown University, Providence.
Zobl, H. 1980. Developmental and transfer errors: their common bases and (possible) differential effects on subsequent learning. *TESOL Quarterly* 14: 469–79.
Zobl, H. 1983. L1 acquisition, age of L2 acquisition, and the learning of word order. In Gass and Selinker 1983a.
Zobl, H. 1984. Cross-language generalizations and the contrastive dimension of the interlanguage hypothesis. In Davies *et al.* 1984.
Zobl, H. 1986. Word order typology, lexical government and the prediction of multiple, graded effects on L2 word order. *Language Learning* 36: 159–84.
Zobl, H. 1987. Categorical distribution and the problem of overgeneralization. *Second Language Research* 3: 89–101.
Zobl, H. Forthcoming. Configurationality and the subset principle. In Pankhurst, Sharwood Smith and van Buren, forthcoming.
Zuengler, J. 1989a. Identity and interlanguage development and use. *Applied Linguistics* 10: 80–96.
Zuengler, J. 1989b. Assessing an interaction-based paradigm: how accommodative should we be? In Eisenstein 1989.
Zuengler, J. 1989c. Performance variation in NS–NNS interactions: ethnolinguistic difference or discourse domain? In Gass, Madden, Preston and Selinker 1989b.

Index

285